FIERY STRONGHOLD

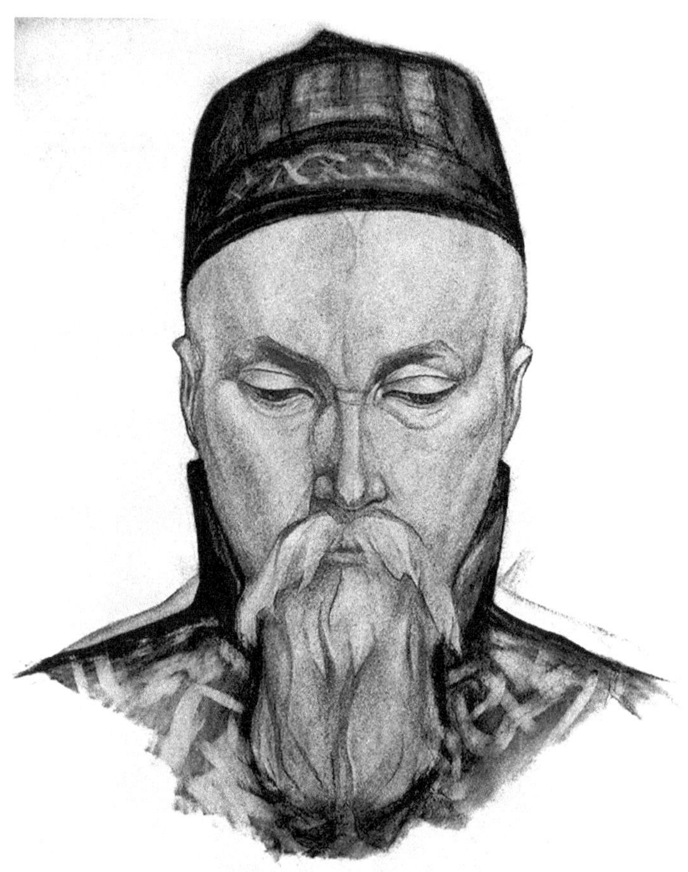

Portrait of Nicholas Roerich by Svetoslav Roerich

FIERY STRONGHOLD

NICHOLAS ROERICH

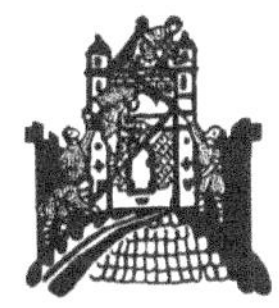

NICHOLAS ROERICH MUSEUM

NEW YORK   MMXVII

Nicholas Roerich Museum
319 West 107th Street
New York NY 10025
www.roerich.org

Cover illustration:
Nicholas Roerich. *Sophia—the Wisdom of the Almighty*. 1932.

FIRST EDITION PUBLISHER'S NOTE

THE present book is the eighth volume of the works of Nicholas Roerich. The seven previous volumes comprise the "First Volume of the Complete Works," "Adamant," "Flowers of Morya," "Altai-Himalaya," "Heart of Asia," "Shambhala" and "Realm of Light." These have been issued by the following publishers: Sytin Publishing Company, Moscow; Slovo, Berlin; Alatas, United States; F.A. Stokes & Co., and the Roerich Museum Press. Several of these volumes have been published in London, in Buenos Aires (Spanish); in Kyoto (Japanese) and other cities.

The present eighth volume is devoted basically to the concept of Culture. With his usual versatility and deep understanding, the author extols the concepts of evolution, Beauty, Peace and Knowledge. In his address, given on the occasion of his election as President of the World League of Culture, Roerich said:

"Culture is the reverence of light. Culture is the love of humanity. Culture is fragrance, the unity of life and Beauty. Culture is the synthesis of uplifting and refined achievements. Culture is the weapon of the World. Culture is salvation. Culture is the moving force. Culture is the Heart.

"If we gather all the definitions of Culture, we find the synthesis of effective blessing, the center of enlightenment and creative Beauty."

The present volume should truly be a friend of each student and teacher. The fruits of the all-embracing artistic and philosophical thought of Roerich are generously disseminated in these tenets of creative labor and vitality. Roerich has been justly recognized by public opinion in many countries, not only as a powerful creator in the field of art but also as a leader of Culture. As the Hon. George Gordon Battle rightly affirmed, "Nicholas Roerich is unquestionably one of the greatest leaders of history. Combined with his extraordinary breadth of mind, there is a sublime sympathy with the opinions of others, and tolerance for their prejudices. He has a wonderful capacity to be the leader of an international movement. He has power not only to plan but to act. He can translate his dreams into action."

* * *

"Fiery Stronghold" has been published for the benefit of the Fund for the Banner of Peace. May this joyous news of Peace, Labor and Beauty ignite young hearts.

CONTENTS

VI. GREETINGS

VII. THE BEAUTIFUL

VIII. BANNER OF PEACE

I

FIERY STRONGHOLD

FIERY STRONGHOLD

I N THE Book, "The Heart," an old Chinese fairytale is related about a giant as tall as heaven, and a dwarf who ridiculed him. It is said that the giant stood with his head above the clouds while the dwarf ridiculed him because the giant could not see the world below. But the giant was unmoved by the scoffing and said: "If I so desired, I could crawl upon the earth but you will never be able to see above the clouds!"

At a university meeting, Crookes made his famous speech on the world-concept as perceived by the giant and the dwarf. The scientist drew a remarkable parallel of the inversion of the laws within the capacities of these antipodes. Similarly antipodal opinions are formulated regarding the idea of creativeness, according to people's personal angle of approach. But as with everything, only the broadest measures correspond to the highest concept of life. In thinking of creativeness one should invoke that which is greatest, most radiant and most unifying. Substance is feeling. Thus, creativeness is an expression of the energy of the heart. How beautiful is this mighty energy when perceived, educated and applied to action! How many possibilities, still unrealized and unutilized by humanity, are hurled into the pit of chaos. People seldom are aware of the fact that creativeness is not only expressed in mechanical manifestations, but also in something far greater and more powerful that is poured forth for the Common Good of the World. Arrows of Benevolence and Beauty are often understood simply as ancient symbols! Humanity has but recently begun to think of the significance and power of thought; and science is only beginning to study the heart and human radiation!

"Children, love one another", such is the ordinance of the Highest and the Best. For love, one should open and cultivate the heart. But what is the approach, if not the key of the Beautiful? Do not spirituality, religious sentiments, attainments, heroism, benevolence, valor, patience and all other fires of the heart unfold in the Garden of the Beautiful?

Not for despair and tears, but for joy of spirit, have all universal evidences of Beauty been created. But joy must be perceived. And how can joy set up its light-spreading haven, if bereft of the language of the heart? Where else, if not in the heart, is the stronghold of joy?

He who has become conscious of the realm of the heart, invariably reaches the shore of creativeness. In whatever way the pilgrim of the spirit expresses his creativeness, in essence it will be the same precious gem of which all the best legends of humanity speak. The inspired Meistersinger, Wolfram von Eschenbach, sings of the same precious Stone of which the age-old wisdom of Tao speaks.

Our meetings are destined somewhere and somehow. Some day we must cast aside all our brute habits. The heart yearns for the Beautiful Temple, for the Celestial Jerusalem, for the Radiant City of Kitej and for all mountain abodes of the Realm of Spirit.

Each departure from the Beautiful, from Culture, has always brought about destruction and decay. On the other hand, all striving towards cultural constructiveness has created brilliant epochs of renaissance.

"To repeat the same things to you is not burdensome for me, but for you it is useful," wrote Paul the Apostle. And this trait of Knowledge of the human spirit is not to be regarded as a sepulchral reproach but as a smile of wisdom. Certainly, until it is burned upon the very brain, one must affirm the necessity of Culture. One must affirm it for all ages, under all circumstances and to all nations.

So long as Culture is a luxury and a Sunday repast, it cannot reconstruct our life. Can the consciousness, in the turmoil of daily life, exist without books, without the creations of Beauty, without the entire multiform Museum —the Home of the Muses?

Culture should become part of daily life, in huts as well as in palaces. This clarified thinking will determine what is most necessary, inevitable, and what is only the alluvia of passing waves. How benevolent is the touch of the wings of Culture, blessing the cradle to attainment and carrying the passing pilgrim to enlightened consciousness. In indescribable, inexpressible ways is the spirit ennobled through the touch of Culture. Not a confused, hazy occultism and mysticism, but the Light of the Great Reality shines where the enlightenment of Culture has taken root.

A friend enters, singing a song. The artist expresses the quality of his spirit in painting. Thus we mutually affirm each other and rejoice at all manifestations of creativeness.

If even beasts are subdued by sound, then how much more are sound, color and form necessary to the heart of man!

Humanity cannot continue to press downward along the way of disintegration and hatred; in other words, he cannot hurry to brutality. Stop, stop! The abyss is already at hand.

Let us gather around the concept of Culture, around the Great Service of Light. Realizing the unity of the Highest Light, we shall also find the power not to reproach, not to belittle, not to slander, but to praise Beauty, the Supreme.

Destructive criticism has reached its limit. The vocabulary of evil slander and humiliation has increased to intolerable dimensions. But even in its dungeon, the human spirit yearns for joy, constructiveness and creativeness.

I remember how Puvis de Chavannes always found a sincere, benevolent word for the most varied creations. But I cannot forget how another famous artist used to go through all exhibitions, with the spume of bitter criticism on his lips. Once I noticed that he took a much longer time while looking at exhibits that he defamed. I noticed that he spent about three-quarters of an hour on abuse and only a quarter of an hour on praise. While accompanying the artist, I said: "I know what makes you stay longer—it is those things that are detestable to you!" And the abuse of this artist was most ingenious; but his praise was very poor and dry. Of course, in his creativeness, Puvis de Chavannes was far higher. Did not the benevolent comments of Puvis also originate from his real creative ability?

Why act with divisiveness and with malice where a general enthusiasm and a united joy of creativeness have been ordained?

The commandments about the Beautiful have been innumerable since time immemorial. Whole kingdoms, whole civilizations, were built following these great Ordinances.

To beautify life, to ennoble and to uplift it, means to dwell in the good. All-understanding and all-forgiveness, love and self-denial are generated in the attainment of creativeness.

And should not all young hearts strive to creativeness? And so they do! How many ashes of vulgarity are required to stifle this sacred flame! How often one can open new gates to the Beautiful by the single call, "Create, create."

What decrepitude is expressed in the fossilized program, "First, I shall learn to draw, then I shall go to color, and after this, I shall try to start composition." Countless are the cases when the flame of the heart became extinguished before the pupil reached the forbidden gates of creativeness!

But how much joy, daring and vigilance is developed in the consciousness of those who from childhood dared to create. How enticingly attractive the compositions of children can be before their eyes and hearts become hardened by the death-inflicting conditions of standards.

In what do the conditions of creativeness lie? In genuineness, in the compelling quivering of the heart which calls forth constructiveness. Earthly conditions are of no importance for the creator who feels the call. Neither time, place nor materials can limit this impulse of creativeness. "Even in prison, an artist will become an artist," was one of the sayings of my teacher, Kuindji. But he also used to say, "If you must be kept under glass, the sooner you disappear, the better. Life has no need for such hot-house flowers." He understood well the significance of the battle of life, the battle of light and darkness.

A clerk once came to the teacher with sketches; the latter praised his work but the clerk complained, "My family and office work stand in the way of my art."

"How many hours do you spend in the office?" asked the artist.

"From ten to five."

"And what do you do from four to ten?"

"What do you mean, from four to ten?"

"Yes, from four in the morning!"

"But I sleep."

"Well, then you will spend your whole life sleeping. When I worked as a retoucher with a photographer, our work was from ten to six, but the entire morning from four to nine was at my disposal. And to become an artist, even four hours a day are sufficient."

Thus spoke the venerable master, Kuindji, who, starting as a shepherd boy, by dint of labor and the development of his talent, reached an honored position in the art of Russia. Not harshness, but a Knowledge of the laws of life inspired his reply, full of the realization of his responsibility, full of the consciousness of labor and creativeness.

The main thing is to avoid everything that is abstract. There is no abstraction in actuality, just as there exists no void. Every recollection of Kuindji, of his teaching, both in the art of painting and in the art of life, always recalls unforgettable details. How necessary are these milestones of experience, when they bear witness to a valor that has been tested and to a real constructiveness.

I remember how, after my graduation at the Imperial Academy of Fine Arts, the Imperial Society for the

Encouragement of Fine Arts invited me to be the Assistant Editor of its periodical. My colleagues were outraged over such a combination of activities and prophesied the end of my art. But Kuindji strongly advised me to accept the appointment, saying, "A busy person succeeds in everything; an open eye perceives everything; but in any case it is impossible for a blind man to paint." I remember how Kuindji once criticized my painting, "The March." But half an hour later he returned, short of breath, having run up to the studio, and said as he smiled, "You must not be grieved. The ways of art are innumerable. The chief thing is that the song comes right from the heart."

Another one of my teachers, Puvis de Chavannes, who was full of benevolent and inexhaustible creativeness, always inspired one with profound wisdom towards the self-expansion of labor and the joy of the heart. Love for humanity and the joy of creativeness were not dead in him, but one will remember that his first steps were not encouraged. For eleven years his paintings were not accepted by the Salon. This was a sufficient touchstone for the greatness of his heart!

My third teacher, Cormon, always encouraged me to carry out individual, independent work, saying: "We become artists when we remain alone."

Blessed are the Teachers, who lead one with a benevolent, experienced hand towards wide horizons. It is a great happiness to be able to remember one's Teachers with the full tremor of a loving heart.

The role of the Teacher in ancient India, the profound concept of the Guru-Teacher, is especially touching and inspiring. Yes; it is inspiring to see how a free conscious veneration for the Teacher exists up until today. Verily, it forms one of the basic realities of India. No doubt the same conception also existed among the old masters of Italy and the Netherlands and among Russian icon-painters. But in these countries it is already a past Beauty, whereas in India it still lives, and I hope, it will never die.

Each spiritual impoverishment is shameful. From the

subtler worlds, the great masters are watching sorrowfully, grieving over the folly of impeded possibilities. In other articles: "Spiritual Values ," "Re-evaluation," and "Agni— The Transmuter," we speak sufficiently of everything that should not be missed at the crossroads. I cannot forget the profound saying of my deceased friend, the poet Alexander Bloch, with regard to the Ineffable. Bloch ceased to frequent the Religious-Philosophical Society because, as he expressed it, "They speak there of the Inexpressible." To be precise, there is a limit to words, but there is no limit to sentiments or to the capacity of the heart. Beauty is everywhere. All pilgrims are in search of the good, all sincere seekers embark at this shore; people may quarrel a great deal and may even become like animals, but still they will be silent in unity at the sound of a mighty symphony and will desist from all quarrels in a Museum or under the dome of the Notre Dame in Paris.

The same love of the heart is evoked when we read of the flashes of Beauty in all ordinances.

The Persian apocrypha about Christ are most touching: "As Christ walked with his disciples, they came upon the carcass of a dog, lying by the roadside. The disciples turned away with repugnance from the putrid corpse. But the Teacher found Beauty also in this case and pointed out how beautifully white were the teeth of the dog."

At the hour of his passing, Buddha the Lord remembered, "How beautiful is Rajagriha and the Vultured Cliff. Beautiful are the valleys and the mountains. Vaisali! What Beauty!"

Besides all his other abilities, every Bodhisattva has to be perfect in art also.

The Rabbi Gamaliel says, "The study of the law is a noble work if connected with some art. This occupation leads away from sin. But each occupation which is not accompanied by art leads nowhere."

And the Rabbi Yehuda adds, "He who does not teach an art to his son, makes of him a highwayman." Spinoza, who attained a considerable adeptness in art, truly answered to this covenant of the harmonization and ennoblement of the spirit.

Of course, the lofty ordinances of India also affirm the same basic significance of creative art: "In ancient India, Art, Religion, Science were synonyms of Vidya, or Culture." "Satyam, Shivam, and Sundaram are the Eternal Triune manifestations of godhood in Man, Immutable, Blissful and Beautiful."

Let us remember the Museum—the Home of the Muses—of Pythagoras, of Plato and of all those great ones who understood the cornerstones of the foundations of life: and let us recall the words of Plotinus about the Beautiful!

Out of the depths of life's harsh experiences, Dostoevski exclaims, "Beauty will save the world!" Ruskin, who has glorified the stones of the past, expresses the same feeling. A well-known ecclesiastic, looking at paintings, exclaimed, "A prayer of earth to Heaven!"

The old unfailing friend of all creative searchers, Leonardo da Vinci, says, "He who despises the art of painting, despises the philosophical and sensitive contemplation of the world, for painting is the legitimate daughter, or rather the granddaughter of nature. Everything that exists has been begotten from nature which has begotten, in turn, the science of painting. For this reason I maintain that the art of painting is the granddaughter of nature and is related to God Himself. He who defames the art of painting, defames nature.

"The painter must be all-embracing. O, artist, may Thy versatility be as infinite as the manifestations of nature! Continuing what God has begun, strive to multiply not the deeds of human hands, but the eternal creations of God. Never imitate. And may every creation of thine be a new manifestation of nature."

Was not the "unyielding austerity" of Leonardo da Vinci strengthened by the clear joy for the far-off worlds, by the firm prayer of the heart in Infinity!

How many of the best of human beings have affirmed the prayer of the heart, the prayer of Beauty, of the Beauty of creativeness, of victories of Light. From all lands, in all ages, everyone has proclaimed the significance of creativeness as the leading principle of life. The ancient monuments have immortalized the glorious images of Egypt, India, Assyria, of the Mayas, and of China; are not the treasures of Greece, Italy, France, Belgium, Germany, really living witnesses to the significance of the highest creativeness!

How wonderful that even now, amidst all the spiritual and material crises, we can affirm the kingdom of the Beautiful! And we can do this not as abstract idealists, but armed with the experience of life, strengthened by historical events and by spiritual tenets.

Remembering the significance of creativeness, humanity must also remember the language of the heart. Are not the parables of Solomon, the Psalms and the Bhagavat Gita and all the fiery commandments of the hermits of Sinai written in this language?

How precious it is to realize that all the covenants lead not to division, limitation, or brutality, but to ascent, to the strengthening and purification of the spirit!

Dr. Brinton has reminded me that on leaving America in 1930, I said to him: "Beware of the barbarians!" Since then many barbarians have invaded the domain of Culture. Under the sign of the financial depression many irredeemable crimes have been committed within the citadels of the spirit.

The scrolls of the dark oppressors, true tablets of shame, have been indelibly recorded on the charts of education and enlightenment. Uncultured despoilers have attempted to destroy and uproot much in the field of education, science and art!

Shame upon shame! Chicago has no funds to pay its public school teachers. A church in New York has been sold at auction. In Kansas, the Capitol has been sold in the same way. And how many museums and schools have been closed! And how many industrious men of science and art have been thrown overboard! Yet the horse races were attended by 50,000 people! Shame! Shame!

The stones of all ancient monuments may well cry out against all apostates of Culture, which is the source of everything blissful and precious. Do not the defilers of Culture trample their own well-being? Even the blind ones see more than these gloomy servants of darkness. "Beware of the barbarians!"

We cannot, however, gather under an unreliable *currency*. We can unite openly upon the steps of Culture, in the name of all that is inspiring, creative, beautiful. It will always be considered a good and noble deed to support everything creative and educational. Ascending these steps, we ourselves become enlightened.

Gathering around the Sign of Culture, let us remember how we addressed Womanhood: "When there are difficulties in the home, we turn to the woman. When accounts and calculations are no longer of aid, when enmity and mutual destruction reach their limits, we turn to the woman. When one is overcome by evil forces, then the woman is invoked. When the statistical mind becomes helpless, then one remembers the woman's heart."

And so now, when times are so difficult for the universal abode of Culture, again we hope that the heart of woman will understand the grief for stymied creativeness, for Culture. She will understand how one may grieve for spiritual treasures and come to the aid of all realms of the Beautiful.

Youth should not be raised on the walls of despair. When we wrote of the predestined Beautiful Gardens, we did not lure into illusory domains. On the contrary, we invoked the strongholds affirmed by life.

In the days of distress we must especially affirm the prayer of the heart for the Beautiful. We must remember that the Beautiful is within the reach of everyone.

To rise from a shepherd lad to an honored master, as did Kuindji, or for a peasant from a remote village to become a beacon light of science, as Lomonosov did, is certainly not easy. Seemingly nothing aided them! Everything seemed to be against them, and yet—"Light conquered darkness!"

As children we enjoyed reading "Martyrs of Science" by Gaston Tissandier. Books such as "Martyrs of the Spirit," "Martyrs of Art," "Martyrs of Creativeness" should also be published.

The life dramas of Van Gogh, Gauguin, Ryder, Vrubel, Mares and many martyrs for the Beautiful constitute an additional unforgettable covenant to guide youth.

In turning over the pages of "Men Who Are Making America," how many beautiful and convincing examples record themselves forever in memory—Edison, Bell, Ford, Armor, Carnegie, Eastman, Du Pont, Schiff, Hammond —a whole host of self-made, enlightened men. How many earthly disasters they overcame, by affirming the truth that labor and creativeness were invincible. Examining the history of Art in America, are we not moved by the strong characters of Ryder, Sargent, Whistler, Thayer, Bellows, Rockwell Kent, Davies, Melchers and all those, who by their creative achievements, erected the walls of the Capitol of American Glory?

"Gratitude is the virtue of great hearts." Let us not only remember the glorious names with gratitude, but let us arm ourselves with the totality of their experience in order to confront all destructive forces of darkness.

The experience of creativeness forges all these invincible "Armors of Light" of which the Apostle speaks.

Now is an extremely urgent hour, when one must be armed with all the experience of the past, in order not to surrender the stronghold of Culture.

Now is the time to be aware of the whole spiritual treasure of creativeness, in order to repel the dark forces of ignorance with this "Armor of Light" and to move onwards fearlessly! *Per aspera ad astra!*

Is it not joyful that, notwithstanding varied partnerships, we can address every sincere artistic group with heartfelt greetings, saying: "Still, despite all kinds of disunity, the human spirit again turns to positive constructiveness, when every sincere effort toward co-operation is appreciated. Are there not numerous kinds of flowers growing upon the spring meadows and are they not superb in their variety? Does not this creative variation of form in its fragrance manifest the Festival of the Spring, which is celebrated by all people since time immemorial?"

Nothing can take the place of divine diversity. As art is the earthly reflection of Divinity, so does diversity also illustrate the bountifulness of the people's spirit. In the midst of human disaster, we feel the value of creativeness even more.

May there be the reverberation of constructiveness and the beautiful desire for the Good, in other words, of those forces which are to be set at the foundation of all of the activities of cultural humanity. Every thinking man feels the oppression of conventional divisions, shocking in their pettiness; he is suffocated by the effluvia of ignorance, by the poison of the absence of culture which disintegrates and putrefies all existence.

All for whom human dignity is precious; all who strive towards a truly preordained perfection must naturally work together, casting off the vocabulary of malice and lies as indecent tatters, remembering that in the vocabulary of Good there are many concepts that are not abstract, but really applicable to life. And how urgently these concepts must be applied in life, in order that the word cease to be an empty sound, but become the true strengthening factor of creative thought!

Everyone who strives towards the good, knows how valuable are all the so-called obstacles, which are only tests of strength to a vibrant spirit, and which by their tension, evoke a new and transmuted energy.

For we do not proclaim what was "yesterday". It is only the reality of the Future that one can proclaim. So long as we ourselves are not convinced, in our hearts, of the radiant constructiveness of the Future, we will remain in a hazy abstraction. It is for the future that trees are planted along the roadside and milestones are set up. The builder would not set up milestones if his heart did not know to where this path leads.

We affirm that the path leads to Knowledge and to the Beautiful; but a Knowledge freed from all prejudices, and irresistibly pursuing the aims of Good. We affirm that this road leads to Beauty; not luxury, nor whim but daily necessity will impel striving and the realization of the Beautiful on all paths. We shall not be afraid of the conception of reality. Those who strive in valor, know all the conditions of the path.

As the wise ones say, "On departing, one does not utter unkind words." The weak one says, "The heart has become weary." But that which lives in infinite love, striving towards realization, with the discipline of the spirit and with Beauty, will not become weary and overloaded. We increase our experience as the result of tension and the burdening of the heart. Let us be guided by the beautiful words of the Wisdom of the East:

"Make Me fatigued now, burden Me even more, lay the burden of the world upon Me.

"But I will multiply my strength.

"Dost thou hearken? The burden will blossom with roses and the grass will be cloaked in the rainbow of the morning.

"Therefore make Me tired.

"When I am approaching the Garden of Beauty, I do not fear burdens."

In wisdom, everything is real; the morning is real, the Beautiful Garden is real and the burden and weariness of the world and transfigured attainment are also real.

One cannot better conclude our contemplation of creativeness, than with the dedication of Count A. Tolstoi's "To the Artist":

> "Be thou blind as Homer and deaf as Beethoven.
> But strain more zealously Thy spiritual ear and
> spiritual eye.

And as if upon the flame of a secret writing, faint
    lines emerge suddenly,
Thus will the pictures suddenly emerge before thee.
And more vivid will become the colors and more
    perceptible the paints.
The harmonious correlation of words will interweave
    in clear meaning.
And thou, at this moment, behold, hearkening Thy
    breath
And afterwards, creating, creating—recall the fleeting
    vision."

Himalayas, July 24, 1932.

AGNI—THE TRANSMUTER

"And then—in the thundering sphere
Of an extraordinary fire,
The luminous Sword will open the gates
Of a resplendent day to us."

ALEXANDER BLOCH repeatedly spoke of his vision of rays of light, and of a fire that transmuted the World. And when Bloch was asked why he ceased to attend religious or philosophical gatherings, he answered briefly, "Because they speak of the inexpressible." I remember how he came to me for a frontispiece for his "Italian Songs." We were speaking about that Italy which no longer exists, but which, by its essence, created so many unforgettable, fiery milestones. Bloch knew these unusual fires, thundering spheres and luminous swords glowing with fire—all these milestones—as something that was absolutely real. He would not speak of them in the terms of an apothecary.

When one recalls the great fires of Reality, one always thinks of Bloch, Scriabin, and of Benois, and Andreev as among recently departed figures. Each in his own way and in his own language spoke and gave advanced notice of the great realities, which again mightily suffuse our lives. Out of a distant past people have often repeated the annals of Amos, the roaring Lion of the desert. Amos, a shepherd from Tekoa profoundly points out:

"And the fire will devour the palaces.
For evil is the time.
And shall not the earth tremble for this,
And all that dwell therein mourn."

We have remembered these words again and have had to transmute the sayings of Solomon, the most ancient covenants of the Book of Genesis, the fiery pages of the Rig Vedas, the flaming chalice of Zoroaster, and the entire extent of the never changing and already historic material which speaks of the same fire, the same dazzling Tomorrow by means of our own inspirations. Certain abysses have already been traversed; the consciousness has already come closer to the Apocalypse in which clear indications of historical and geographical significance are expressed.

People now remember, with special eagerness, the once-forgotten Nostradamus. Suddenly, as though the seals which covered his meaning have now been removed, people have become convinced, due to a series of undeniable historical facts which have taken place and are taking place under our eyes, of that which this seer foresaw 300 years ago. The visions of Swedenborg have become part of our scientific records. An Austrian professor has published a work on "Paracelsus."

Through gates opened anew, people are approaching ancient and eternal treasures of Covenants. Instead of a repulsive intolerance which leads nowhere, save to evil and dissolution, flashes of creative synthesis have appeared. A sense of the great truth, which exists forever and which has been expressed in manifold eternal metamorphoses, is apparent. Following the depressing aspect of condemnation, the understanding of the Heart, of Fire, and the Infinite, in which the structures of all enlightened souls are primarily contained, is now evident.

Tolstoy used to say, "Did you ever cross a swift river in a boat? You must row beyond your desired destination, or you will be carried downstream. So also, in the domain of moral necessities, one must always aim higher; life, in any case, invariably carries one downstream." . . . "Let him steer his rudder high," Tolstoy used to admonish my "Messenger,"* "Then he shall attain."

"Do not look into the running water," say the Mongolian

---

* The painting "The Messenger," by Nicholas Roerich is in the Tretyakov Gallery in Moscow.

lamas. From our experience in crossing the rapids of the Blue River during the thaws, we know how imperative it is not to look into the swift current, filled with cracking ice-floes. One must choose some distant point in the horizon in order not to lose one's balance. These two principles: "aim as high as possible," and "as far in the distance as possible" have always presented themselves before mankind and they do so just now with special clarity.

Ah—those rushing ice-floes are sharp, so sharp! The cold, crackling floes which startle the horses, as if ice-covered human hearts, cracking and groaning, were attempting to slash the firm steps of those who walk "more firmly and higher." Is it not against these very ice-bound hearts that the human consciousness at present turns with such swiftness towards fire? What is better to drive these ice-floes and the frozen, mirage-like torrent back, if not fire? That illuminating and warming fire upon which the resplendent swords are forged? The search for that glowing warmth, those creative and ardent torches which are so truly expressed in recourse to the great Mother of the World, also will leave their enlightening seeds after our time. In the search for warmth, for recourse to the great heart of womanhood, we also turn to the search for the center. In the heart, we shall feel that it is impossible to live any longer at the fringes; impossible to live a divided life, but that one may create only by realizing the center, the very same center, that very resplendent citadel, which has been depicted in all manner of symbols.

It would seem as though the Apocalyptic Angels had already poured out their chalices. If the most bitter of these chalices does not stir the human heart to awakening, whence shall the great flame itself turn? Must it not turn to searing? Will the awakened heart be able to transmute this burning flame into a purifying fire? And if humanity fails to realize in the name of Whom it should powerfully assemble, it will be carried along like the cracking ice-floes "of the great Blue River of Life." If these breaking ice-floes are in the Blue River, how muddy and terrifying must be the currents of the Yellow River which constantly carries away many corpses! Both the Blue and Yellow Rivers symbolize for us examples of the focus, the loss of unification, the loss of that most simple and healthy thought of spiritual enlightenment and accumulation.

On the one hand we have historic examples, and on the other the inspired writings of the poets. Nor is this metaphysics, nor abstraction—this is the very same concept in whose name the stormy and supplicating voices of the prophets resounded, as with their most glowing and evocative images, they warned mankind, who had forgotten what was "beyond" and "above."

And so mankind has entered a crisis. Mankind has none to whom to sell its wares. Mankind is ignorant of where its labor lies; nor does it find its labor. The question of unemployment has become a horrible seal of our age. Unemployment first of all is the loss of meaning of existence, a consequence of the horror of fastening one's being to the rushing ice-floes which are destined to thaw.

Man has become "specialized" in learning to screw in one little screw, thus diverting him from a realization of the meaning of existence. In his decline, man has reached the coarsest forms of life, at times coarser and more formless than stone age implements. And in the impoverishment of his spirit, man does not even attempt to withstand the current of the destined ice-floes which will carry him into the shoreless oceans of chaos.

In horror, man takes up arms against the Beautiful. He tries to impugn, to demean all that has been created, sometimes by the true transport of the spirit. Man tries to destroy Temples. Thus, it is just like the ice-floes that cut the feet of the swimming horses. Men have ceased to read and regard in wonder, when groups of youths—not modern in their opinion—nevertheless turn towards the great covenants. It would take long to enumerate all the ice-floes which are creating the terror of contemporary existence, those ice-floes which in their rage are trying to destroy everything upon their frozen path.

But no times were ever hopeless, because hopelessness would contradict Infinity. Like a great torch-bearer, the powerful Fire rises that can transmute each icefloe into a purified energy. Therefore great is the time. It is threatening but in balancing the ice with the inexhaustible fire, one may also know the way out. Of course every one is free to choose between the ice or the creative fire. One is also free to remain in that shameful middle state which causes the most suffering. "Neither cold, nor hot, but lukewarm," is said of the outcasts.

The spheres which have found the focus have begun their song, for chaos cannot sing. The music of the spheres is there where rhythm is already achieved, where the number is already found, and in this lawful arithmetic, the great rhythm which opens hearts is being born. The heart which does not know rhythm will be easily consumed, but the co-worker who creates the rhythm of existence recreates that flaming heart that becomes inexhaustible and eternally ascending, like the same great Fire of Space.

Today is the twenty-fourth, a very remarkable date. One wishes in spite of all the disturbing newspaper reports, to think of Fire, of creativeness, of the ardent heart, and of fiery thought.

"The one who is not afraid to be misunderstood by others is with Us. The one who is unafraid to build links among the great currents of the teachings is Our friend. The one who is not afraid to see the light has an eagle's eye. The one who is not afraid to enter the fire is of fiery birth. The one who is not afraid of what he cannot see can pierce the darkness. The one who is not afraid to travel the world is ready to strive to the far-off worlds. The one who is not afraid to know the teachings of wisdom is with Us.

"We renounced and thus acquired. We gave away and thus received. We deprived ourselves and thus freed ourselves from temptation. The one traveling the path of knowledge walks like the lion of the desert. Who will respond to the roar of a lion? Only another lion, free of fear.

"Where then are the bonds? Where then are the chains? Knowledge of the far-off worlds will forge the crown of achievement." (Agni Yoga, 481.)

"Three flames. Then the Chalice of Attainment." (Agni Yoga, 465.)

Thus Agni Yoga calls towards Valor and Knowledge.

Urusvati, Himalayas, January 24, 1932.

THE RESISTANCE TO EVIL

"DEPART from evil and create good," ordains the Apostolic wisdom. In this short canon are contained two definite actions: "Depart" and "Create." Here "create" does not mean only a departure. No! "Depart" *and* unfailingly "create good." The departure from evil alone is but half the work. But one must also "create," make, build well, as a counterbalance to evil. It is indicated, thus tersely and absolutely, to create bliss. Without action, without consciousness, without striving of the spirit, there can be no achievement and fulfillment of the covenant. But how often for the sake of self-satisfaction, this vigorous and commanding covenant has been transformed into a bitter departure, inflexible in essence! If one departs, is the good already created? No, dear readers; would this not be too easy? For the good, it is necessary also to exert all the forces of spirit and body. The good is not a nut, demanding only a strong tooth. Good will be created, not out of thoughtlessness nor a lethargic consciousness. The plowed lands of good must be sowed and harvested according to the covenants of the Apostle, in the true omniscient Knowledge of life. And let us raise another question: When is there more sweat upon the brow—during the season of sowing or of harvest? The very same untiring call toward active labor is spread through all the apostolic calls because evil by its nature is active. It departed from good and by this departure it already manifested the substance of activity; this means that the counterbalance must also be active. Evil is self-assertive because it cannot otherwise attract to itself. So also must good and bliss assert themselves, because without works, these are dead.

The Apostle ordains that one must not battle with evil, thereby exalting the enemies, but one should creatively build bliss. Light does not battle with darkness but consumes it and forces it out. But for such a victory, an attacking swiftness of light is demanded. And what swiftness and irresistibility!

The Apostle ordains a noble resistance to evil through the construction of an act of great bliss which like light, pierces and disperses the darkness of evil. Of course without resistance and aggressive action, evil will inevitably overtake retreating bliss, because all space is filled. By retreating we therefore enlarge the field of the enemy.

How then to define evil? The Eastern wisdom defines it in the following way: "The resistance to evil is manifested as one of the fundamental qualities of those who seek Hierarchy. No physical property offers resistance to evil, but the spirit and the fire of the heart create an armor before the cunning of evil. But how to understand evil? Of course, it is, first of all, destruction. But the replacing of a new and better house for a crumbling one is not destruction. Destruction means decomposition which brings a chaotic condition. One must know how to resist such decomposition. It is necessary to find strength of the spirit to conquer the fear which is characteristic of non-resistance to evil. Thus let them be ready to resist evil."

So also wisdom forewarns: "Are there not enough earthquakes? Are there not enough disasters, storms, frosts, and excessive heat? Has not the fiery cross been raised? Have not the stars shone by day? Has not the fiery rainbow glowed? Are there not enough signs which continue to multiply? But mankind does not wish to know the manifestation before the reality amidst chaos. Thus Let us not insist upon a visible sign when doubt has blinded the people. But amidst the blind and deaf ones are the children of Fire. To them we are sending the signs by which they should discern the approach of Light."

Thus without the realization of what happens without activity, we shall again succumb to evil. Again we shall touch the senseless destruction with the disgusting return to what is amorphous and unmanifested. Who has the right to return into the darkness of chaos that which has already been manifested by the greatest creativeness? Who in the name of darkness can then extinguish the light?

And was it not indicated to form and deepen one's consciousness by means of actions? Without consciousness, how shall we understand where is bliss? Sir James Jeans has remarked that if typewriters were given to monkeys, perhaps, in a million years of unceasing and accidental thumping, they would also type out a sonnet of Shakespeare. But what would be the value of this unconscious thumping?

A blind archer who shoots his arrows into space may also sometimes get his prey but he shall not be party to this success.

For millions of years mankind has filled space with arrows, but only a few of them are sent consciously in the name of bliss. And therefore, instead of crowding out the darkness, the disturbance and self-destruction is great. Let us examine with full conscience whether mankind has solved its daily problems. Just the opposite. All are in debt, materially and spiritually; all are over-mortgaged, so one cannot even establish where is the end and the beginning of this universal mortgage. Even materially-minded people have lost account of their possessions because they have subjected them to an unlimited amount of burdens invented by themselves. It is as though wishing mechanically to foresee all possible conditions of a business contract, they had calculated five-fourths instead of four-fourths to a whole. Without the realization of bliss the meaning of outlines is being lost.

What then is bliss? If evil is decomposition and lethargy, then bliss must be construction, creativeness, complete understanding of general usefulness. The same wisdom ordains: "Labor, create bliss, revere the Hierarchy of

Light. One may inscribe Our canon even upon the palm of a new-born child. Thus the beginning which leads to light is not complicated. In order to accept it, one must have a pure heart." And still further: "I shall tell the zealots and hypocrites about treason. They regard treason only as a matter of thirty shekels, but they forget that it exists in every blasphemy and slander. One should not think that a hateful word is not treason. Namely, malice is often inseparable from treason and slander. The same black tree nurtures these shameful branches. And the fruits shall be as black as the roots of shame. It is necessary to tear oneself from the horror of malicious words."

Thus is the darkness of evil distinguished from creative bliss. One of the most interesting chapters in technological studies is the one concerning the resistance of materials. One can easily translate these calculations into the language of human relationships and receive instructive conclusions about the vitality of resistance. Whoever wants to die shall die most easily of all. Vitality is comprised in wholeness, in motion, in the permeation of space. Permeating the space with bliss, with the sendings and thoughts of bliss, we receive cosmic re-enforcement for our resistance to evil. In this magnetization is received an energy which grows unlimitedly: therefore bliss-creation is the most worthy and practical occupation. And how many possibilities, great and small, measurable and immeasurable, in themselves contain bliss-creation! And how many purely medicinal values the prophylaxis of bliss contains in itself! Besides, in its substance, bliss-creativeness, like progressive energy, directs us unalterably forward. In this sacred progression, no darkness is feared.

Let us not forget that the very same apostolic wisdom which speaks about "the consoling spirit," also affirms "the indignation of spirit." Without this sacred indignation the waters will not revolt and no healings will occur.

You know that at night the most active safeguard against leopards and tigers is a powerful electric light. The spawn of darkness retreat in dread and disappear, when the flood of light is directed unflinchingly into their eyes. The human heart irradiates a still more powerful light: This ray transfixes darkness, if the indignant spirit has lanced it unwaveringly without gray doubts.

The "deadly eye" of the Yogi is indomitable when he defends Bliss. But the Yogi is not a Yogi if he falters in bliss. The chief thing is not to extinguish the "electric" light of the heart. Before its glow, all the spawn of darkness will retreat. They will retreat and bring upon themselves all that they prepare against Bliss. Resistance to evil will be that noble action which was ordained by the highest Teaching. From the noble magnetization of energy is born that exalted refinement which is manifested by the foundation of Culture.

Kyelang, July, 1931.

RE-EVALUATION

IN the remote Himalayas, newspapers have reached us.
In one we read that more than two thousand banks in
the United States have discontinued operations. Another
informs us of the failure of a powerful bank in Switzerland.
The third announces the closing of banks in Ger-many,
Austria and Hungary. And finally the news that the gold
standard has been abandoned.

Well, well! Let us remember what we wrote ten years
ago about "heaps of valueless banknotes," in the full
meaning of this word. Is it not time to remember the tales
related of the first revolutions in Germany and Russia;
when people who had huge fortunes in paper money, suddenly realized to their horror that their assumed fortunes
were in fact only paper when instead of spending money to
print labels for beer bottles, the brewers preferred to paste
banknotes of high denominations on their bottles. And in
our collections we still have German postage stamps of a
face-value of twenty billion German Reichsmarks. How
much further may one go?

These are not fairytales, but living facts. Yet even
during these times of paper disaster, good old Rembrandt
never betrayed his collectors. And it never entered anyone's head to label beer-bottles with original creations of
artists. Thus, even during the most difficult times, the
human spirit never forgot the true, irreplaceable values
of mankind. Perhaps humanity remembered these values
only dimly as in a dream, overcoming with reticence the
entire heritage of prejudice and ignorance; nevertheless, it
did recall them. And even persons of the most desperately

negative character, although remaining silent, never dared to contradict that which constitutes the whole meaning and purpose of human life.

Until quite recently humanity professed an unusual reverence and esteem for bankers. They were at times even elected as members of Governments. True, these Governments did not last long and passed without a trace into oblivion. Financiers should not take this statement to mean that we are altogether against them. Among them we know quite a number of very cultured persons who devote much of their time to educational problems. And one should not forget that these cultured representatives of the financial world have responded very quickly to true values at times. I remember how one of them told me, "And yet I would prefer to have a collector of art objects for a son-in-law; after all, it is safer."

Of course when we speak of collecting an object we should understand its inner quality. We do not mean the common purchasers of art objects who show their outer prosperity by a certain display of furniture and bibelots which are brought to their home by obliging antique dealers. We mean of course those true collectors who build up their treasury in the name of the beautiful, in the name of the imperative demand of their dynamic spirits, those who impress their individuality upon the characters of their collections, thus proving themselves to be true co-creators. We should take off our hats before such preservers of values.

One may only wish that all storms of life should pass by such collectors without affecting them in any way and that each revolt of ignorance should bring them new possibilities and new energy.

We cannot follow the laws of life of artistic creations. Beyond the boundaries of seeming coincidences, we invariably meet the great Cosmic Justice. Amidst dazzling snow-white peaks it is difficult to discern which is higher and stronger, but each of them is subject to unchanging laws. This is similar with human creations. Who can follow this most intricate complex of the conditions of creativeness? But it is not for us to judge them. We should but rejoice and be uplifted in spirit while approaching the constructions of Beauty. With great care, we should guard their existence, for we cannot think like those who consoled themselves: *"Après nous—le déluge!"* We are responsible for these creative treasures.

Someone interposes, "We already know all this." No, my dear one you do not know this; for if you knew it you would construct your lives differently. But if you do know this and do not apply this valuable Knowledge into life, the worse it is for you. For your sake, let us think that you are not aware of these values. But if you insist that you knew all this long ago, we must regretfully classify you as ignoramuses! For only the ignoramus lightheartedly judges and condemns. And the same ignoramus is primarily most gullible; he accepts all paper values, each beer-label, just because his grandfather drank from the same bottle or because the beer-labels are bought by gentlemen in shiny top-hats and ladies who, despite their figures, annually change the fashion of their dress.

What further disasters are needed in order that the gullible and light-minded should listen to the voices of their hearts, which in some sleepless hour of dawn, whisper to them that truth is not interwoven with top hats, nor with a new fashion of dress that makes even walking difficult.

But the laws of life forge an immutable evolution. It is the greatest happiness to see how, despite all prejudices and superstitions, life builds its steps and evinces the significance of creative labor.

By speaking of the re-evaluation of values, we perhaps use an inexact expression. We should simply say evaluation of values, for by re-evaluation we imply the acknowledgment of values which after all have never really been accepted as such.

How useful is the study of history, especially when we can liberate ourselves from preconceived, conventional ideas and purify our thinking for a true understanding. Again and again, let us remember precisely what monuments and what types of deeds the history of the world records as worthy and transmits as its heritage to future generations. Unbiased history has long ago given us a true appraisal of values. Then why make up and whisper conceitedly about changed conditions of living? The value of the heart, the value of the Beautiful, the value of Knowledge is always identical and precious. History does not preserve beer labels; through all its appealing symbols, it untiringly teaches us where the true, indestructible value lies. Each bit of news about the crash of conventional values is nothing save a new knock of fate at the door. Remember those persistent knocks of fate in Beethoven's Symphony. Just as inexorably will Cosmic Justice knock at the doors of mankind until the human heart opens towards the joyous realization of true, indestructible values.

But let us never conclude with regrets. Not all people care for top hats, not all are devoted to the conventionalism of their attire. We know that the hearts of the great masses of humanity are striving to move from the conventional to the real, are striving instinctively and often semi-consciously towards the covenants of sublime Teachings. And not only the hearts of the widespread masses, but also the child's heart is always open to the Beautiful as long as it is not besmirched by the experiences of life. In the name of this child's heart which is open to the assimilation of everything beautiful, which is ready to accept true values, we send our best thoughts. And great is the host of these striving co-workers, visible and invisible. Therefore, neither the crashes of thousands of banks, nor a tempest of cancelled and cremated banknotes, can upset us; instead they will fill our consciousness with the radiant dawn of true values.

THE URGENCY OF THE HOUR

IMITATION and simulation are signs of a demand; copying is the answer to a necessity. From the very inception of our cultural institutions, we had no doubt that, with their success, we would see all kinds of imitations of them as well as the borrowing of their ideas. By this method, men express their homage. During the very time when the dark, uncultured forces acutely resent everything which reminds them of the existence of that Culture which they so despise, other elements, desiring to identify themselves in some manner with the movements of culture, begin to imitate whatever has already expressed itself in life. A limited mentality is often wrathful at imitation and simulation; but this is precisely unworthy of the realization of culture. On the contrary, one should rejoice at each evidence of simulation and imitation. Permit all kinds of cultural centers to grow. Some may be enriched with money; others grow through a deepened consciousness and fire of the heart; Let each one progress accordingly, if only they avoid deadening limitation.

It is not simulation and imitation which are terrible, and which we can observe and over which we can rejoice. Terrible are the breeding places of ignorance where the pronunciation of the word "Culture" is forbidden—where, because of the limitations of the mind, the desire to destroy all who think and express culture dwells. It is sad that these fossilized monsters of a prehistoric epoch still survive. By their dark powers, they try to harm culture as well as those who are its representatives. To our sorrow, we have evidence that such dark forces still exist. And not only do they vegetate under the cover of their casually-acquired social positions, but they even attempt to consider themselves the "Voice of the people," thus indicting humanity with the heinous and unjust stigma of ignorance.

The true voice of the people is the expression of the people's consciousness. In its substance this consciousness is always progressive, because all civilization has been created precisely through its offices. Of course, under the term "people's consciousness" we do not refer to something quantitative; it is expressed through quality and through the minority. But such a minority seemingly appears as the hidden potentiality of mankind, and therefore these leaders, this sacred legion of Heroes, must be verily regarded as the treasure of the people. For in due time, in the hour of difficulty, the people's consciousness invariably puts forward and leans upon these Bearers of its pan-human, heartfelt wishes.

Special signs mark these focuses of the heartfelt thought of the people. The dark forces, which fundamentally spread disunion and destruction and a return to chaos, are especially incensed at the glowing manifestations of Light. The stake of Jeanne d'Arc; the guillotine of Lavoisier; the burning of Giordano Bruno; the martyrdom of Hypatia, and of all other countless evidences of the inexplicable wrath against the heroes of culture, appear to us as contemporaneous signs of recognition by the dark forces of that which threatens their dark kingdom with destruction.

It is time for us to have lists, not only of the friends of Culture but also of its enemies. Their oblivion does not permit the adequate picture of the true circumstance of things for history. It is not enough to assume that the dark, anti-cultural forces were active; one should be aware of their forces. Unexpectedly among them, names eminent in the various branches of life will appear. Such information will facilitate the precision of future historical writings. It is useful that history has preserved the name of the destroyer, Herostratus.

Without succumbing to truisms or sentimentality,

we must admit that the present upheavals threaten the destruction of all cultural concepts. It is a sad fact that a general financial and economic crisis is usually reflected first upon the entire domain of education. The people fear to reduce or do away with the manufacture of poisonous gases, but with distinct ease they are ready to close educational institutions or, at least, to reduce the salaries of the hard-working employee in the field of education. One may quote many of the saddest instances in human history, where the numbers of the unemployed and starving greatly increased, while at the same time the precious seed was destroyed and the ingress to national riches was closed through fear of overproduction. Yet overproduction itself is no more than a sign of petty thinking and the back of observation. But conventional standards are so greatly shaken that even the Golden Calf, the Valuta of Gold, is wiped away without the substitution of some other conditional sign. The shaking of such a conventional stronghold as gold, only indicates the degree of obsessed agitation and confusion.

It is precisely now, notwithstanding all the assaults of the dark forces, that the thinking circles of humanity must urgently turn towards the realization of culture. This is not the time for the workers and for those striving for culture to permit any barriers between themselves. This is not the time for dogmatic discussions, for rivalries, for quarrels behind each other's backs. This is the time for the urgent building, construction, assembling of all forces which, though done only partially and imperfectly, can be carried out in the name of culture. It is necessary to forget all the crudeness, the attacks and conflicts. Why think of these?

It is necessary to hasten, with all means, to replace the ragged standards with vital and strong foundations of creativeness and of high quality. It is sad to see how at times those who might be in agreement, often seek to resurrect the memories of dead, malicious offenses and contentions. He who in himself finds the spiritual force to forget all pettiness and discomfort for the sake of general construction shall thereby express the most vital need of the present hour.

The necessities of our life, which at times could have been expressed in terms of years, now, because of their acceleration, must be measured by a day or even an hour. In the same hastened way, the striving towards the unification of all those who can think of Culture, who dream not of abstractions, but who feel inwardly the potentiality of applying this creative thought in action without fearing all the bovine derision, the venomous darts and the cudgels of contemporary barbarians must also be measured.

Hence, he who within himself finds the strength of construction and of unification will express the urgency of the Hour.

1932.

SYNTHESIS

ONLY the most all-inclusive and most clearly understood synthesis can create the benevolent cooperation of which humanity is at present so greatly in need. From the highest representatives of our spiritual world to the most materialistic shopkeeper, everyone agrees that without real co-operation, no activity can be created. We see in the Culture of whole countries, that wherever a broad synthesis is understood and allowed, the creativeness of the country bears fruit and advances beautifully. No separation, no chauvinism, can create such progress as is attained by the radiant smile of synthesis.

Let us not regard this statement as a useless truism. At this time many concepts have been totally perverted through misunderstanding or through a personal desire to give some casual meaning to the concept. Beginning with the very highest concepts, one may say, even of God down to the smallest personal feelings, how often ideas are maliciously mutilated and misconstrued!

What should humanity do in such cases of evident distortion of its fundamental conceptions? Should it not purge them immediately and restore them to their simple, original meanings? One may certainly create entirely new conceptions and expressions, but it is absolutely inadmissible to attach to old conceptions, established centuries ago, new meanings inspired by egoism. If the latter be permitted, life, instead of becoming more refined and more fittingly designed, will turn into unbearable chaos and into a confusion of tongues, of which the Bible speaks so symbolically in the tower of Babel. Of course, everything progresses; life requires new definitions for its discoveries and for the circumstances created by them. We have new names for rays, gases, various energies, planets and for everything that was unknown yesterday. Let us create these new definitions, being careful that they be expressive, impelling and beautiful. Perhaps some entirely new language will be created. This may be so, and we will understand and accept it; but it would be a great mistake to give new, arbitrary and often presumptuous meanings to old concepts, created and ordained to us by the Culture of the past; this would lead to regrettable and prolonged consequences. This would be a peculiar move towards disunity and decomposition, whereas it is the duty of every thinking being to serve the creation of synthesis, co-operation and the construction of Good.

A study of all misused and perverted expressions would no doubt form a considerable scientific work. Let us hope that someone may work on this subject, which is of such importance to humanity. Just now I would like to clarify the definition of two concepts that one meets daily. We often speak of those significant concepts: Culture and civilization. To our surprise we find that even these thoughts, which seem to have such subtle roots, have also already been subject to misrepresentation and distortion. For example, up to now, many people consider it fit to replace the word Culture with civilization, forgetting completely that the very Latin root *Cult* has a very deep spiritual significance, whereas civilization has as its root a civic social structure of life. It seems quite clear that every country passes through certain social steps, viz. civilization, which in its highest synthesis forms the eternal and indestructible concept of Culture . As we see from many examples, civilization may perish, they may be altogether annihilated, but Culture creates its great heritage upon indestructible spiritual tablets which sustain the future generation. Every maker of standardized articles, every manufacturer is of course already a civilized person; but no one would insist that the owner of every factory is necessarily a cultured person. And it may easily happen that one of the subordinate workmen in the factory may undoubtedly be the transmitter of Culture, whereas the owner himself may still remain only within the bounds of civilization. One may easily imagine a "Home of Culture," but a "Home of Civilization" would sound absurd. The concept of "cultural worker" is quite definite, but "civilized worker" means something entirely different. Every university professor will be very satisfied to be called a "cultural worker," but try to call the honorable professor a "civilized worker"; every scholar, every creator would feel an inner uneasiness with this title, if not even an offense. We know the expressions "civilization of Greece," "civilization of Egypt," "civilization of France," but they do not in the least exclude the concept, far greater in its immutability, of the Great Culture of Egypt, Greece, Rome, France. . . .

In a previous article on Culture, I defined Culture as the Cult of Light. After all, we need not give up this definition. *Cult* will always remain the adoration of the principle of Good, and the word *Ur* reminds us of the old Eastern root, which always means Light, Fire. But perhaps I am too enthusiastic about the concept of Culture; therefore let us turn to more prosaic definitions of dictionaries and encyclopedias. Webster defines civilization as a civic act or a civilized condition, and as a relative advancement in social culture. The same dictionary defines Culture as an act of improving and developing by education, discipline, etc.; the enlightenment and discipline acquired by mental and moral training; refinement; the characteristic attainments of people or social order, as "Greek Culture."

Hastings' "Encyclopedia of Ethics" omits the word civilization altogether, as not entering into the sphere of higher ethical concepts; he devotes the following lines to "Culture": "To Bacon the world is indebted for the term, as well as for the philosophy of culture (Advancement of Learning, 1605, 11 XIX, 2). While of itself, the notion of culture may be broad enough to express all forms of spiritual life in man—intellectual, religious and ethical—it is best understood intensively as humanity's effort to assert its inner and independent being. This effort is observed in a series of contrasts, due to the division of man's functions into intellectuality and effectiveness. The most general contrast is that between nature and spirit, with its dualism of animality and humanity. With the ideal of Culture, man is led to live a life of contemplation, rather than one of conquest, while his attention is directed towards the remote rather than towards the immediate. Viewed socially, culture is contrasted with industrial occupation, the two differing in their valuation of work."

Thus we see that in speaking of Culture as of the adoration of Light, we have but synthesized the existing definition.

Should someone ignorantly insist that the concept of Culture is connected only with Physical Culture, he will simply show his limitations. If anyone will recollect some previous unfortunate misuse of this lofty concept, he will simply cut off all possibilities of development, refinement of consciousness and containment for himself. We have met with a very definite understanding of these two concepts among people. The masses consider everyone who wears a white collar a civilized man, often even mispronouncing this word, which they have heard somewhere; every literate person is already civilized; thus, although in primitive form, the first principles of a civil state are correctly understood. But above this civil state so easily reached, all people of the world feel the existence of something higher to which every searching human spirit invariably strives. For this higher concept even the most primitive peoples have their own word, which will tell you of mutual understanding, of a more elevated spirituality, of higher knowledge and of joy of the spirit. Those will not be merely clerical conceptions, but they will correspond exactly to our concept, inherited by us from great discoveries of the Latin Culture. Perhaps we might take the same concept from Chinese or Tibetan writings, but the West has been enlightened by Latin sources of this great concept; therefore we can at present pervert it only to placate those who would like to willfully use or distort it.

For some reasons everyone easily understands the definition of a "World-Day of Culture," but a world-day of civilization may be interpreted in a rather strange way and perhaps even comically. The example of the relationship of these two accepted concepts, Culture and Civilization, reminds us how many such correlations have been forgotten or misused. We know how many ancient commandments require a new translation, since many definitions of our recent past turn out to be either vague or primitive because we must not forget that the end of the 19th century did not contribute much towards the refinement of scientific and philosophical terms. But now we are at the gates of a most significant time, at a time of conscious synthesis, when no distorted, temporary conglomerations should obstruct our striving towards Light and towards unconstrained Knowledge.

Some feel that the pronouncement of the word Culture implies conceit and vanity. But this is not so; on the contrary, all that strives towards perfection is in itself opposed to ignorant conceit. He who is conceited, being self-centered, does not move, but one who is searching strives and is ready to defend culture against all attacks of ignorance, if only to move untiringly along the Path of Light. This Light is not an abstract concept. The discoveries of our great scientists now tell us of immediate possibilities, which only a quarter of a Century ago appeared as an unattainable utopia, and evoked, even in the scientific institutions of that time, smiles of pity. There are unfortunately too many examples of this. But we are happy to see how the evolution of humanity, even proceeding through peculiar paths, rapidly alters the meaning of the whole contemporary civilization. This step will be followed by a growth of the accumulations of Culture. And if men will begin to think of Culture, begin actively to introduce the sacred concept of Culture into daily life, this certainly should not be considered as conceit, but as proof of their readiness for higher containment.

This benevolent synthesis will help to bring into life elevated, healthy concepts and will teach us to absorb and apply all which yesterday seemed to be an abstract absurdity, an inapplicable awkwardness, or simply ridiculous from the point of view of conventional habits, prejudice and superstition. Has not prejudice and superstition spoiled so many beautiful concepts? And the young generation now has to valiantly uplift the forgotten treasures, in the name of a better and more radiant life!

Himalayas, December 6, 1931.

TESTING STRENGTH

RISHI NARADA undertook the difficult role of the great debater for himself, provoking an interchange of opinion, thereby proving the strength of his heroic effort through the practice of resistance. Ancient history in its various aspects has repeatedly disclosed the significance of forces which oppose the forces of Good as a means of consciously evoking the tension of energy necessary for the process of creation. The blacksmith needs an anvil to forge the sword which serves as a weapon of achievement. The tension of the anvil which eventually results in the sure stroke of the sword, is as significant as the labor of giants who bear the burden of the whole universe on their shoulders. It would be unwise to attribute these manifestations of conscious opposition to the good only to the realm of Evil. Evil as such may feel as disturbed over such manifestations as it does over those of Absolute Good. For evil understands that the basic meaning of these is Good. Thus the underlying principle is invoked as an immediate tool to be utilized for constructive work, whereas the principle of evil has as its purpose only deterioration, in order to increase chaos. If Good means the loftiest art for art's sake, then conscious Evil to no less a degree desires to destroy and decompose for the sake of decomposition itself, since decomposition is accompanied by decay.

When we speak of enemies—and not only speak of them but also feel the pressure of their assaults—let us first examine them well and be sure that we do not mistake decomposition and decay for the anvil. There may be a certain resemblance between these two ideas in many of their manifestations, but in their inner significance, as proven by the immediate deed, they are entirely different. When the so-called basic principle is Good, it multiplies the sparks caused by the forging of the sword, and as such, it frequently disappears without a trace, merging ultimately into the volume of accomplished constructive Good. But the evil forces do not willingly disappear; they remain in themselves a constant force for breeding of evil, leaving unmistakable traces of the virus of deterioration, ultimately resulting in chaos and inertia. What then, is it that Evil wants to cause? Not a stronghold of achievement, but the effluvia of decay. It tends to transform the human spirit into a swarm of creeping worms, which in their crawling, slimy inchoateness drag that which has already begun to take shape from out of the chaos into the mire. Of course, each of us is aware of the difficulties and travail of the task of creating out of chaos, and in comparison, how swiftly the shameful process of retrogression into the original formlessness is accomplished.

Let us apply all that has been said thus far to our own circumstances. No one must imagine that I would attempt, even in the slightest degree, to compare the problem of Rishi Narada with the blackmail attempted by some of our discharged employees and other disseminators of darkness. Let these ignoramuses be relegated to the function of the "Turk" at the fair in the market place who challenges people to try their strength against him. Let them be mere "testers of strength" and serve after their own fashion to strengthen the principle of Good. Verily, testing stones and building materials are multiform. All sorts of pipes, shavings, and anvils find their way into the walls of a building with the Knowledge of the builder, but let us not express glee over the numerous testers of strength who present themselves. It is only the passer-by at the fair who boasts that his strength forced the "Turk" to stick out his tongue. Builders are not in the least concerned about the kind of convulsions that contort the features of these ignoramuses. Such contortions may even give them grounds for thought, making them think of things that might otherwise have never occurred to them. The builders must hurry to complete the building so as not to leave the building uncovered when winter sets in with its rains and severe storms. The efforts of the challengers of strength are one thing, but the negligence of leaving the gates unlocked by night belongs in an entirely different category. Let the Guiding Will send as many testers of strength as necessary, but let us not try to waste someone's energy only by forgetfulness or light-mindedness.

There is a great and lofty responsibility in wisely utilizing the tests of our strength without permitting any negligence or disrespect toward the thing which we ourselves consider within the scope of the desired Culture. Let us take, for example, the history of entire States. What do we find? Have they sustained injuries solely from external enemies or did they themselves primarily contribute to their disparagement and destruction by their own inner measures? "Seek more closely"—these wise words are the utterance of sages. Why should so many hopes be set and accusations heaped upon the testers of strength? Are there not circumstances instrumental in creating troubles right in the house and at its very hearth, which add difficulties to the conditions? When the ancients decreed: "Keep your hearth in cleanliness, keep it in holiness," they certainly did not intend it to apply solely and literally to the hearth. Indeed, this was one of the wise indications of the significance of spirit with its many accumulated strata that are ofttimes hardly noticeable when segregated, but which lead to irreparable and often severe consequences. Thus, first and above all, seek closer. And if anyone, instead of making the "Turk" stick out his tongue, smashes his fist against him without achieving the desired results, let him not blame the tester of strength, but the inaccuracy and inadequacy of his own stroke. Even at a fair, a more experienced passer-by, before preparing his blow, looks well, so as to gauge the distance and not become the laughing-stock of the onlookers. When soldiers are training with clay dummies, it is noticed that very often the inexperienced warrior breaks his weapon against the soft clay dummy without any effect. To this, an experienced observer would remark: "Why, you idiot, your stroke is like a wood-cutter's; it is not the force of the stroke that counts, but its skillful aim." The novice, after breaking his weapon, puzzles over how the sharpened blade could split in striking such a soft substance. But he soon learns that it is much more difficult to cut flexible rods than the dead branch of an oak tree. Hence, remember examples of war even in times of peace for strategy is an accomplishment of life itself and not one that should come from without. And finally, again seek more closely to you, especially when you want to look into the distance.

The good does not imply formlessness, "gelatinousness" nor day-dreaming. It means striving, determination, constructiveness of the mind and heart, as well, in all it, Infiniteness. And in this Infiniteness so many things find a new place for themselves. It is precisely the heart with its broad understanding that will appreciate where the indisputable, constructive and creative effort exists.

THE CLOSED EYE

A CHARACTERISTIC episode in the field of Archeology comes to my mind: Twenty-five years ago when we found anthropomorphic images of the Stone Age, within the boundaries of the Novgorod and Tver districts, Professor N. Veselovsky, at a session of the Imperial Russian Archeological Society, pronounced the exhibited objects as false. Not having any proofs for his assertion, Professor Veselovsky mentioned that discoveries of such great significance had never been previously made, and that the workers during their excavating could have planted them. Neither the delicate technique of these objects nor my contention that the planting of them could only have been carried out with a mercenary aim, while our workers did not even examine and certainly did not understand the meaning of the discovered objects, served to influence the elder member of the Imperial Archeological Commission, and Professor Veselovsky; he maintained his own opinion. But the next year, unhindered by the usual ethics, Professor Veselovsky with a group of archeologists, went to the sites of my excavations and discovered similar anthropomorphic figures amongst the Stone Age objects. When, however, at the session of the Archeological Society, Professor Veselovsky announced his remarkable discoveries, I, following his example, asked whether the honorable professor did not regard his discoveries also as false? Naturally, Professor Veselovsky indignantly began to support their authenticity and the great significance of these discoveries. I was therefore compelled to ask him again whether his opinion was correct this year or last.

I also remember another episode, this time in the field of the collection of paintings. Once a painting was brought to me which suggested Rembrandt not only because of its signature but also because of the technique. Seriously doubting its authenticity, I showed it to the eminent connoisseur of the Dutch School, a member of the Imperial Council, Semenov Tan-Shansky, who not only pronounced this painting an original, but also expressed the most enthusiastic desire to buy it. The same attribution of this painting was also made by another known collector, S. Since the owner of the painting demanded an immediate decision, it was necessary to buy the painting without further consideration. But my doubts did not subside and after a detailed examination of the painting, I became convinced that the board did not correspond to the period and that the painting itself, although made by a talented artist, did not belong with the signature which it had. However, the painting was not hung.

But my friends did not forget the matter. One day the collector S. insistently asked: "Where is that Painting?" to which I answered, "Unfortunately it is not an original."

"Splendid," replied my friend. "If you consider that it is not an original, then sell it to me, because I know how much you paid for it."

"The board is not sufficiently aged," I answered, "and in any event I could not sell a painting which I do not regard as an original."

My friend replied, "In the first place, the painting could have been transferred onto a new board and, in the Second place, well, good-bye, I am in a hurry."

Two hours had not passed after this conversation when a messenger arrived with a letter from my friend and two paintings of the Dutch School. My friend wrote, "I ask you to accept from me, as a gift and a memento, the two Paintings sent herewith. If, however, you would care to reciprocate, do not refuse to give me the very painting which you do not regard as original. I would want to have only this gift."

There was no choice but to fulfill his stubborn wish and the collector became very proud of this new addition to his collection, about which he spoke to all friends who gathered at his home. Winking at me, he would always announce, "And this painting Nikolai Konstantinovitch considers as not original," whereupon he made a belittling gesture with his hand.

Such episodes are also found in the field of painting: For example, I once saw a beautiful Jan Victors with a complete signature transformed into a Rembrandt and with written credentials. Also in the world of archeology: A bronze idol was once found in a kurgan with a museum number. One could quote very many similar episodes in all countries. The Epic of the Tiara of Saitaferne and the Kluzelski findings, or the inscriptions in an unknown language from Afghanistan, are alone sufficiently characteristic.

I recall these instances not for the purpose of saying that Professor Veselovsky or Semenov Tan-Shansky or Solomon Reinach or Aurel Stein are poor judges. Certainly not. We do not live by condemnation. One only recalls the inexhaustible possibility of mistakes that are especially unavoidable when jealousy and partiality dominate what should be an impartial research work and judgment. Just now the newspapers announce that an expedition has found a Chaldean tribe in the Himalayas! How many such winged idle tales flutter over the world distracting minds and dragging with them the possibilities of what might have led to important discoveries. One must not undermine people's confidence because all enthusiasm has to possess the element of confidence, but how necessary it is to weigh this confidence with truth in order not to undermine reality by even the smallest violation of truth.

Here, for instance, Mr. H-r and similar "art connoisseurs" say that I could not have painted all my paintings. Its error, substance and its ignorance make this statement not only ridiculous but stupid. But if we look back, to our amazement, we find similar occurrences more than once. Of course all these curiosities remain in the category of historic anecdote, but they show how uninventive is the thinking of slanderers who, since ancient times, have worked according to the very same formulae. Most curious of all is that not only H-r and his inspirers have invented such ideas, but I must say that a similar invention was made more than once, and most curious, from the time when I attended the Academy of Art. Already at that time it was alleged that some unknown person was painting my paintings for me. Already—at that time with regard to this legend—I had to say, "Of course; why to trouble myself when one can order paintings to be painted by outstanding artists?"

Yaremitch in his article, "At the Sources of Creativeness," tells the interesting fact of how an art critic once stated that I made use of one of the paintings of Vasnyetzov. As a matter of fact it appeared that my painting was completed prior to the work of Vasnyetzov; neither Vasnyetzov nor I would have presumed otherwise, as also was established by Yaremitch. I remember how my teacher Kuindji always smiled when such tales reached him. And he had a full right to smile indulgently at these legends, because a unique legend was also invented about him: It was whispered that he had killed the reputed artist Kuindji and seized all his paintings. But that he himself probably knew nothing about the art of painting, and that he was not Kuindji. The end of this legend also touched me, when in London in 1920 "authoritative people" informed me that I had died in Siberia; and there also, exactly ten years afterwards, one scientist asked me in great secrecy, "But, your name is not Roerich, but K—?" And such mistakes happen! It is even a pity that we cannot trace the original sources of such fiction. Probably one would be amazed at the page of such original creativeness. Probably they are altogether not unlike the Tibetan nam-tar[*] about us, which praised our valor; which related how we, unscathed, advanced in the face of all bullets, baring

---

[*]   A Tibetan Ballad.

our chests—even such detail is included—in order to show the absence of a protective armor. And this invention was not discovered in an ordinary way. A British colonel gave us this information from Lhassa.

Quite acutely, evil intention, error, legend, and credence are converging. Sometimes it is impossible to define the border between well-intentioned belief from subtle, evil intent. One is reminded of Hoffman's "Errors" with their fantastic good humor. Well, let creativeness blossom. At the end, the chaff is separated, but let the consciousness safeguard one from errors which can only contaminate space.

Looking back at the roots of error, let us not forget that one of the most formidable among them is the "closed eye." Examples of "closed eyes" are sometimes astonishing and if they did not actively appear in life, it would often be inconceivable to admit such possibilities

Let us close with an instance from our archeological journeys. While studying an ancient monastery which was lying outside of the usual byways, we found in the middle of the monastery courtyard, an ancient stone cross half-buried, but with beautiful carvings that were well-preserved. I asked the abbot of the monastery to let me have this cross for the Museum, since, although it was in a central place, it apparently invited no one's care. The abbot was very much surprised and first said to me, "There is no ancient cross in the monastery courtyard." I continued to insist and invited the abbot to go with me to the courtyard. The abbot, accompanied by the Treasurer and other members of the Brotherhood, went to the courtyard and stopped before the cross in open amazement. Thereupon, the abbot made this unforgettable statement, "Cross! Certainly a cross! Lord, for twenty years I have walked on this spot and never noticed the cross." For a monastery and its head not to notice a cross is a remarkable sign of "closed eyes." Similarly, in one very distinguished home, I pointed out that one picture was apparently hung upside down. But the venerable owner of the house for a long time contradicted the possibility of this, saying, "I assure you that for ten years no one has rehung the pictures."

In another home, with wonderful Dutch portraits, I mentioned to the woman who owned them my regret that the eyes on one portrait had been absolutely rubbed out. She also answered me that this was impossible because no one had taken the picture down from the wall. However, insisting that the portrait be taken down from the wall, I pointed out the irreparable damage. The lady, thereupon sighing, admitted the evidence with the words: "Probably it was cleaned with sand for the holidays."

In all these cases, and many other instances, there was no ill-intention or even any neglect as such, because they valued the pictures. It was simply the "closed eye." And speaking of culture, first of all, the eyes are opened by cultural actions in order to see reality. Perhaps the most important and irreparable acts of vandalism were done without ill-intention, but it is precisely because of the "closed eye" and all the errors to which artificial blindness gives birth. Blindness and deafness verily do not limit themselves to the lack of sight and hearing but they are also there where these faculties have been obscured by ignorance. Beethoven was deaf and Homer was blind, but these characteristics did not hinder their names from remaining in the ranks of honor of the light-imparting culture. If a moment could be devoted in the schools to give warning about the "closed eyes" and about all the irreparable misfortunes that are born because of this, one more danger of destroying the treasures of the human spirit would be eliminated.

Himalayas, February 17, 1932.

TOLERANCE

THE inscription of King Ashoka reads: "Do not denounce other sects, nor deprecate them without cause, but render honor to other sects for whatever in them is worthy of honor." The Great Akbar and wise Jodha Bai, in building the Temple of United Religions, filled with the spirit of Tolerance, had in mind the same great containment.

When the Bhagavan Ramakrishna participated in all religions and performed the tasks of all castes, he did so out of the same great feeling of esteem towards everything that existed. It was in the name of great Tolerance that the Gates open to the radiant constructions of the Future. And when Saint Sergius advised Prince Dmitri to exhaust all possibilities of peaceful negotiations and to use utmost friendliness before beginning any military actions, he acted in the name of the same great Commandment of Tolerance. Does not each manifestation of crass intolerance leave us with the same unpleasant burdensome feeling? Are not all the numerous historical examples sufficient to indicate how the greatest of human heritages were destroyed through ignorant intolerance? Verily, intolerance can be identified only with ignorance, the daughter of darkness.

"Agni Yoga," in the Book of the Heart, says: "Intolerance is a sign of ignobility of spirit. Intolerance contains embryos of the most evil activities. There is no place for the manifestation of spiritual growth where intolerance nests. The heart's potential is unlimited; how impoverished a heart must be to deprive itself of the Infinite! One has to eradicate every sign, every indication that might lead to the idolatry of intolerance. Humanity has invented all sorts of obstacles to ascent. The dark forces are trying in every way they can to restrict evolution. Naturally, their first assault will be an action against the Hierarchy. Everyone has heard about the power of a Blessing, but out of ignorance they have turned this beneficial action into a superstition. And yet the power of the Magnet also lies in its ability to strengthen someone with a Blessing. Much is said about cooperation; thus, with every creative act it is necessary to assert awareness of the Higher World. And what strengthens the power with more immediacy than the Ray of the Hierarchy!"

It is indeed instructive to note what is the chief target against which crass intolerance is directed. In the first place, ignorance hates co-operation and Hierarchy. According to its ignoble understanding, a forceful union between co-operation and Hierarchy is absolutely incongruous, but on what else are we to base our progress'! It is especially strange to notice how those who are full of intolerance, being unaware of it in themselves, establish their own Hierarchy. And even if it be the Hierarchy of destruction, it still remains a Hierarchy. The dark Hierarchy is a tyranny, whereas the Hierarchy of Light is based primarily on conscious co-operation. Tyranny is violence, fear, terror, slavery. True Hierarchy is constructiveness, in which every positive ability finds its application and grows in a continuous process of improvement.

Let no one think that while speaking against tyranny, we admit at the same time intolerance. For tyranny, as we have already said, is the root of decomposition and becomes the gateway to chaos. Besides, tolerance does not mean the tolerance of evil and of criminality, but refers of course to all endless branches of constructiveness.

And let us not attach the concept of tolerance and intolerance to some exalted nebulous regions. Let us not consign them to something superhuman or supernaturally great, beyond the horizons of normal, everyday life.

Why go so far, when both these qualities are evinced in daily life? We must look for the expressions of our nature in small, habitual actions.

"And Jesus answering said, A certain man went down from Jerusalem to Jericho, and fell among thieves who stripped him of his raiment, and wounded him, and departing, they left him half dead.

"And by chance a certain priest passed by that way: and when the priest saw him, he crossed to the other side.

"And likewise, a Levite, when he was at that same place, came and looked on him, and passed by on the other side.

"But a certain Samaritan, as he journeyed, came upon where the man was, and when he saw him, he had compassion on him.

"He went to him, and bound up his wounds, pouring oil and wine, and set him on his own beast, and brought him to an inn, and took care of him.

"And on the morrow when he departed, he took out two pence, and gave them to the host, and said unto him: "Take care of him; and whatsoever thou spendest more, when I come again, I will repay thee."

"Which now of these three, thinkest thou, was neighbor unto him who fell among the thieves?

"And he said, He that showed mercy on him. Then said Jesus unto him, Go, and do thou likewise." (Luke, X, 30-37.)

Not from the summit of a throne did the good Samaritan pour the healing balm into the wounds of the unknown traveler. No, the Gospel presents the parable in the surroundings of daily life. A lonely road, and a perishing, lonely, wounded man. Not a few crossed his way and hastened to pass by. Who knows who he might be? Perhaps he is of foreign faith? Perhaps to help him would mean to become entangled in an unpleasant affair? A servant of the Church once confessed that he could not help a certain sick woman, because he did not know to what faith she belonged. But the good Samaritan, by his example, censured all hypocrites of intolerance. And Saint Martin also, when presenting his cloak to a naked beggar, would hardly have held an inquest as to his faith and social status. Examples from both Testaments speak of the highest and most beautiful Tolerance.

An intolerant person is primarily unmerciful, and consequently ungenerous; he does not know the meaning of confidence. Each incipient intolerance should be uprooted in childhood from the very day when the consciousness is awakening. An experienced educator should notice the first signs of negativity, and should immediately supplant it with positive containment. What a mass of prejudice and superstitions would be removed from life! How many dramas would be solved by a benevolent command of all containment!

From the first day, the broadest enlightened attention and containment must be patiently instilled, with great care in each school, no matter in what specialty. Extreme care will be given to thought-development, because, with few exceptions, humanity has forgotten to exercise the great power of thought. Despair, the devil incarnate of intolerance, will be replaced by the boundless realization of creativeness. The dark "impossible" will be replaced by the "possible," ennobled by true education.

Reminders about Tolerance are as old as the first pages of the Testaments, but the lack of attention to them makes them as new as if they were meant for tomorrow. What little effort is required in order to turn this tomorrow into a radiance of many achievements which are possible in the case of sincere co-operation!

Even in our days of extreme intolerance, such unifying institutions as the World Postal Union and International Red Cross are possible. Even the most intolerant hypocrites do not protest against these institutions...then, what slight expansion of consciousness is needed to reach co-operation and trust! And is this so difficult?

Since antiquity, psalms and folk-sagas hail the most unifying and uplifting human aspirations, as noble acts of heroism. Do not young eyes sparkle at the sight of beautiful heroic achievements? And no machine, no standards, will crush the sacred tremor of the heart that faces the beautiful Infinite. In the schools, let there be untiring reiteration about heroism, generosity, and unceasing mental creativeness. Even a small shifting of consciousness will already show the radiance of Light from behind the shadow. And the shifting will turn into an achievement.

Let us remember the instructive example from a Chinese legend about artists:

"A famous artist was invited to the Court of the Emperor in order to paint his best possible painting. The expenses connected with remuneration and travel of the artist were great, but the Emperor, the Protector of Art, wanted to have the best masterpieces and spared no effort to give the artist the best conditions. The artist agreed to complete the picture within a year. Special apartments were allotted to him. Here he spent day after day in contemplative thought until everyone became worried as to when, after all, he would begin to paint. All material was long ready, but the artist apparently had no intention of starting work on the canvas. Finally in view of the approach of the deadline, they decided to ask the artist, but he merely replied, 'Do not disturb me.' And two days before the expiration of the year, he got up and with precise touches of the brush accomplished his greatest masterpiece, stating afterwards, 'To create does not take long, but one must first visualize what one desires to create.' "

It seems that sufficient time has elapsed for humanity to realize the impracticality, the baseness and meanness of intolerance. Let us hope that past centuries have already taught us to see and realize the harm that is continuously done. Let us hope thus, in accordance with the saying of the wise Chinese artist: "to visualize takes a long time, but to do takes little."

Thus the shifting of consciousness can be transmuted into achievement.

Himalayas, January 7, 1932.

[66]

DIVERSITY

WE receive letters from the Academy of Creative Arts, Spinoza Center, our Latvian Society, our Women's Unity, the European Center, from far-off Argentina, China and the entire varied group of our Institutions. What strikes one most, when receiving all this news, is its diversity. One may imagine that if in jest, all these communications would be reversed for a minute, there would at once be chaos. However, all these organizations think of culture and undoubtedly they all strive towards one and the same high aim. The diversity of thought is a most benevolent sign. The wide embrace of the concept of Culture already affirms a great multiformity. One cannot imagine that Culture all over the world could be clothed in a single uniform. There may be identical strivings of the heart. There may be identical feelings of human dignity, but outer forms will of course vary.

It is already a correct approach to Culture to learn to value this multiformity. Imagine for a minute the deep distress if because of differences of outer signs and garbs, there would arise misunderstandings as to the nature of the sacred concept itself. All our coworkers should train themselves to this broad understanding in order to guard, with sacredness, the dignity of culture. Each quarrel is in itself an anti-cultural sign. Each doubt as to the righteousness of a brother is in itself somewhat anti-cultural. Each effort to compel others to think according to one's own recipe, cannot in itself serve as a sign of culture. No, our brothers, whether they come from South Africa or Finland, Tahiti or Belgrade, will be bound and spiritually united by an entirely different foundation. The striving to high quality, to a heartfelt devotion to every evolutionary construction, creative labor, veneration for Beauty and esteem of Knowledge—this will unite all the blessed pilgrims of the spirit. These foundations of Light cannot be obstructed by the differences of creeds, not by the peculiarities of languages, nor by traditions, however ancient they may be. The understanding of the evolutionary constructive basis of life, of broad striving beyond all conventional boundaries, will so broaden the consciousness that the containment of even the most startling multiformity will take place benevolently. Where there is a basic goodwill, there will also be Bliss, by which spirit-creativeness and straight Knowledge will be strengthened.

Therefore diversity is not an unwieldy quality, which is difficult to manage, but on the contrary it manifests, seemingly countless vigilant eyes, hands and feet, indefatigable in its true vigilance, flexibility and resourcefulness that will build this Co-operative. In other words, diversity becomes an invulnerable, noble armor. In old fairy tales we read of the united group of Bahadur—heroes in which each one had some special quality. And only in co-operative unity, complementing each other, could they achieve the most difficult and seemingly unfeasible tasks. If despite their might, they would have had one and the same quality, they would undoubtedly have been defeated.

Mutual respect takes into consideration, first of all, the safeguarding of individuality and the encouragement of personal initiative. Tyranny, against which the human spirit inevitably revolts, is only an uncouth expression of selfishness, and an ignorance of the value of individuality. If all past tyrants of the world would not have erroneously forgotten the value of personal initiative, they, as the heroes of fairytales, would have assembled around themselves an invincible and benevolent legion of builders of life instead of revolts and defeats. I emphasize benevolence, because I trust that the complex of the best human strivings in their widest scope, is always constructive, and everything constructive is already benevolent in itself.

In the name of this constructive benevolence, we have to encourage diversity among our organizations, although I know this surprises certain ignorant people who cannot grasp the basic idea of constructiveness. If the foundations of Beauty and Knowledge are vital, then they shall protect this benevolent multiformity as the basis of creativeness. Everyone who has tried to analyze life thoroughly will remember how elements most varied and, according to human convention, seemingly opposed, were blended into benevolent, cordial understanding, when their spirits felt the selfless constructive principle. The same constructive principle teaches mutual control of our armor. This will bring about a better result of the spiritual battle, but neither for condemnation, nor for mutual embitterment. Containment is born out of the same spiritual growth and straight-Knowledge. And it comes to life not in a painful birth, which furrows the forehead in wrinkles, but easily, with a joyously conscious smile, which adds one more altar to the Temple of Beauty. And this altar will not be without form, but it will harmoniously enrich the whole structure. Every city may expand either without order and in rivalry and hatred, or it may be beautifully balanced. Even the most ancient stones, in the hands of an experienced master-mason, find their dignified and predestined place amidst modern contemporary structures.

How beautiful it will be if a city so domestically unified retains its full diversity, which is but a natural outlet of the inexhaustible might of the human spirit.

Our cultural organizations should also be based on the foundation of true freedom. As nothing else, it is liberty which is organically related to the conception of multiformity. Freedom is the dream of all mankind; she leads beautifully, resplendently winged, if her foundation is the true understanding of Culture. Anti-cultural liberty is only revolt—rude and chaotic.

And thus fate has given us, as co-workers, such precious

concepts as the true freedom and diversity of creative manifestations. The best feelings of the heart grow upon this all-embracing field. And true cordial sincerity is the first banner of Culture. Only in this armor may one pass all abysms of darkness. There are many such murky passes, where ugly monsters prey upon peaceful pilgrims. But in the ancient fairytales, it is ordained: "Let he who has found and taken the treasure, walk on without glancing back." What treasure may be more precious than the achievements of Culture? Everything spiritual is synthesized in Culture, everything heroic, everything constructive and creative. To call friends and co-workers to the festival of construction and cordiality is full of dignity and Beauty.

Let us safeguard with fullest care the benevolent multiformity, which is so generously sent to us from all ends of the world.

Himalayas, October, 1931.

ARMOR OF LIGHT

VERILY blind are those who do not wish to see! During my practical studies in Roman Law, our old professor once assigned a thesis on the prosecution of slander. Discussing the subject we came to the conclusion that slander and defamation, in their essence, were not sufficiently prosecuted. And we asked the professor why the giving of false statements was not prosecuted by any of the laws. I remember how the kind-hearted professor smiled and raising his hands, exclaimed, "But, then, practically nine-tenths of mankind would be in jail!"

These student dreams of protecting humanity against lies and falsehood often come back to mind. It would seem that the very accumulation of circumstances, so destructive for humanity nowadays, indicates what attention should be paid to the vast currents of false invention, which are mostly directed to evil.

None of the contemporary laws, even though aiming to put a stop to harmful slander, have sufficient power to counteract the whispering of lies. Someone may say that such lies are identical with slander, but in fact, a great deal of evil gossip would not come under the category of slander, and still would be a source for spreading the most harmful consequences. Even if we would try not to pay attention to every lie which people, like birds, thoughtlessly chirp, not realizing the terrible condemnations that are often passed along in the irresponsible twittering of a drawing-room; even if we would not pay attention to these, the essential harm caused by them would not diminish.

For besides this irresponsible chirping, a mass of consciously false inventions which have the sole, full-intentioned aim, of causing harm by dissension and devastation has grown up in the world.

If we would put on record all the statistics of harmful falsehoods which we daily encounter, it would make a huge "Tome of evil". Sometime the making of picklocks, thus impressing the minds of weak-willed spectators with all sorts of harmful ideas, is also depicted on the stage. To record such malicious inventions of the mind would be harmful in itself, but from time to time one should take the trouble to ponder about the colossal amount of lies parading in life, which in their path destroy the most valuable and often irreplaceable possibilities.

Now people often leave their churches, after the most evocative and uplifting sermons, refreshed only for new slander. By the most touching psalms, souls have become inspired only to evil whispering. The heroism of the best dramas now often results in paroxysms of suspicion. And does not even prayer become a threat? Is this not so? And is this proper? To be venomous, a snake need not be large. The coral-snake and viper are small, and the poison of even a small scorpion may be fatal.

The deceiver dreams of cheating. The traitor lives by treason. The coward is tormented by terror. Everyone in his own way: "Tell me what you think and I will tell you who you are."

Certainly, if laws are meant to protect the safety of the citizen, then they should be adequate to counteract slander and lies. When humanity sees that the torrent of evil is increasing with such invention, it is strange to fight these giants of evil with the antiquated, ancient Roman Law, or the *Codex Justiniani* or even by the *Codex Napoleon*, which many of the current lawmakers imitate.

If evil has created new formulae, then the remedies must also be adequately renovated. If every slanderer would realize that he is not only imitating the chirp of a winged-sparrow, but his act is already foreseen in the criminal code, he would ponder a Second time as to whether his cherished whispering of evil, would not cost him too dearly.

It is quite natural that the increased numbers of blackmailers and of infant kidnappers in America have resulted in the enforcement of corresponding laws. Probably at this hour, Lindbergh smiles sadly, realizing that this stronger law has not helped him. On the contrary, after the enforcement of the new law, he even suffered from worse blackmail which had the air almost of scoffing. Does not such cruel mockery prove how greatly evil has increased and how legal measures against it are already too late?

Is this not like a gangrene, which the knife of the surgeon tries vainly to overtake? Do we not again have to return to the same solution, which has already been proposed by us also for other walks of life? Is it not high time to introduce into all schools without delay, from the earliest grades, the foundations of practical Ethics?

Unfortunately this most essential subject is now regarded as something abstract, of which it is not even customary to speak because it would be considered antiquated, not of proper social grace, and would arouse the severe derision and the resistance of the allies of conscious evil.

But if the beautiful ancient concept of "Ethics" is not to be blamed in itself, is it not we who are guilty in having eliminated all discussions about good, blissful things from our social life?

We arc all guilty of having garbed the vital foundations of ethics in a dull gray toga, while allowing the slanderers to utilize the most vivid pages of the human vocabulary. In our social life, do we not regard enthusiasm, this radiant flame of the heart, as something unfit and childish? Praise and admiration, these flowers of the Beautiful Garden, are considered almost as a sign of ill breeding. And adoration, instead of its inspirational significance, assumes the form of conventional hypocrisy and is admitted as such.

Well-brought-up children should ask for nothing,

should strive for nothing and should dull their creative strivings, blindly following the standards of those educators to whom, in their turn, no one ever taught anything blissful and constructive! And there are many such pseudo-educators!

Dusty are the gray togas in which we have garbed Ethics and each lofty mark of creativeness. And these have been replaced by accusations, malicious whispering and the spreading of falsehood. It is strange to witness how faces brighten up at the very mention of an untrue story. Then vocabularies become enriched and even the most silent guest becomes a brilliant speaker. And often his brilliancy increases when he is certain that he lies.

A liar is inventive also in suspicion. Judging by himself, and entering this murky field he feels like a fish in water. His malicious experience encourages him, because he knows that all his attacks will remain unpunished. And should you remind him of the text of the Gospel: "With what measure ye mete, it shall be measured unto you," he will only wave his hand self-contentedly and will say, "*Après nous—le déluge!*"

A bad conscience whispers to him, that his defense lies only in evil, and without evil he will, like the fish out of water, lose his vitality. A profound atheism is also expressed in his basic malice, in his suspicions, and in his desire to besmirch all.

The liar has not before him the Highest Image, in the presence of which he stands ashamed. His poor imagination can show him no vista of his own future, when he will be called to an accounting of his actions, or rather when he will set himself in the place he merits.

It is a wise motto: "Do unto others as you would have others do unto you."

But for this, one must have at least some imagination. And such imagination should be cultivated in order that it may guide one beyond the limitations of the day. People are very much afraid of illness, poverty and of every kind of misfortune. The most impertinent liars and slanderers often turn out to be the most primitive fetishists. They hazily know of "unlucky signs," but they do not wish to hear that the reverse side is simply the return of their own boomerang. Karma!

Anyone who has watched the throwing of a boomerang may remember how sometimes an inexperienced and careless thrower will shriekingly try to avoid being hit by his own weapon that mercilessly surprises him and strikes him with mathematical accuracy of the force he himself used. Experienced boomerang throwers call such victims, first of all, fools. Verily, there is no better denomination for the malicious ignoramuses than fools! The ignorant slanderers, are, above all, fools! No matter what imitative gilded words they invent, no matter what they do to placate their naive listener with disgusting narratives, they still remain fools! Each of their lies gathers impetus with perfect accuracy and at an unexpected moment strikes them the harder; each garden grows, whether it be dark or light.

It is indeed unbelievable that our earth should have existed for countless years, only so that now we should be faced with the urgent necessity of descrying the immense evil caused by lies! But one need only take any newspaper, the events of any single day, in order to prove what terrifying limits have been reached by men in their efforts to harm one another.

Just as we reprimand children not to fight during their play, so one wants to advise the grown ups: "Try to pass a single day without doing harm to one another!"

It almost seems that if men could pass but one day without inflicting evil on one another, some great miracle would occur, some beautiful healing force would visit us as naturally as a kind smile of the heart, or as a fertile shower over parched fields.

A woman once said to a priest, "When I pray, the sacred Image smiles at me." And the wise priest answered, "your heart smiled and the smile of the Savior responded!" Is it possible that this smile of grace, of the truth, the smile of blissful offering and self-sacrifice is no longer possible?

Is it possible that egoism, this nearest kin to lie, has actually been victorious?

No, it is impossible—since ancient times wise Commandments have been given.

Let the children, from their very infancy, from youth, march by the new paths of great co-operation with creative Bliss, not with the boredom of Ethics distorted by misunderstanding, but with the joy of Ethics, transmuted by the fire of the heart!

History gives us remarkable examples of how, not only the still unspoiled mind of children were often transmuted, through the art of thought, but how even the most apparently inveterate criminals became enlightened. Such examples of enlightened criminals have always been given in the Great Ordainments; thus nothing is lost. Consequently one may fortunately reach the best results by an enlightened consciousness and not by mere threat of the law.

A scholar once said to me, "We have no more formulae." What nonsense! All the most beautiful formulae remain in their full vitality. It does not demand so much courage to turn to these beautiful and blissful formulae. This purifying teaching is called the science of the heart. Of course this annunciation of Good Will should be clad in garments of Light; as the Apostle Paul ordained: "Let us array ourselves in an Armor of Light!"

In such effulgent garments, in radiant armor, through the luminous torches of the heart, it will not be difficult to stay awake throughout the long night awaiting the dawn.

No one has ever believed that festivals were not needed. On the contrary, the true Festivals of Enlightenment, the Festivals of Labor and Truth, are most inspiring! And how easily such a sacred Festival is possible, in the simplest places, but as well as in a palace.

Let us overcome everything, even the most dark and most evil, by a creative constructiveness, which will afford humanity a true Festival of the Spirit. By this we abide!

Himalayas, May 1, 1932.

QUALITY

D URING a certain period of production, an imposed curtailment of its volume is not necessarily harmful if this reduction is utilized to synthesize the quality of the results. Quantity, as is known, is effective as a messenger for the masses, and is at times admissible in works of the highest Culture; but the movement of Culture never made its imprint either through quantity or through the majority.

A high quality and refined minority were always the impetus for real achievements of Culture. Very often, even in splendid addresses and writings regarding Culture, it is made evident that Culture begins where people know how to utilize their leisure time. This can be true only in as much as we ourselves determine the concept of leisure. If by leisure we understand the period outside of our routine work, or as we have sometimes called the period of work—pranayama, then so-called leisure becomes a concentration upon finding high quality in our activity. How beautiful is the sound of these concentrated strokes of an accumulated energy of high quality, and how their resonances awaken the hearts of the masses who were previously stimulated only by quantity!

Quality also awakens another characteristic, indispensable to evolutionary processes. It arouses a real sense of responsibility for all that happens, be it even a single affirmation or warning, or even if it appears as a new phase of refinement in something already known. The greatest drama often hides in our presumption that something is common knowledge. This "known" is entered into the category of the habitual, about which people no longer think; in other words, not only do they fail to refine it, but they do not even elevate this concept.

Striving to quality will lead us to many axioms of life which must be stated as problems for solution because they demand refinement, accuracy and striving from new angles of our existence. *"Non multa sed multum"*—this wise counsel was also given at certain periods of activity. One cannot begin the glorification of Culture with silence. The hermits departed from the world for their silences only after a certain activity, when their silence itself became a thundering spiritual call and a cure for ailments.

How beautiful is the concentrated and responsible motion of the sculptor's chisel, when, after the crude modeling, he begins to sculpt the subtlest features in which the most minute inexactitude in the precision of the hand may result in an irreparable distortion. As long as the sculptor works in the province of the fundamental forms, his hand is permitted the use of either a deep or shallow curvilinear stroke of the chisel, but as soon as he reaches the final interpretation, any distortion would mean a return to chaos. Thus his creative enthusiasm becomes more exalted, combined with a great responsibility for each motion of his hand. At such moments, the sculptor frequently stands away from his work to view it from various positions in order, when coming closer, to impart the inimitable touch to it. Whereas, during the early days of his work, the sculptor could express his intentions in words, during the final strokes he is more silent, more deeply penetrative, knowing his responsibility for that which he completes.

The quality built up by the entire complexity of circumstances infuses into the work of construction a special spiritual joy. In crossing the mountain stream one cannot afford to make a single false step. Likewise, when crossing an abyss upon a rope, we seem to lose something of our physical weight, and when we are attached by the heart to the spiritual threads, we almost fly over perilous abysses.

Whether we term it enthusiasm, spiritual upliftment, or perfection in the quality of movement and thought, or a lofty solemnity in all our feelings, there is no difference in definitions. For he who does not understand solemnity in love and the exaltation of quality, all other definitions are like stones rolling in the mountain stream. The judgment of high quality does not consist in the resonance of loud words. In a concentrated solemnity of the heart, this judgment of eternity is resolved. If we dare to pronounce the word Culture, it means we are primarily responsible for quality. The root of the word Culture represents the highest service towards perfection, and this is also our duty with regard to quality.

In the aggregations of quality, nothing remains unforeseen, nothing remains forgotten, and of course, nothing is distorted through reasons of self-interest. Great or petty self-interest is so enrooted in the life of humanity through centuries of perversions and denials, that it has become one of the chief enemies of everything achieved above the personal quality.

There have been discussions in the press as to whether the heroic achievements recognized by humanity were prompted by self-interest. The question was raised as to whether or not the deeds of the shepherdess Jeanne d'Arc and the fact that she set herself to the thought of the salvation of an entire nation, was impelled by egotism. Such thought could occur only to the minds of those who are themselves essentially self-interested. In their opinion, not only these achievements, but also the deeds of daily philanthropy are of course called forth only by various degrees of egotism and self-interest.

Such is the canon of the heartless who, judging only by their own natures, suppose that each good act is performed either for self-interest or for some other material personal benefit, forgetful that these earthly flowers endure but a single day, like the brilliant blossoms of the cactus. By condemning everything to self-interest, those who are inherently self-interested begin also to assault Culture.

They say: "These sanctimonious paths are inaccessible to us," as if the functions of Culture demanded some sacred achievements.

Those who disparage always consign the reality which they hate to the clouds of inaccessibility, in order thus to be rid of it more easily. With pleasure they promote boxing matches, bull fights and contests for speed records. They will bring forward the crudest physical manifestations, in order to erase, at least partially, everything subtly creative. They are ready to surrender the Temple into the hands of the money-lenders, confident that in line with the era in which we live, there will be none to expel them from the Sanctuary and to sustain that by which the human spirit exists.

Happily, the paths to perfection and the highest quality are, in their essence, outside of the hands of the money-lenders. The minority thinks of quality. The young heart can think of quality as long as it remains unsullied; no matter along what byways humanity wanders, the process of the enhancing of quality nevertheless continues. Because heroism inhabits the heart of a refined spirit, the accumulations of refinement are beyond the recorded laws.

But let us not enter into the spheres that are inexpressible. Now one must reiterate precisely about the concrete concept of quality in all actions and in all productiveness. Those who do not strive to quality had better not speak of Culture. Culture is not a fashionable concept. It is the deepest basis of life attached by the most sensitive silvery threads to the Hierarchy of Evolution. Hence, those who have realized the striving to quality are not afraid of derision and they repeat the words of the Apostle Paul: "When you think us dead, we are nevertheless alive." And not only alive, but each one striving to Culture or in other words, to quality, finds within himself an inexhaustible source of strength and opposition to everything wrathful and destructive. He can repeat the wise saying, "Blessed be the obstacles, through them we grow."

For him each manifestation of an obstacle is a possibility to elevate quality.

Through what else, then, will the coarsest forms be conquered, if not through the radiation of the spirit which is reflected in the quality of each action, each day, each thought. Thus, striving to the highest forms of civilization, daring to think even about Culture, let us not forget that the vitality of striving is created out of the high quality of all action. Our responsibility for Culture lies not in dreams, but it is manifested in life. And this responsibility verily extends not only to dreams beyond the clouds of some rare festival days, but must be imprinted in everyday life. Quality, Beauty, Solemnity in love in all its impetuosity and limitlessness, weave the unbreakable wings of spirit. Quality, quality, quality, in everything and everywhere!

Of course there will also be found satanic elementals who will hiss at everything spiritual and beautiful. "To hell with Culture, place the cash on the table." The sad fate of such satanists is not enviable. Happily, "Light conquers darkness."

But, what heartfelt expressions of salutation one can send those who fight for Culture in a disinterested and self-sacrificing manner! How, then, to greet those who through their noble battle help the State to inscribe unforgettable pages of the best achievements. For this battle, as a battle with the densest darkness, is unusually difficult. But at the same time it is that true achievement which will remain imprinted for ages and which represents the best guiding milestones for the young generation.

A noble battle also creates the inexhaustibility of strength and cultivates that radiant enthusiasm with which the eyes glow and the human heart resounds. In the name of the fathomless Beauty of the human heart, let us gather and become strong in the luminous victory of Culture.

Himalayas, June 17, 1932.

THE YOUTH MOVEMENT

DEAR YOUNG FRIENDS: In your Letter of November 23, 1931, you asked me to become your Honorary President, Teacher and Leader of your Youth Movement. So it shall be. You do not err in your conviction that everything young and aspiring is close to my heart.

If you take a few of the titles of my articles from the "Realm of Light," you will see that they were written seemingly for your Youth Movement, and that, at various times, they concern the same youth and the same future constructiveness. "The Beautiful," "Creative Thought," "Blessed Hierarchy," "Love Unconquerable," "Despite All Difficulties," "Spiritual Values ," "Sacred Principles," "The Realm of Culture"—all these contain that through which I aspire to kindle young hearts. Through these calls I would like to awaken courage and heroism and achievement and that limitless constructiveness which transforms life into a luminous holiday. This is not a holiday of indolence, a holiday of so-called rest. No, this is a festival of spirit and an untiring striving to Light. You have read in all my articles about this Light which is not an abstraction for the refined heart. It is a living Light, as living as are all subtlest energies of nature.

Youth does not like nebulous suppositions, but facts and action. And this is the pledge of eternal Youth. Likewise, in all our works, we turn first of all to facts, to the immutable reality, even though it be behind the boundaries of primitive evidence. In my address to our Washington Society I spoke of physical and spiritual health. These concepts are indivisible. There can be no physical health without spiritual health. You gather in the name of culture, in the name of spiritual health from which all other benevolent conditions and possibilities will be generated.

Should any doubts or confusions arise within you, annihilate them at once. Without tarrying a moment, go to the source and investigate, for what can be more harmful or darker than petty, desecrating doubts? It is very dear to me to see that in your letter you do not create any narrow boundaries for your movement. You speak about the courageous transport, about the universal cultural movement, which means the true achievement of youth. We are not bigots and zealots and we know the significance of enlightened labor, which may rest upon true co-operation. No movement is possible without co-operation. And co-operation develops upon the foundations of the discipline of spirit. When youth understands how harmful each aspect of slavery and of tyranny is and when it realizes the radiant Hierarchy of Knowledge, youth will build a true legion of light of its groups, beautiful in spirit as well as in body. The conception of physical culture is very often distorted among the falsely understood foundations of civilization. Not only is this conception falsely understood, but it may, in addition, bring harm to the future generations if there be no synthesis.

Read my thoughts about synthesis in the article of this title which I have sent to your friends. Read also the article, "Artists of Life" and "Tolerance" which are likewise dedicated to the multiform expansion of consciousness. It is precisely youth who create the style for the future life. It is precisely youth who must and are introducing the nobility of spirit which has perhaps been clouded by narrow materialism, commercial interests and standards which are so contrary to individuality. Seemingly representing one great universal being—spirit and body—youth will realize how to treat the spiritual values in an extraordinary way.

Youth will understand why we raise the Banner of Peace. Youth will realize that this is not an impotent pacifism, but that it is the spirit-creativeness of the New Era. In this Era, peace is necessary first of all for intense discoveries and constructions. War must be eliminated, as well as each quarrel, lie, slander, and each meanness which impedes the progress of humanity.

I am happy that you are not insulating yourself within a conventionally outlined program. Your motto must be an exalted, healthy young generation that creates, with the song of joy, success and Beauty. It is precious to see that in our days in various countries the same hearths of culture are being kindled and that after the misunderstood calamities and clashes the human hearts strive again toward benevolent quests.

Not so long ago people were speaking of a great shifting, but now the next step has already taken place and the thought about a shifting has been transformed into a luminous thought about achievement. You must not think that your movement will not encounter difficulties on its path. These little difficulties will arise, and with time you will bless them, for they will open reality still further before you. For you begin your organization at a difficult time. You are gathering together at a time of material as well as of spiritual crisis, at the time of overproduction, a time of unemployment, a time of mutual suspicions and various conditions which hamper the progress of humanity. But it is precisely these difficulties that will inwardly prompt you to gather and to unite in one courageous and enlightened unit. When it becomes dangerous for travelers to proceed alone along the desert roads, they gather into communities and these united caravans easily conquer all obstacles which would be unsupportable for any individual participant.

Now it is not only a difficult time but it is also a great time. Youth must not think that its destiny was to manifest itself only during a difficult time. No, it has come here during great days, when a new world is being forged, when the human consciousness is being transformed with unusual speed. When from the crossroad, a multitude of people enter upon the straight path in order to receive the beautiful, destined revelations and transformations of life.

In the name of the great newly-realized, transfigured Culture, I greet you, young friends! When we speak of great concepts, we need not fear great words. If you will hold through upon the crest of the courageous call of Knowledge and creativeness, if you will beware of brutal quarrels and unbefitting arguments, you will perform a great work. And you will find limitless young forces, ready to stretch out their hand in a true *cultural co-operation.*

In spirit with you! God speed!

Himalayas, January 12, 1932.

GOD

"Oh, Thou Infinite One,
Existing in the very vortices of matter,
Primordial, in the tides of time,
Impersonal—Triune Divinity!—
Spirit, Thou One and Omnipresent,
To Whom there is no dwelling, no cause,
Who no imagination has yet conceived!
Filling all with Thy presence,
Containing, creating, preserving all,
And Whom we glorify as God!"

SUCH is the literal translation of the first verse of the immortal poem of the first Russian poet, Derjavin, written by him in 1784.

"And in heaven I see God!"

exclaimed another great Russian poet.

The Credo begins: "I believe in One God, the Father Almighty, the Creator of Heaven and Earth and of all things visible and invisible."

Towards the Highest of the Highest, to the Breath of all that is Breathing, to the Atman of all Existence, all nations in all languages bring their sacred and immutable effort. Each within the limits of his heart, within the limits of his understanding of the Beautiful, addresses the best names to Elohim. Although these sacred Names be manifold, gathered into One, they sound in an inspiringly touching symphony of all that is best, of all the highest that the human mind can express and which the embodied hand may inscribe with all the most Sacred Hieroglyphs.

The sacred permanence of God, the Almighty, is born in the brain of each child, when he first sees the splendor of the stars and thus turns his thought toward the infinite worlds. This enlightened thought brings one to the same eternally radiant conception: "My Father's house has many mansions." And another formula, as limitless in its greatness, is affirmed: "But the hour cometh and now is, when the true worshiper shall worship the Father in spirit and in truth, for the Father seeketh such to worship him in spirit and in truth" (John IV, 23-24).

The title, "Has Science Discovered God?" a symposium compiled by A. H. Cotton, has just appeared. In this book the opinions of the foremost scientists about God are collected. Among the renowned names we see: Millikan, Einstein, Oliver Lodge, Thompson, Byrd, Curtis, Eddington, and Mather, and each one of them in his own way glorifies this Highest all-unifying Concept, without which the very idea of the greatness of Infinity would be impossible.

The time has already passed for the great Realities to be refuted in the name of a false scientific materialism. In the history of humanity, atheism appeared as the paroxysm of despair when man, due to his own faults, found himself in complete darkness and lost all understanding of his surroundings, of the great forms, of the meaning of fundamental principles. The last generation still held at times to the conceited formula that nothing existed besides themselves. To them, all the far-off worlds were only lamps, for their own delight, and even the sun was of course only an instrument for their personal comfort.

Noted for his atheism, Bazarov stupidly exclaimed that after his death only burdock would grow from him! Yet, such nonsensical exclamations were not peculiar expressions of modesty; on the contrary, those who pronounced them intended to establish their physical and material finiteness, filled with conceit about their relative and materialistic Knowledge. Such a negative type is described by Turgenev in his famous novel, "Fathers and Sons"; Turgenev understood well the fallacy of such ideas. Another Russian writer, Dostoevsky, approaches the same subject in presenting a type of peasant pseudo-atheism.

This writer describes a soldier atheist, who, desiring to perform the extreme act of desecration in order to convince himself of the nonexistence of God, places a most sacred ecclesiastic object on a pillar and shoots at it. At the instant of his sacrilege, he sees a vision of Christ Himself, appearing in its very place. A peculiar evocation of God is described in this example of pseudo-atheism: the prayer for a miracle, for a holy sign, which has always existed in the depths of the heart. Thus, the human heart understands in its inmost depths, that every form of destruction is negative.

We have before us a significant book, recently issued, of the miracles which have occurred during recent years. In this book, facts are compiled that have been certified by many witnesses and that have also been mentioned in the press. These subtle manifestations are detailed at length, with particulars about the quality of radiation occurring during these phenomena and with all their effects and impressions upon the many witnesses. Elsewhere there are similar records about the miraculous cures at Lourdes. And again, we have information that in 1925, in the town of Kostroma, on the Volga, an aged monk passed away in whose papers were found the records of a path to the sanctuaries of the Holies of the Himavat. And the Siberian Old Believers still go on pilgrimages to the sacred Belovodye ("White Waters") and strive to the highest communion with God. On the same path one meets the "don-dam donpa," the highest form, so-called, of the Understanding of the Buddhist-Tibetan consciousness.

As soon as one eschews the path of senseless negation and strives to the Path of Good, to the path of radiant creative thought, one is overwhelmed by the innumerable facts and signs among all peoples of the entire world, the value of which were perceived immediately by the pure heart. All nations seeking God and manifesting God, know in their hearts also of a glorious future. Messiah, Maitreya, Kalki-Avatar, Muntazar, Mitolo, Saoshyant—everyone in his own way, and according to the best of his understanding, awaits this radiant future, sending his heart-felt prayer to the One God Almighty. In Isfahan, the White Steed is already saddled for the Great Advent. A Rabbi, in Hamadan, will say: "You are also Israel if you search for the Light!" Brahmins come to you in order to celebrate great Shri Krishna together, among the spring flowers. Each one, striving in his own way toward the good and the Blessed Future, knows God.

In a remarkable book, "On Eastern Crossroads," by Josephine St. Hilaire, an inspiring saying is quoted about the veneration of the Guru:

"I recall a small Hindu who found his Teacher. We asked him, 'Is it possible that the sun would glow to you, if you would see it without the Teacher?'

"The boy smiled: 'The sun would remain as the sun, but in the presence of the Teacher twelve suns would shine to me!'

"The sun of wisdom of India shall shine because upon the shores of a river there sits a boy who knows the Teacher."

In this heartfelt veneration of the Hierarchy of Light is manifested an unwavering faith in God. Even beyond this, there is manifested not only a belief, but even a realization of God, which leads not only to God-seeking, but to the manifestation of God. The Knowledge of the omnipresence of God, existing in each grain of sand, not only does not minimize the Greatness, but on the contrary, bends reality to all the subtle conditions, to all the far-off worlds, to everything perceived by the human eye and moreover, to everything that the human heart knows in its innermost depths. The Heart—the Sun of Suns—this Altar of the Almighty! Verily, science and the great religions have not been parted. All the new discoveries of energies, rays, waves, rhythm and all glories invisible to the eye, treasurers of the actual Might of God, again attract each honest study which inevitably leads along the infinite Hierarchy of Light ascending toward the highest beautiful regions, where neither petty earthly divisions, nor malice and hatred exist, but where the Great Agni-Fire of Creative Thought eternally shines. And in the radiance of the great Thought of the Almighty, human thought is also enlightened by the flame of the awakening Heart.

Up to now, Western science has attributed only physiological functions to the heart, ignoring its higher meaning as the transmuter of the subtlest energies which incessantly pass through, nourish and refine the consciousness. From the old traditions, the Hindus know that the great Manas has its abode in the heart, and it is not without cause that the Hindus, when speaking of thought, place their hands on their hearts. Thus the apparatus of the brain, sometimes forcibly separated from the activity of the heart, again becomes a true worker of reality. And, this turning to co-operation again expresses the great Conception of the omnipresence of the Spirit of God. The conception of cooperation destined to humanity for the glorious future, is indeed close to the true Realization of God. Those strong in spirit, were not frightened at the responsibility of the formula of the Imitation of God. "Of the Imitation of Christ," by Thomas à Kempis, contains nothing of conceit, but is a call toward highest co-operation!

The East with its ancient traditions, has watched, with amazement, the attempts of science to separate itself from the Highest. For it was in the East that the heart was acknowledged as the first conductor to the Altar of God. The Hermits of Mt. Sinai, all Prophets and all Rishis, imbued by their striving to God, knew the highest possibilities of our spiritual guide—the human heart.

Swami Vivekananda justly says that some of the modern thinkers, because of the diversity of understanding of concepts, have raised the question whether it is not necessary to replace the word of God by another appellation. But, of course, the wise Swami arrives at the conclusion that so many of the highest human strivings are concentrated in this term, that its deep reality should not be touched. Indeed, any blasphemous substitute would be analogous to primitive searching, when the human mind, still bound by numerous crude conditions, tried to bring the concept of Infinite Greatness to its own earthly conditional understanding and definition. The concept of God, this infinite aggregate of the highest qualities, is of course inexpressible with our limited earthly vocabulary. But the Heart, in its own unlimited language, knows this highest wisdom of Infinity, the rays of which play on the Lotus of Consciousness. I remember how one of my dear late friends, the renowned poet Alexander Bloch, ceased to attend the Religious Philosophical Society. On being questioned about the reason for his absence, he answered: "Because they speak there of the Inexpressible!" This great Ineffable, Indescribable, was for him a reality. And indeed, with his fine sensitivity of a poet, he felt the crudeness of verbal disputes regarding such a Lofty, Fine, so Infinite a concept, which resounds only in the Heart. Every word about God already inflicts some blasphemous limitation to this Inexpressible Greatness.

Now it is especially timely to remember God, to remember the Commandments of old Ordainments, to remember the Indescribable, the Unutterable, the Undefinable, the Infinite and at the same time to remember what is so near to us, what saturates every human heart when it thinks of the Common Good. How beautiful is the Divine Omnipresence expressed in the best Commandments!

The world is shattered by all kinds of crises. In this misery, in this poverty, the great Concept is once again raised, which if, only partly realized, would transmute human life into a beautiful garden. A breaking away from God, a breaking away from the free, unbound, radiant Knowledge, a breaking away from the predestined joy of perfection, would turn the significant life of this world into an Island of Tears. Yet, our lot is not misery, nor is unhappiness predestined; the highest joy, the creative tremor of thought, the fragrance of the Altar of the Heart are ordained. Not an Island of Tears, but a Beautiful Garden, a garden of transformed Labor and Knowledge is the domain of all people who turn toward God.

Derjavin concludes his poem "God" with the following lines:

"Creator, I am Thy creation!
I am the being of Thy Wisdom!
Thou, Giver of the Blissful Source of Life,
Thou Spirit of my soul, and King!
In Thy Wisdom it was fit
That my immortal Be-ness pass
Through the abysses of death;
That my soul be clad in mortality
And that through death I should re-enter
Thy Immortality, O Father.
O Indefinable! O Ineffable!
I know that the imagination of my soul
Is helpless to trace even Thy shadow;
But since glorification be a law,
Then impotent mortals
May not better articulate their adoration,
Than by exalting themselves even to Thine Image,
To merge in Thine Infinite form,
And pour forth their tears of gratitude."

Himalayas, May, 1932.

II
CULTURE

WORLD LEAGUE OF CULTURE

I

The Heart of Culture

CULTURE is reverence of Light. Culture is love of humanity. Culture is also fragrance, the unity of life and Beauty. Culture is the synthesis of uplifting and sensitive attainments. Culture is the armor of Light. Culture is salvation. Culture is the motivating power. Culture is the Heart.

If we gather all the definitions of Culture, we find the synthesis of active Bliss, the altar of enlightenment and constructive Beauty.

Condemnation, disparagement, defiling, melancholy, disintegration and all other characteristics of ignorance do not befit Culture. The great tree of Culture is nourished by an unlimited Knowledge, by enlightened labor, incessant creativity and noble attainment.

The cornerstones of great civilizations support the stronghold of Culture. But from the tower of Culture there radiates the jewel-adamant, from the loving, discerning and dauntless Heart.

Love opens these beautiful Gates. As with each true key, so also must this love be true, self-sacrificing, daring, and fiery. Where we find the sources of Culture, they are fiery and issue from the very depths. Where Culture has once been born, it cannot be killed. One may annihilate civilization, but Culture, the true spiritual treasure, is eternal.

Therefore the field of Culture is a joyful one. Joyful even during arduous labor. Joyful even during the tense battles with the most obscure ignorance. The flaming heart is without limitations in the great Infinity.

The Festival of Labor and Constructiveness! A summons to this Festival means a reminder of eternal labor, of the joy of responsibility and of human dignity.

The labor of the worker for Culture is like the work of a physician. The true physician is acquainted with more than one disease. And not only does the physician cure that which has already occurred, but his wise foresight anticipates the future. The physician not only eradicates the illness, but he labors to improve the health for the whole of life. The physician descends into the darkest cellars in order to carry light and warmth there. The physician is not forgetful of all the amelioration and beautification of life, in order to give joy to the understanding spirit. The physician not only knows of the old epidemics, but he readily acquaints himself with the symptoms of new diseases, which have been induced by the decay of the foundations.

The physician has sane words of counsel for the young and for the old, and is ready to give everyone encouraging advice. The physician does not cease to extend his Knowledge, otherwise he could not answer the needs of the present. The physician does not lose patience or tolerance, because a restraint of feeling would repel the suffering ones against him.

The physician does not fear the sight of human ulcers, because he is concerned only with their cure. The physician collects various curative herbs and stones; he knows the research for their benevolent application. The physician is not weary of hastening with aid for the suffering ones at all hours of day or night.

All these qualities are also inherent in the worker for Culture. He is equally ready at all hours of day or night to contribute his help. The worker for Culture always beneficently answers: "I am always ready," like the motto of the Sokols. His heart is ever open to everything in which experience and Knowledge may be useful. While helping, he himself continually learns, because "in giving, we receive." He is not afraid, for he knows that fear opens the gates of darkness.

The worker for Culture is always youthful, for his heart does not wither. He is flexible, because in movement there is force. He stands vigil on the parapet of Bliss, Knowledge and Beauty. He knows what true co-operation is.

All co-workers for Culture are united by threads of the heart. Mountains and oceans are no obstacles to these flaming hearts. They are not dreamers but builders and smiling plowmen.

In sending this greeting of Culture, one cannot do so without a smile, without the call of friendship. Thus we shall meet, thus we shall gather together and labor for Bliss, Beauty and Knowledge. And we shall do this without delay, without losing a day or an hour, in blissful constructiveness.

September 1, 1932.

WORLD LEAGUE OF CULTURE

II

Culture: Co-operation

RECIPROCITY is the most cordial definition of co-operation. If for long, we have dreamt of ways of reaching the best of co-operation, now actual circumstances urgently impel us along these paths of the heart.

At last, one more co-operative body has been formed, based upon our sincerest striving to common welfare and reciprocity. Our acting committees, which embrace a wide program in their scope, can live and mature on the basis of warm co-operation, in other words—on reciprocity.

Our most heartfelt wish is not only to attract co-workers to our activities, but to give them the full possibility to become fellow-creators, fellow-builders of the new steps of Culture.

Simple co-ordination of work is one thing, but infinitely higher resonates co-creation, co-operative construction, in which no one in any way loses oneself. On the contrary, in Cultural Infinity everyone forges his realm and stronghold, precious for everybody but created by him according to his individuality. By what else, if not by heartfelt reciprocity, can individuality be kept up?

The Festival of Culture shall come on that day, when each will imperishably bring to the Great Service the best accumulations of his experience, of his vigilance! Through all our manifold Societies, Institutes and Organizations, the possibility has been given for self-development along the most varied aspirations, if only these are directed towards the sacred stream of Culture. Each suppression of the sacred feeling of the beautiful is alien to us.

Now in the growth of construction, the World League of Culture is towering. This is the hyper-unifying conception, before which all other divisions, definitions and denominations have no place. Unity and general good-will is expressed in the word "League". The conception of universality requires no explanation, because truth is one, Beauty is one and Knowledge is one. About this there can be no further discussion. In the same way no educated mind will argue about the concept of Culture, because the Great Service of Light, refinement and the upliftment of the heart are universal.

The realization of the long-desired possibility of the World League of Culture is in itself most significant.

In the present difficult hour, at a time of utmost world tension, the possibility is offered of uniting around a noble unifying concept. Culture is the testing stone of inexhaustible youthfulness of the heart. Neither age, mindless education, nor other superficial divisions are in order, nor can there be mutual harm where the ancient *Ur* shines. The inextinguishable Light cannot have any enemies within the flaming beautiful domain.

Of course darkness and ignorance, always striving to disperse and to destroy, will again attempt to outrage and to oppose. But gathering in the name of the thrice-blessed conception of Culture, we should not burden our hearts with fears about darkness. It is true that darkness exists, but it is also true that Light conquers darkness. This old axiom is also indisputable.

In its wide scope, the World League of Culture must sponsor everything beautiful, everything within the sphere of Knowledge. All ways to ennoble the young generations, whose hearts in essence always respond to heroism and attainment should emanate from the World League of Culture.

In contact with Culture, we need empty words least, and most of all we bind ourselves to enlightened actions. It is necessary not to impede, not to limit, but first of all to mutually combine, respond sincerely with fiery actions, in tirelessness, in valor, in the kindling of hearts and in incessant labor for the realization of the General Good—this is the aim of Culture.

Let everyone in his own field gather and bring to the one hearth the very best of which his experience and creativeness is capable. Everything good and enlightening, is so needed and should be welcomed. In this greeting, from the depths of the heart, in unbreakable striving towards co-operation, in blessed reciprocity, let us begin our new endeavor.

Let us send our greetings to all our visible and unseen friends and co-workers. To be one with the whole world already means Infinity, where, for every laborer, the beautiful Garden is preordained!

At the right hour! On the right Path!

Himalayas, July 24, 1932.

WORLD LEAGUE OF CULTURE

III

The Word of India

BEFORE us we have a vast number of periodicals published in India. They are most significant, both in regard to their quantity and variety, justly in keeping with the characteristics of this great continent. We will mention several names outside of the stupendous number of publications in Bengali, Urdu, Tamil and other Hindu and Moslem dialects.

Here is the voluminous "Kabyan," devoted to the highest spiritual concept. Here are the publications of the Visva-Bharata, permeated with the noble enlightened spirit of the great poet of India—Rabindranath Tagore. Here is the "Modern Review" with its wide response, under the experienced guidance of its revered editor, Ramananda Chatterjee. Here is the "Maha Bodhi Journal" directed by the benevolent hand of the venerable Sri Devamitta Dhammapala and the "Ceylon Buddhist" of the Y.M.B.A. where P. Siriwaredkhana works untiringly. Here is an entire series of good journals of the Ramakrishna Mission, such as the "Prabuddha Bharata" in Mayavati, "Vedanta Kesari" (Madras), the "Morning Star" (Patna). Here is the "Scholar" from Palghat, with its wide, cultural artistic and scientific program. Here is the evocative "Dawn," saturated with the religious and cultural teachings of the esteemed Sadhu Shri Vasvani. Here is the beautifully edited "Rupam," of which O. Gangoly can justly be proud.

Here is a legion of periodicals, indicating the best educational aims: "Kalpaka," "Educational Review" (Madras), "Young Folk," "Upasana," "Student," "Trivent,"

"Indian Educator," "Orient" (Bombay), "Theosophist," "Young Builder," "All-India Trade Magazine," "The Field," "The Singalese" (Ceylon), "Current Science," "Journal of the Geological Society," "Journal of Mining and Metallurgy," "The Forester," "Indian Science," "Literary Review" of D. B. Taraporevala, various organs of the Botanical Survey, of the Archeological Survey, the "Journal of the Bombay Society of Natural History," publications of the Bose Institute, "The Annual of the Biological Chemists' Society of India," "Indian Historical Quarterly," "Journal of the Asiatic Society of Bengal," "Journal of the Bombay Branch of the Royal Asiatic Society." . . .

It is impossible to cite in its entirety the complete colorful multitude of equally useful publications which guide cultural thought. The Indian Year-Book indicates that there are 5,362 printing presses, 1,378 newspapers, and 3,089 periodicals. During one year, 2,117 books in English and other European languages, and 14,276 books in Hindu, Moslem and other vernacular tongues were published. Amidst the world ocean of the press such strongholds of thought constitute a beautiful island.

Of the entire educational asset, even these few mentioned titles already characterize a whole world of philosophical, scientific and social thought, majestic in its traditions, millenniums old. In our days of diffusion and perversion, it is precious to witness the depth of existing living thought!

Often people speak of the past and only of the past. And we seem to be ashamed of the present, especially when it concerns philosophical and scientific thinking, which by many of our contemporaries is regarded as something remote, abstract.

Too many persons at present believe that religion, philosophy, culture, science, the art of thinking are abstract and that to dwell on them at present is untimely, and that the so-called true realities are trade, industry and accounting.

Therefore it is such a joy to see not only books devoted to the true values, but also monthly and weekly periodicals where the daily thought pulsates in all its incessant untiring strength. You know how monthly and weekly periodicals require continuous kindling and concentrated labor.

Only recently I wrote you about friendliness, as the adamant of the world. In these manifold editions one notices there are no malicious polemics. One observes the predominance of facts of research and a profound philosophical approach to questions of vital necessity. Even such an apparently specialized journal as the "All-India Trade Magazine" heads an issue with an article, "The Cultural Mission of the Modern Merchant," and concludes it with a beautiful quotation from Goethe. In this way the co-operation of commerce and culture—a relationship that is so often mutilated in the concave prisms of contemporary life, finds a dignified solution.

One immediately notices the absence of vulgar jokes and all the trash attached to the perverted notion of a so-called "good-time."

One also notices that instead of crass intolerance, a benevolent treatment of a neighbor's point of view can often be found. Certainly, we always select the kindest and the best, because in the domains of Culture one may only travel along positive milestones.

The milestones of evil and darkness have already lured humanity into the labyrinths of black magic, from which neither nudism, golf, gambling on the stock exchange, races, nor record-breaking matches can help to find a way out. Whither will it lead, this pugilistic speed? A human being may also slip downhill towards the precipice at terrifying speed. This would also be extraordinary speed!

The number of serious articles devoted to women's movements, to youth and to experimental research, also makes one rejoice. Constructiveness and seriousness of exposition also indicate the demands of the reader. And these thousands of publications—in reality the number is even greater than that given—have their circle of readers. They somehow exist, are regularly issued, and in most cases probably are published by people who know what labor is and who are usually not wealthy.

At a time of general depression, in the midst of all sorts of upheavals, it is truly precious to record the facts of steadfast spirit. Let these be multiform, for Culture as such also has infinite aspects, yet it remains One is its radiant, creative foundation.

It is always necessary to look for facts without prejudice and conventional limitations, facts in which the human heart resounds. Our duty is to collect and to record these facts of the accumulations of the spirit. Thus are the treasuries of true values erected. In the hours of depression, one may primarily renew one's strength, unbreakable vigor, patience, joyousness and all the creative principles of life from these true treasures.

It is infinitely inspiring to see, with one's own eyes, this multitude of serious publications which expand and sensitize the consciousness, and which exist as the best indication that they are needed and welcomed by many millions of hearts.

Please convey to all our Societies, Institutions and Committees, the thought that each of them in its own country should collect and present a brief digest and description of the press and publications. Let all our European, Chinese, Japanese, South American and South African Societies give such reports; they will constitute a most valuable symposium on the direction of contemporary thought.

Let no one attach too much attention to negative matters. Every expression, ugliness and ignorance is contagious and depressing. May all our co-workers proceed by positive, radiant paths. And as always let us remember that only the sparks of positive constructiveness kindle hearts, and awaken creative joy.

Himalayas, November, 1932.

WORLD LEAGUE OF CULTURE

IV

The Radiant City

"TO regard the Beautiful means to improve" (Plato). "Man becomes that of which he thinks" (Upanishads).

"Comprehend the uncontrollable, console the faint-hearted, defend the weak, have patience in everything" (Apostle Paul).

"Illumine yourself with the Light of Knowledge" (Hosea, 10-12).

"Man has to become the co-worker of heaven and earth. . . . All beings nourish each other. . . .

"Consciousness, compassion and courage are the three universal qualities, but sincerity is needed to apply them. . . . Does there not exist a panacea for everything that exists? Is it not love towards humanity? Do not do unto others that which you do not wish to be done unto you . . .

"If man could govern himself, what difficulties would he meet in governing a state? . . .

"An Ignoramus proud of his knowledge, a nonentity excessively desirous of freedom, a man who returns to ancient customs, are subject to unavoidable calamities" (Confucius).

How old all this is and how greatly it is needed now! Perhaps it only seems to us that there is such a necessity not only in faith but also in the professing of faith? No, friends, this is not merely seeming to be so. The news of each day shocks one in its reflection of the turmoil of the world.

Apostle Paul and Plato and Confucius give courage

again, because they passed through all the horrors of spiritual turmoil, and Solomon the Wise confirms: "And this will pass."

Verily, it will pass. Pilgrims are going to Shambhala and Belovodye. No abysses can stop the striving of spirit. Known are Prester John and Gessar Khan and the Lord of Shambhala. Behind the White Mountains the bells of the abodes are ringing.

Among the spiritual movements born of the past few years, the pilgrims of the "Radiant City" especially resound. Brother Alexis speaks thus in his teachings of their pilgrimages: "Amidst the mire of the world's untruth, amidst the jungles of false Knowledge, avoiding the rocks of human stupidity, thou wilt reach the plains of Thy searches and the eight roads which lead to them. And in its midst is a lake of living water. The path to it lies in the circles of pilgrims. Thou will become a pilgrim in order to awaken within them the longing for perfection. Say whether thou art willing to respect all quests. Dost thou wish to penetrate into the quests of others? Dost thou wish to seek the light of perfection? Has thou answered: 'I so wish?' Pilgrim, thou art accepted into our circle. Here is a staff with wings for thee. Proceed, Flower of the circle of pilgrims—buckthorn.

"Thou who hast understood the longing for the provisions to be upon all paths everywhere along the road, and yet never to know whether or not you are on the path—here I give thee the blue star of a corn-flower, Let it lead thee. The blue stars of the corn-flowers bloom upon the gold of the rye fields. But thou who hast come, what fields hast thou sown? Do not pass by the fields longing for love, sow them with the gold of free strivings. Take an ear; in it thou wilt find seeds for the sowing. From each seed, sown by thee, let there grow a new Radiant City. And they are all one. Fruitless are the unwatered fields. . . . Then Let the ruby-colored carnation bloom upon Thy chest. Go. I shall meet thee on the path.

"The Radiant City stands upon a pure lake. Four

Brotherhoods lead to it: The Oriental Brotherhood of John—a brotherhood of religious creativeness and preaching of the spirit; the Northern Brotherhood of Boyanov—the brotherhood of the magic of art; the Pythagorian Brotherhood—a western brotherhood of science and philosophy; the Southern Brotherhood of Mikula—the brotherhood of love and sacrifice.

"The pilgrims went upon a pilgrimage and informed each other about it during their spiritual repasts. In certain places the pilgrims met, and partook of their common repast consisting of bread, wine and fruit under the open sky."

Are not such quests wondrously beautiful? Is it not significant that the word Culture now rings out in all magazines? People are attracted to this panacea from all ends of the world. Here is a call of Culture from Bulgaria, there is one from India, one from Estonia and one from Buenos Aires. In heartfelt striving, people realize where the panacea lies.

But of course, there are just as many voices afraid of this light-bearing word: But without this condition, there would be no Armageddon, there would be no calamities which disturb not only the markets, the bazaars, but which also destroy the Temples. To those who fear the word Culture, we shall refer the article of Dr. Cousins, "The Salvation of Civilization is Through Culture," or to the book of Proctor, "Evolution of Culture," or to Bacon, who underlined the significance of this concept. Only recently a Professor of New York University, Dr. Radosavljevitch wrote beautifully about Culture—the Reverence of Light. Swami Djagadisvarananda, speaking of Culture, concludes: "Similar to religion and science, Art and Culture are universal beyond the boundaries of all ignorant limitations." Shri Vasvani dedicates his beautiful book, "Religion and Culture" to the same concept. On the other continent, Louis Madeleine speaks of Culture as being "very humane," and also speaks of its power and attraction. How many beautiful voices, how much mutual understanding and how many pledges for true constructiveness they contain!

Let us not fear all those who are frightened and let us proceed courageously by the path of collecting all beautiful and eternal beginnings.

Let us remember about co-operation in all its manifestations. Let us attract the most diverse workers towards the future labor so that there will be no negation and extinction. For, everyone can manifest in his own life the highest measure of friendliness. Everyone knows in his heart where there is evil and ignorance, and he thus will be firm in counteracting evil.

"All for one and one for all." According to this old formula, let us find inexhaustible strength.

"It is not better in the world", verily it is so! The world structure is cracking. But where there are pilgrims, where there are stone masons, where there are creators, hope itself is being transmuted into straight Knowledge. This Knowledge speaks of the urgency of the hour. Let us hasten and be not afraid.

The book, "Fiery World," thus ordains the courageous constructiveness:

"468. The manifestation of the loss of co-operation makes people quite helpless. The loss of concordance of rhythm destroys all possibilities of new achievements. You yourself see what difficulties are engendered through disunion. Such a state is very dangerous.

"472. Poor is the master craftsman who does not make use of all the riches of nature. For the skillful carver, a bent tree is a precious treasure. A good weaver uses each spot for the embellishment of his carpet. The goldsmith rejoices at each unusual alloy of metals. Only the mediocre craftsman will deplore everything unusual. Only an impoverished imagination is satisfied with the limits set by others. The true master develops great acuteness and resourcefulness in himself. The blessed spell of his craft frees the master worker from discouragement. Even the night does not bring darkness for the master, but only a variety of forms of the one Fire. No one can entice a master toward aimless speculations, because he knows the inexhaustibility of the essence of being. In the name of this unity, the master gathers each blossom and constructs an eternal harmony. He regrets the waste of any material. But people far from mastery lose the best treasures. They repeat the best prayers and invocations, but these broken and unrealized rhythms are carried away like dust. The fragments of knowledge are turned into the dust of a dead desert. The human heart knows about Fire, but the reason tries to obscure this evident wisdom. People say, "He was consumed with wrath; he withered from envy; he was aflame with desire." In a multitude of expressions, precise and clear, people show knowledge of the significance of Fire. But these people are not master artisans, and are always ready thoughtlessly to scatter the pearls they themselves so need! One cannot understand the human prodigality which destroys the treasures of Light. People do not deny themselves a single opportunity for negation. They are ready to extinguish all fires around them, only to proclaim that there is no Fire within them. Yet to extinguish fires and admit the darkness is the horror of ignorance.

"476. The fiery consciousness gives that invincible optimism which leads towards Truth. In its essence Truth itself is positive. There is no negation where fire creates. One must accept the conditions of the world according to the level of fiery consciousness. The conditions of the manifest life often impede the fiery consciousness. It is difficult to be reconciled with the conventionality of the vestments of constructiveness. The course of life with its many details impedes the assimilation of fire. But if one contacts the Fiery World at least once, then all the husk becomes unnoticeable. Thus one should be guided by the higher level, without being disturbed by the imperfections of the surroundings."

WORLD LEAGUE OF CULTURE

V

Exchange

DEAR FRIENDS: Recently I have heard from you that apartments in New York are sometimes exchanged now for goods or products, In the *Literary Digest* for February, 1933, the following note has also appeared:

"Paris and Middle West seem to be competing in leadership to bring back the age of barter.

"The first places its emphasis on art, the second on foodstuffs. In Paris, paintings at an estimated value of $100,000 have been exchanged without the use of a single sou. Shoes, automobiles, wines, and even surgical operations were the medium, Thus the *United Press* reports:

" 'In a barnlike structure at the Exposition Park, just outside the Portes de Versailles, the Salon des Exchanges has flourished for two months.

" 'The Modernistic Painters, Osterlind and Ramey, received enough new shoes to last them twenty years each. Vera Rokline, formerly of Petrograd, will no longer have to worry about hats. Bompard, a noted gourmet, has fillet in his cellar with Chablis. One fortunate Parisian, S.H.Moreau, obtained an automobile.'

"Other items listed in exchange for paintings were:

"A physician's services for the artist for a year; a surgical operation; rare Chinese embroidery; half a dozen washing machines; rooms in a hotel, and life insurance. One artist accepted an elaborate camera for a couple of his paintings."

"Five Americans were represented. One, Harry Stillman, turned down an offer of a Montmartre cabaret for free champagne for himself and his friends any time they wished to visit the place.

"Other Americans who took part in the show are Frederick Kann and Davis Kerkman, dynamic painters, and Minna Harkavy and Anne Wolfe, sculptors."

On the following page, under the headline, "The Growing Barter and Exchange Movement," there are also many useful suggestions and a description of how these are already practically applied. The author states: "An important by-product of the movement is the improvement of the morale of the community. By offering the means whereby men provide for their physical needs through their own toil, co-operative bartering is preventing moral collapse."

These significant descriptions reminded me of several episodes from my own life when I was collecting Old Masters. For example, one well-known antique dealer asked an enormous sum from me for an old Dutch painting. And when I pointed out the absurdity of such a price to him, he smiled and said, "It is strange for you to speak of price, when you yourself are making real bank-notes. Just give me one of your paintings in place of a bank-note."

A similar thing occurred when I approached a well-known Court physician of the Emperor for treatment. He refused to state a fee, but asked for a sketch instead. There are many such examples and they not only show the vitality of art, but are also exceptional and powerful examples of all kinds of exchanges in the cultural field, replacing the conventional and fluctuating bank-note with the value of labor.

Voluntary exchange which provides a new impulse for multifarious production, spreading through large masses, is especially useful now when the material and spiritual crisis has upset the equilibrium of normal progress for a long period.

It would be desirable to facilitate such co-operation in every way. I would like to hear the opinion of our friend Leon Dabo about this. With his tremendous experience and customary brilliance he always comes to assist the solution of the most arduous questions of creativeness and progress.

A highly cultured outlook will protect this vital exchange from any vulgarity which might introduce a disintegrating note.

I should be very glad to hear the opinion of Mr. Dabo, as his judgment, always impartial, would help to avoid many complications which should be dispelled in so delicate a question as the exchange of cultural creations.

In the "Sphere" we have also recently read of an interesting undertaking in England of a whole co-operative-barter settlement for the unemployed. Within the shortest period these co-operators not only succeeded in establishing a firm foundation but even built their own theater and other public cultural institutions.

In the days of crashing bank-notes and even of the very universal almighty golden idol, every new co-operative that upholds human labor as the true value, is indeed most welcome. And it is especially welcome when the concept of human labor is accepted without conventional limitations, in its true, real meaning. This proves that at last people have understood that intellectual, creative labor absorbs more energy than muscular work, a fact sufficiently corroborated by science.

Verily, the value of multiform labor is a true constant of human interrelationship, if labor will be understood in its whole powerful creativeness.

The quality of labor, without egotism, in continuous self-improvement, solves many financial problems which already are beyond antiquated conventional practices. Interchange of labor, perfecting of labor and cordial co-operation should be immediately encouraged by the World League of Culture.

Himalayas, April, 1933.

WORLD LEAGUE OF CULTURE

VI

The Anguish of the Planet

THIRTY-TWO years ago, I wrote an article, "To Nature." A third of a Century has but confirmed all the calls to Nature which I then expressed. But everything is now accelerated; hence, the "call to nature" has already also changed into "the anguish of the planet."

In 1901, after my travels through Europe and Russia, I thought: "Strong is the unconscious striving to Nature in man, the single direction of his life; so strong is this striving, that man does not hesitate to use pathetic parodies of Nature—gardens, and even indoor-plants, forgetting that sometimes he is as droll as someone who carries with him, the hair of his beloved.

"Everything impels us towards Nature; our spiritual consciousness and aesthetic demands, as well as our bodies, have been awakened and propel us towards Nature. We, have become armed with vanity and have lost faith. Of course, as in the presence of everything natural and simple, we often become stubborn; instead of steps towards real Nature, we try to cheat ourselves by false and created simulations of it. But life, in its spiral of culture, immutably carries us closer to the primary source of all things, and never as yet, have there been heard so many different calls to Nature as now.

"And one must say that the demands for a solicitous attitude towards Nature and the safeguarding of its characteristics is nowhere as easy to be applied as with us. What character of their own can many of the European districts have now? To give character to that which has lost it is already impossible. And, at the same time, what, if not originality and character, is valuable everywhere and in everything? Without touching upon the principle of nationality, let us, nevertheless, state that national products are valued, not so much because of their unique utility, but because of their character.

"Unfortunately, the consideration of a careful attitude towards Nature cannot be superimposed, nor can one be imbued with it forcefully. By itself, it can enter unnoticeably into the daily life of each one and, although unnoticed from without, it can turn into the impetus of a creator.

"People will say: 'Must we also worry about this? Should we waste time for consideration as to the character of Nature? As it is, we have too little time, and besides, there are not sufficient funds for it.'

"But again, because the question of expenses is always so acute that even its phantom impels fear, I say, for the third time, it demands no means, and the conversation as to time and extra labor reminds one of a man who does not wash his mouth after a meal, because of back of time. But if the excuse is made that it is because of frank unwillingness and disinclination to live in the manner of one's grandfathers (although these same people will instantly start something of a character of which grandfathers never dreamt), then this is another matter.

"In order to care for something, one must naturally primarily know the object of his care.

"Do we desire to know Nature?

"It is not apparent.

"Is it customary for us to become acquainted with Nature?

"No, this is not customary.

"One especially always expects much—and in this one rarely errs—of a man, who in his youth had close communion with Nature, or in other words, who came out of Nature, and in his elder years, returns to it.

"Sprung from the earth, and returned to earth.

"On hearing of such a beginning and end, one always

presupposes an interesting and richly full middle-age, and rarely, as I say, does one err in this.

"It also happens that sometimes, towards the end of life, a man who has no possibility of returning physically to Nature, at least returns to it spiritually. Of course, this is not as complete, but it nevertheless adds a fine conclusion to a life fully lived. . . .

"People who spring from Nature, are somehow instinctively purer; at that, I do not know whether the ever-goal-fitting Nature whispers to them, or whether they are healthier spiritually, but they usually better allocate their energies, and it will be rarer for you to ask the man who has sprung from Nature: 'Why does he do that, when the period of activity has long passed for him?'

" 'Drop everything, go to Nature,' one tells a man who has lost his equilibrium, physical or moral; but his bodily presence alone in Nature will have little meaning and the result will be effective only when he will succeed in merging spiritually with Nature, in being imbued spiritually with its Beauty; only then will Nature give to the suppliant strength, and a healthy and quiet energy.

"The City which emerged from Nature, now threatens Nature; the City created by man, now dominates man. In its contemporary development the City is already a direct contrast to Nature; Let it then live in a Beauty directly juxtaposed, without any unifying attempts to co-ordinate that which cannot be co-ordinated.

"But there is nothing terrifying in the contrast of the Beauty of a City and the Beauty of Nature. As the tones of beautiful contrast do not kill each other but produce a stronger harmony, so the Beauty of a City and Nature go hand in hand in their juxtaposition, accentuating the mutual impression, producing a powerful triad, the third note of which will sound out the Beauty of the unknown."

Thus I thought thirty-two years ago. Since then much of the "good earth" has become the "bloody earth." Many harvests have been wiped away. The extension of the deserts has not ceased, the farmers have begun to abandon their very nurturer and have been attracted to the cities, only to increase the army of the unemployed. In the service of the value of the stock market, hecatombs of grain, coffee and other valuable products have been sunk somewhere in the ocean or burned away. In some places the depletion of cattle products occurred, in other places forests have been razed, and in still others, the deadening sands have extended their conquests.

The City has apparently conquered Nature. In smoke, the City has drawn its conjurations upon the sky. We have erred in expecting only hundred-storied houses. The dwellings of the cities yearn to become still higher in order to entice and shelter all of Nature's deserters. Moloch—the stock market—more than once has fiercely chastised all its devotees. But an easy though illusory gain nevertheless distracts the confused human mind from true values. The City attracts the weak in spirit, and leaves to Nature either the outmoded old-believers, or the tourists who arrogantly crowd along the beaten tracks. Everyone recollects the sight of a forest after its holiday visitors. The refuse lies about in piles, and the nature-dweller whispers sadly: "Again they have scattered rubbish about!"

A speedy, almost dazzling passage through Nature does not mean co-operation with it. And now, during the days of Armageddon, in the midst of confusion and in days gripped with anger, one must recognize true values. It would seem as if Nature were inexhaustible; yet the castrated spirit, the robot, the mechanics of technocracy, can cover even the greatest spaces with their debris. And no one who cuts down a tree, ever thinks of planting a new one.

Only with general culture, which will recall the true values may one primarily attract the farmers again to the soil. Then Knowledge, education, broad Tolerance, reconciliation will recall joyous labor again instead of merry pastimes.

The excesses of the urban crowds will become apparent to the peaceful spirit, and the machine itself will begin to converse under a loving hand. Each lack of co-measurement is opposed to the Highest Creativeness. But what can be more un-commensurated than the deterioration of a giant city, and the pollution by ignorance of the desert which once was a flourishing expanse.

If man is not always capable of creativeness, nevertheless he can always inflict pain. And he may do this, not only to people, not only to animals, but also to the whole of nature and to the entire planet. Great is the responsibility of mankind; not one to make man vain, but one which humanity must accept sacredly. In essence the human make-up is positive, creative, and the decaying elements are nothing but the products of ignorance. For this dark ignorance defiles the mind, dries the heart, and soils and withers the entire planet.

"How beautiful!" were the last words of the departing Corot. He who had loved Nature, in the moment of his great passage across, was worthy of perceiving something truly beautiful. We speak of peace, of disarmament, but it is by spirit that the swords have to be beaten into plows.

"Peace unto you," Christ ordained to us. "I leave my peace unto you; my peace do I give you; not as the world gives, do I give unto you."

"Peace to all beings, peace to all worlds," chants the hermit of India before prayer.

"Having known Me as the mighty Ruler of all the worlds, and as the lover of all beings, the Sage goeth to peace" (Bhagavad Gita, Fifth Discourse).

"Where the chosen ones gather," says the Koran, "there resounds but one song, the song of peace."

"Let every living thing live," says Buddhism.

Every orthodox liturgy begins with the exclamation of the great liturgical prayer, "Let us pray to the Lord for the peace of all the world."

Everything creatively beautiful, everything exalted, invokes peace. But this quietude descends upon us amidst Nature. Thus the Book of the East, "Fiery World," commands:

"529. A common error of people is to cease to study after leaving school. The Pythagoreans and similar philosophic schools of Greece, India, and China furnish sufficient examples of continuous study. Truly, limiting education to the prescribed schooling indicates ignorance. Obligatory learning is only the entrance to real knowledge. If we divide humanity into three categories—those who are altogether unschooled, those whose education is confined to compulsory schooling, and those who continue their education—the number of the last will prove astonishingly small. This primarily shows indifference toward future lives. In their decline of spirit, men are indifferent even to their own future. There should remain a record that in the present significant year it is necessary to remind people about that which was useful a thousand years ago. In addition to elementary education one should further the education of adults. Several generations exist simultaneously on Earth, and they are all equally indifferent in striving to the future which they cannot evade. Such negligence is astonishing! Learning has become an empty shell. Yet for a simple holiday people like to dress in their best. Is it possible that they do not think it behooves them to secure an attire of Light for the solemn Abode in the Fiery World? One should rejoice not in bigotry, not in superstition, but with an illumined mind, and not only at the schools for children but also at the uniting of adults for continuous learning.

"530. It is right to repeat about the sickness of the planet. It is right to understand the desert as the shame of humanity. It is right to direct one's thinking toward nature. It is right to turn one's thought to the task of cooperation with nature. It is right to recognize that to plunder nature is to squander the treasures of the people. It is right to rejoice at nature as the refuge from fiery epidemics. He who does not think about nature does not know the Abode of Spirit."

The evocation about culture, about peace, about creativeness and Beauty will reach only an ear strengthened by true values. The understanding of life as the process of self-perfection in the name of the people's bliss, will be crystallized there where the reverence for Nature is strong. Therefore the League of Culture, amidst the fundamental work of enlightenment, must by all means expound the wise attitude toward Nature, as the source of cheerful work, wise joy, continual knowledge and creation.

Himalayas, March 24, 1933.

WORLD LEAGUE OF CULTURE

VII

The Role of the Teacher

WE have news before us from Chicago that the salaries of school teachers have been frozen. This sounds strange on the eve of the opening of the Chicago Century Exposition.

In the *Literary Digest* for March 18, 1933, under the title of "The Teachers' Battle for the Schools," the following most striking facts are given among many others: "Education must be deflated so the order of the economists goes forth. . . . 'We are on the battle-line,' is the cry from thousands of educators gathered at the Convention in Minneapolis of the Department of Superintendents of the National Education Association. . . . 'Already,' Dr. Cooper declares, 'thousands of children in such Sections are virtually without schooling. Two hundred districts in Arkansas are able to give but sixty days of school in a year, or about two years' education in eight. And similar situations prevail in Alabama, Oklahoma, and Idaho.' . . . 'We would prefer to make personal sacrifices,' states Prof. J. K. Norton of Teachers College, 'rather than have children denied their educational birthright. It is this loyalty that has won the admiration of parents for teachers in many communities, and that has paved the way for effective cooperation in defense of the schools.' . . . 'What will it profit the nation if we maintain the credit of industrial corporations and deny education to America's children?' asks the report of the Committee of Toledo, Ohio." . . .

In the last issue of the *New Haven Teachers' Journal* there is a complete itemization of the most remarkable information about the same plight of educational matters. In the leading editorial we read the following: "The crisis confronting public school education in New Haven is now in such an alarming state that one does not hesitate to say that we have arrived at the point where we feel each impending decision may be the fatal one." The article concludes with a call for uncompromising justice. The following article, "Human Rights versus Money Rights," states, "Taxpayers are groaning under the weight of the expense of the Government compared to their reduced incomes. . . . It has become increasingly evident that what was called in the beginning 'the Depression' has now become 'the Banker's Panic'."

A third article of the same Journal, entitled: "The Citizens' Conference on the Crisis in Education," is most characteristic for our present-day disturbances and gives among other items, a "Declaration of Policy," which affirms the importance of education for the nation, protesting against the intervention of politics in school life and again calling attention to the necessity of proportionate salaries with regard to the cost of living. The declaration is compelled to repeat old axioms, apparently because there is sufficient reason for their repetition. Thus the fourth paragraph of the declaration states: "Education is a necessity, not a luxury, since the growth of the child cannot be halted or postponed during an economic emergency." And the thirty-third paragraph remarks quite correctly, "If the State is to have institutions adequate to serve its needs during the coming generation, it must not now unwisely weaken the human foundations of those institutions."

Such significant statements are found in a copy of a Teachers' Journal sent to us. But even without this, we have lately read an endless list of various "necrologies," about the curtailing and cutting, especially of educational institutions. Verily, not in one country but everywhere, people seemingly have agreed not to think any longer of the future and to discontinue the growth of educational undertakings. The condition of the teaching staffs, under the constant threat of sudden curtailments, has become altogether unstable, thus bringing harm to the education of youth.

Everywhere there are special Ministries of Public Education, Departments of science and art; it is strange to observe that such institutions, which would seem to be the most essential for the progress of a cultural country, are the first to be subject to continuous cuts: As if they were a luxury and not the most essential public necessity, without which all other ministries and departments could not even exist! People do not dare to discuss the curtailment in salaries of many other departments, but it has become a general trend of mind to suggest the cutting of teachers' salaries which are already meager. The teacher, who, as a rule, has no savings, must exist in some miraculous way, and yet he must manifest full kindheartedness, satisfaction, balance, and all those qualities which are primarily demanded of a teacher. Depressed by worries about to how to make ends meet, the teacher must wear the mask of endless patience and the smile of wisdom, when at the same time his family may not know how to balance their daily needs. Why is such exceptional civic heroism demanded only from the teacher? Why should we expect continuous, endless sacrifices just from those who are most of all in need?

A country which is aiming at construction and the positive solution of life problems, cannot ignore the condition of its teachers. To ignore them would mean to ignore the destiny of its entire future generation. Of course the teacher who is absorbed in educational work which requires special concentration, is the least protesting element, unless he be compelled by some hopeless hardships. People desire that teachers should not only teach well and should not only continuously bring their Knowledge up-to-date, but also that the teachers should arouse the love of their students. Love is inseparable from reverence and the nation ought to create an especially esteemed position for its teachers. It is impossible to divide the teachers arbitrarily into lower and higher ones, for the synthesis of Knowledge is high everywhere and one must apply a great deal of time and concentrated effort to become assimilate and remain on the crest of the synthesis of Knowledge.

The teacher is a friend of a positive, creative government, because the teacher exists for continuous constructiveness and for the affirmation of human dignity. Who else will tell the young generation about the most beautiful, the most creative, the most powerful, the most heroic and about progressive Knowledge? Verily, we expect from the teacher the Knowledge of the highest concepts. We expect from him endless patience, incessant labor and continuous improvement, and at the same time we do not exercise care, that these elevated conditions and demands are sufficiently guaranteed.

For twenty years I myself was at the head of educational institutions. Among thousands of students and hundreds of professors and teachers, one could observe the complex of human interrelations in full diversity. Indeed, the teaching profession stands high, but it is also difficult. In the continuous flow of the school's elements, one has to retain a great equilibrium and must always inexhaustibly provide joy to the young spirit which must enter life full of the real hopes and high aspirations, and to which task the teacher has pledged himself.

The concept of teaching widely permeates the whole of life, beyond school hours; how valuable if we can safe guard throughout our entire lives, in our hearts a love and reverence towards our first teachers and guides! If the students, entering life would realize afterwards that their teachers had suffered undeservedly and had been overburdened, many regrets would occur in the name of love and friendliness, which are the foundations of education.

For the sake of these fundamentals of public life, in other words for the sake of the foundations of Culture, one should give special attention to questions of education as the most precious, as the most sacred. If, in the time of its greatest welfare, the nation must give the greatest care to the solution of educational problems, then during the time of material and spiritual crises, the conditions of educators must definitely be safeguarded.

The safeguarding of the foundations of education is the primary aim of the League of Culture. Without care for education, the very existence of the League of Culture becomes useless. One may unite in the name of knowledge, in the name of the beautiful, in the name of sincere co-operation. Therefore, one must ask all members of the League, each in his own activity, and each in his own field, to draw the most sincere attention to the plight of the problem of Education.

Let us not feel relief that after all education still exists and that teachers exist somehow. This is not sufficient. Education must thrive beautifully and teachers should be in good circumstances, as befits a progressive, positive nation. If everyone, according to his ability, will apply thought and care to this essential problem, then I assure you that much good will result for the benefit of a truly national necessity.

In my book, "Shambhala," I paid tribute to teachers in the following passage of an essay entitled, "Guru—The Teacher":

"Once in Finland I sat upon the shores of Lake Ladoga with a farm lad. A middle aged man passed us by and my small companion stood up and with great reverence and took off his cap.

"I asked him afterwards: 'Who was that man,' and with special seriousness the boy answered, 'He is a teacher.'

"I again asked, 'Is he your teacher?'

" 'No,' answered the boy, 'he is the teacher from the neighboring school.'

" 'Then you know him personally?' I persisted.

" 'No,' he answered with astonishment.

" 'Then why did you greet him with such reverence?'

"Still more seriously my little companion answered, 'Because he is a teacher!' "

Verily in this little boy, who bared his head before a

teacher, is contained the healthy seed of the nation, which knows the past and knows the significance of the word "to build."

Let us close with the following lines from the Book of the East, "Fiery World": "A mother was relating to her son about a great Saint: 'Even a pinch of dust from beneath his feel is already great.' It came to pass that this holy man came through the village. The boy followed his footsteps and took a pinch of this earth, sewed it in a bag and began to wear it around his neck. And when he recited his lesson at school, he always held this holy relic in his hand. Thereupon the boy became filled with such inspiration, that his answers were always remarkable. At last, when he left the school, the teacher praised him and asked him what it was that he always held in his hand. The boy replied, 'The earth from underneath the feet of the Saint who passed through our village.' The teacher added, 'The earth of the Saint serves you better than any gold.' A neighboring shopkeeper who was present, said to himself, 'What a foolish boy, to take only a pinch of this golden earth. I shall await the Saint's coming and shall collect all the earth from underneath his feet. Thus I shall receive the most profitable goods.' And the shopkeeper sat at his doorstep and waited in vain for the Saint. But the Saint never came. Covetousness is not in the nature of the 'Fiery World.'

"Shame on the country where teachers dwell in poverty and want. Shame on those who know that their children are being taught by a man who is in need. Not only is it shameful for the nation that does not take care of the teachers of its future generation, but it is a sign of ignorance. Can one entrust children to a man who is depressed? Can one forget what emanation is created by sorrow? Can one be ignorant of the fact that the spirit which is depressed will not evoke enthusiasm? Can one consider teaching an insignificant profession? Can one expect of children the enlightenment of spirit if the school is a place of humiliation and offense? Can one feel the construction during the gnashing of teeth? Can one expect the fires of the heart when the spirit is silent? Thus I say and repeat, that the people who have forgotten the teacher have forgotten their future. Let us not lose an hour in order to direct one's thought towards the joy of the future. But Let us take care that the teacher should be the most valuable person in the institutions of the nation. The time approaches when the spirit must be educated and derive joy from true Knowledge. The fire is at the threshold.

"One must soften the hearts of teachers, then they will abide in constant Knowledge. The hearts of children recognize that which is aflame and that which is extinguished. Not a prescribed lesson, but the mutual striving of the teacher and disciple discloses a world full of wonders. To open the eyes of disciples means to love the great creation together with him. Who does not agree that one should stand on firm ground in order to aim at the far-off distance? The marksman will verify this. Thus, let us learn to take care of everything that affirms the future. The fire is at the threshold.

"Every abuse of the Savior, Teacher, and all Heroes is a thrust towards savagery and a plunge into chaos. How is it possible to explain that chaos is very close; there is no need to cross an ocean to find it. It is equally difficult to explain that savagery has its inception in the most minute. When the treasure of solemnity is lost and the pearls of knowledge of the heart are scattered, what remains? One may remember how people mocked at the Great Sacrifice. Has not the whole world become responsible for such savagery? One may see how the latter is reflected in shallowness. There is nothing worse than shallowness. I affirm—be blessed in all energies, only not to succumb to the marasmus of dissolution. Thus Let us remember all Great Days!

"One may imagine how beautiful can be the co-service of multitudes of people, when their hearts aspire to one ascent. We shall not say impossible or it is rejected. From Power one may borrow and from Light one may become enlightened only to realize in what lies the Light and the Power. Some one already roars with laughter but he laughs in darkness. What can be more horrible than laughter in darkness! But, Light will abide with him who desires it."

Urusvati, Himalayas, April, 1933.

THE CONCEPT OF CULTURE

WITH our friends lives Tizi-Wizzi. This is not a human being but a parrot and a most unique bird. Besides all his other philosophical views, Tizi-Wizzi, having learned about the success of the nudists, has decided to follow their example and has shed all his brilliant plumage. He did not even have mercy on his long trailing tail, and he began to walk around naked, not at all concerned about his gigantic beak and tiny body. This happens also with the nudists. Tizi-Wizzi became so converted to the ideas of nudism that he immediately pulled out each little feather that appeared. During the numerous conversations with his owners, Tizi-Wizzi sometimes whistles in the strangest way as if he wants to imitate the word Culture.

Oh, often, very often, this sacred word is being repeated with whistles and squawking. As with nudism and other styles, some people will soon consider it very stylish to repeat this inspiring word twenty times a day without reflecting whatever upon their former habits.

During the long periods of so-called civilization, humanity has become accustomed not to associate its own deeds with the conceptions pronounced. People go to church and are touched by the words of lofty teachings; they admire sermons about casting aside tortures and about reiterating: "Before God we are all animals"; they go home in order to hastily to fill their stomachs, drink too much, poison themselves with all kinds of narcotics and pronounce blasphemy. People go to theaters and weep over the sad fates of the heroes; they become imbued with the highest ideas and hasten home in order to prepare the same fates for the heroes of contemporary life. People listen to music, and try even to introduce it into their daily lives, but observe these connoisseurs of sound when the stock market does not meet their hopes! Thus we manage to fill our lives with the most absurd contradictions, but with one pretext—the upliftment of spirit is of fleeting duration, whereas bestiality naturally saturates life. In their insincerity, people have even achieved a certain subtlety. Thus one liar, intent on cheating, always filled his eyes with tears. And another one, ruining numerous people, tried to cover his estate with constructions of temples and magnificent buildings, hoping that the souls of the stifled ones would not shatter the foundations. And in other branches, even close to science and art, one could often encounter an innate hypocrisy. When it became stylish to investigate antiquity more deeply, how many irrelevant and superficial words were pronounced! New connoisseurs were ready to guard that remote antiquity in a creative way; but when it came to more frequent attention to antiquity, which depended upon their own involvement, the entire enthusiasm for the past evaporated. Antiquity became something annoying; perhaps some "unavoidable business" distracted yesterday's exponents of idealism.

When we turn to the concept of Culture, to this concept so near and vital and urgent, one involuntarily recollects all the hypocritical excursions of humanity, when some persistent supplication was forgotten swiftly, like yesterday's tempest.

Sometimes one is frightened—what will happen if Tizi-Wizzi begins clearly to squawk the word Culture? And what will happen if somebody, repeating this word, will invent new possibilities of oppression? And what will happen if a conference against narcotics will sanction the sale of narcotic raw materials, while benevolently affirming the harmful effect of the poison? Take any newspaper files for a whole year and you will find the most unique examples of hypocrisy, bigotry and falsehood made under the pretext of lofty tasks.

Certainly, these excursions into hypocrisy have already complicated contemporary life sufficiently. People have become involved. They carried guns into the Christian cathedrals to be blessed, but this special measure did not help either. Persons of the theological profession tried to speak of the invalidity of obligations which were only orally pronounced. But these desperate ones did not thereby improve either their own situation nor that of their parish. And amidst this contradictory entanglement there suddenly and imperatively arose a motto—Culture. One must admit that this call broadly penetrated among the masses, among those masses which have always aroused in us the best expectations. Organizations were formed, dedicating themselves to the quest and striving for Culture. We know such organizations, where laboring youth, instead of going to some vulgar vaudeville performance, turn to heroic achievement for the betterment of life in the cause of the most lofty names and concepts. No accusations of hypocrisy or comparisons to parrots apply to these sincere and striving people. It means that before us lie two definite tasks. On one side, one must with all measures help and unify and ease the destiny of sincere seekers of Culture. On the other hand, one must watch with fire in one's hand, lest the precious conception of Culture should fall into the lists of stylish headlines, lest it become a fashionable, but unrealized, conception of drawing-room gossip.

Two kinds of work are before one: educational and protective. It means that circles, societies, organizations, who have realized the value and meaning of Culture, must see that no vulgarization and debasement should begin to disintegrate this precious and salutary concept. Of course, not watchmen, but the enlightened warriors of culture must gather and support each other, cementing the space through the highest and most beautiful, thus advancing these real values in life. The nudists for the sake of their idea are not afraid to exhibit their ugliness publicly. Then let the workers of Culture be unashamed to exhibit not ugliness, but the Beauty of Spirit.

When we incorporated the organization, League of Culture, it was difficult to foresee how this organization would progress. But the Banner of Peace was raised; it was realized that this Banner is needed not only in time of war but still more in daily life. The concept of the Banner was linked unconsciously and hastily with the realization of the League of Culture. It is a universal selection of that which is best, conscious, and enlightened. Not so long ago it would have been a delusion to dream of such a union. But apparently, the wheel of life turns swiftly, and the wheel of the immutable law brings us again to an equality based upon the highest. It is touching to note that thus far, happily, this union proceeds without any vulgarization. The people wish to gather in a better way, spiritually as well as publicly. This upward striving contains in itself the solution of a multitude of social problems, because in an enlightened union, evil is uprooted, and rust is wiped away; the inspired spirits do not have to fear ugliness. We have just reproached the nudists for ugliness. If they could eliminate ugliness then half of the attacks on them would disappear. But the carriers of Culture, revealing the most beautiful sides of their spirit, will perform an unusual transformation of life. For humanity must turn away from ugliness. In the very word ugliness, is comprised the formlessness, chaos, and aggrandizement. But our spirit strives to lofty constructions, clarity, Light. Who, then, works in darkness?

Thus let us beware of parrots: Let us beware of those who distort and of blasphemers because it is unbefitting for us to return to the stage of birds, and it is incompatible to bark like animals. There is so much immediate work before us. There are such profound currents of the past, one must as yet find and link them with the currents of the future. Thus Let us conscientiously and with striving learn to respect each other, and in this, learn to respect human dignity. For in daily life, people do not know how to do so. They know better how to impede, than to facilitate and help.

Vast is the problem of the League of Culture: Everything beautiful, everything enlightening, everything educational! This is not an outer intellectuality—this is a heartfelt striving to Light, to mutual health and usefulness. Somebody will smile, remembering the old cynicism, "Man is a wolf to man." To this one must reply: "Then go to the wolves; and with all these wolves and under the covenant, 'push him who falls.' You become old-fashioned and ridiculous, and what can be more ugly than to fall into ridicule?"

Thus the League of Culture will first of all fight against the ugliness, oppressiveness and the decay which have crept into our lives. For, the feasibility of advancing action demands, first of all, order, organization and voluntary spiritual discipline. But Culture as such, in its very essence, already contains refinement, understanding, and creativeness. And there where construction rises in the name of enlightenment, there is no time either to look back or sigh, or regret. Let us remember again, "When the construction proceeds, everything advances." Let us not forget that every construction in itself contains joy. And in the name of this creative joy we gather together and respect each other, and can look into each other's eyes with benevolence.

When the treasure troves were searched for the most essential words of farewell, these were found to be, "Do not look back." Likewise we shall say here, "Away with turmoil, away with all quarrels and outworn accounts; when the construction proceeds, all advances."

THE PANTHEON OF RUSSIAN CULTURE

(To the Russian Association of the Roerich Society in Paris)

MUCH of the news which we receive from Europe is not quite clear, due to distance. Thus, for instance, vague rumors have reached us saying that the tomb of Diaghilev on the Lido is neglected. On the other hand, we have had reports about the foundation of a Diaghilev Museum. Thus, it is after all rather difficult to judge the measures that are being taken to preserve the name of this eminent Russian.

I always think of Diaghilev as of one of the representative figures in the history of Russian Culture. Leaving aside all paradoxes and circumstances arising out of present day conditions, let us bear in mind that we must try indefatigably to throw ever more light on the universal significance of Russian Culture, which in its interpretation of the Orient and the Occident has created such a perfect and unforgettable whole. In the flashing of Mongolian swords, Old Russia hearkened to the enticing fairytales of the Orient. It was on the shields of the Vikings that the runes of the Romanesque were first carried into Russia, leaving their noble imprint on the walls of Russian castles and cathedrals. Yet, Russia was sustained not only by the East and West; she derived her potential energies from North and South as well. Here we have Byzantine mosaics combined with the style of Amsterdam, all of which contributed the beginning to a synthesis that, above all temporary problems, should show each Russian where the real values lie. Not through destruction, but through constructive creativeness, has Russian Culture brought into the life of the whole earth an element which impelled the attention and esteem of the entire Western World. The outstanding performances of Diaghilev in various lines of artistic endeavor showed the world what we possess.

Even at this very moment a whole galaxy of Russians of renown participates in the cultural work of Europe and the other continents, as servants and interpreters of the Beautiful. We can assert without any exaggeration whatsoever that it is the Russian group that so whole-heartedly joined in the cultural work of all countries of the world, thus upholding the heartfelt threads of spiritual contact between Europe and America.

Russian Art, still unknown to the world only a quarter of a Century ago, not only has found complete recognition and a permanent place in world consciousness, but a friendly co-operation and solidarity with local cultural workers has developed in many fields. It is a precious feeling to realize that names like Dostoevsky, Gogol, Tolstoi, Chekhov, Moussorgsky, Serov, Rimsky-Korsakov, and Scriabin have found their affirmation as an integral part of the universal mind. As is fitting, the pride of Russian culture has become a universal pride. And now we have before us a remarkable galaxy of living examples of the universal unity, living creators in the name of Beauty. For, is Chaliapin not universal, and has not his unforgettably subtle creativeness and artistry become a symbol of truly great achievement? Has not such an astute a writer as Merezhkovsky brought into literature a combination of cultural understanding of the past and insight into the future that is still unparalleled? Without exaggeration, are there many other writer-creators who can touch on problems of universal foresight with so much profundity and wisdom? And Remizov, Bunin, Grebenstchikov, do they not appear as the most remarkable interpreters of the Russian essence, so convincing in its typical diversity? And with what gentle care we ought to treat such outstanding cultural figures as Alexander Benois, who, in their own creations, as well as in their indefatigable pursuits of Knowledge, are following the highest paths, the highlights of Culture. We must not forget that the names of those who now constitute some of the brightest pages of the History of the Arts, the names of Somov, Yakovlev, Dobuzhinsky, Bakst, Bilibin, Maliavin, Sudeykin, Grigoriev, Petrov-Vodkin, Borisov-Musatov and the entire brilliant group of such strong and wonderful living creators, active in their most diversified respective fields, will always remain dear and invaluable to the understanding of world culture. The powerful Konenkov is also among the living, so is Steletzky, and their work has found its way into the most diverse circles and countries of the world. Who does not know Stravinsky and Prokofiev, whose names appear on the programs of every important musical event? And what far-reaching assertion of Russian art has been achieved by the great Pavlova, Karsavina, Nijinsky, Mordkin, Bolm, Myasin and the entire splendid group of the Moscow Art Theater!

We can go on forever enumerating the names of the proponents and interpreters of Russian Art, and yet you will sense immediately that many a splendid name has been left unmentioned. It is in this abundance of wealth that the powerful spirit of the Pantheon of Russian Culture finds its expression. Our list would be incomplete if we were not to mention the mighty pillars of culture erected by those laboring in the field of scientific thought: Pavlov, Mechnikov, Mendeleev, Metalnikov, Lossky, Miliukov, Rostovtzev, Kondakov and all those who, disregarding the hardships and obstacles which present-day conditions seem to put in the way of all cultural endeavor, introduce radiant pages into the cultural refinement of the universal consciousness.

The younger Russian generation, and in fact all future generations, should know about these builders of a culture, which so buoyantly pursues its goal amidst the confusion which has taken place in the minds of our days.

The young people must not only know about these culture builders, but they must be able to derive new strength and inspiration by listening to the voices of the untiring and great creative forces. We mean the presence of an unquestionable element of achievement and heroism, i.e. precisely what needs to serve as the guiding principle in the building of a vast and brilliant future.

Our French Society has for its purpose the encouragement of the forces of the great culture of France. It is but right that our Russian Association should endeavor, to the best of its ability, to commemorate and pay due tribute to its impressive purpose by means of various cultural activities, thus impressing the younger generation with the wonderful landmarks of the great path.

Our program of proposed lectures, of which I have previously written, should devote much attention to Russian cultural achievement. It is easier for you who are right there to know where to begin and what cooperation can be established with what is already being done in the name of Culture.

That which holds true for all other occasions, applies here also, namely: the main thing is not to quarrel, not to split unnecessarily, not to permit suicidal dissension. The unifying idea of Culture must be sufficient to eliminate all disturbing elements and converge all the aspirations, deeds and consciousnesses into one brilliant creative channel.

I am eagerly looking forward to hearing from you as to what you have decided to do about my project, whether you have decided to give the lectures by consolidating your cultural endeavor in the hall of our European Center or in some other place,. The where and how are utterly immaterial, as long as one more beautiful effort has been accomplished without any delay in the name of Culture.

I am enclosing another thousand francs to be added to the fund of our activities in the name of Culture.

Urusvati, December 24, 1931.

LOVE THE BOOK

AMONG the arts which adorn and thus improve life, one of the most ancient and most expressive is the art of the book. What is it that has impelled humanity since the most ancient days of graphic symbols to lend such a refined and highly expressive appearance to the cuneiform characters, hieroglyphics, Chinese magic signs and to all multicolored manuscripts? This solicitous and loving attitude sprang of course from a realization of the importance of a fixed impression. The best of Knowledge, the best of strength were brought to the creation of these significant monuments, which justly occupy their place with the most elevated creative works. According to the essence and exterior of the manuscripts of books we can judge the very epoch which produced them. Not only because people had more time for writing in script, but the spiritualization of the instructive memorabilia gave an uniquely elevated quality to these imprints of human strivings and achievements.

However, it was not only handwriting that gave its high quality to a book. Printing was inaugurated, and can we not say that this availability of manuscripts to the masses did not give many memorials to high art which served the development of many people?

Not only in the sensitive editions of the 17th and 18th centuries but in contemporary editions as well, the lofty traditions of a refined taste have been safeguarded. The quality of paper, the refined conviction of type, the attractive lay-out of sentences and the whole composition of the page, the value of frontispieces, and finally the fundamental firm armor of the beautiful binding made the book a real treasure of the home. The possession was as firm as the strength of the binding of the book, which did not bend with any tempests of life.

It is said that the quality of present-day paper will not last longer than a Century. This is deplorable and scientists ought of course to occupy themselves with the invention of truly durable paper for the protection of the best human imprints, rather than to invent "humane" means of warfare through gases. But even if such paper were invented, we would again have to return to sensitivity in the creation of the book itself. Verily, even the best covenants can be printed in a repulsive way. The human eye and heart aspire to Beauty. Whether this Beauty be in spacing, in the arrangement of the text, or in the attractive frontispieces and significant decorative end-pieces, this complex ensemble of the book demanding thought, is a true creation.

Only ignoramuses presume that it is easy to print a book. Certainly it is not difficult to throw together a bad book, which, due to its careless broken lines and irritating irregularities, is soon recognized as such by people who then throw it on the lower shelf of a unbefitting, unsuitable bookcase with disdain. Or else, they send it with pleasure to a friend, following the proverb: "I offer Thee, Lord, what I need not." A good book is not easy to create. The names of the editor and publisher of a good book are verily esteemed names. It is he, the thoughtful toiler, who gives us the possibilities not only to acquaint ourselves with the book, but also to preserve the true treasures of the sparks of human spirit. The book remains seemingly like a living organism. Its exterior will reveal to you the entire character of the editor and the other participants. Here is an austere book of eternal covenants. Here is an untidy book. Here is a superficial reasoner. Here is one that is concerned only with externals. Here is an eloquent gabber. Here is a profound scholar. . . . Knowing all these subtle reflections of book production, how sensitively and attentively we should handle everything that surrounds the book—it is the mirror of the human soul.

But everything is created only in true co-operation. We deeply respect the editor-artist at his work. But he also may expect from us that we shall love the book. Sometimes under the guidance of our contemporary interior decorators, no room is ever found for bookcases. In some homes of great wealth, we have seen bookshelves against the walls with imitation books. One may imagine the amazing hypocrisy of the owners of these empty book-bindings! Are they not an eloquent symbol of an empty heart and spirit? And how many uncut books lie mysteriously on the little tables of boudoirs?! And their hostesses speak with delight about the famous name printed on the cover. How often among inheritances the books are destroyed first of all, thrown like household junk on the scales of the junk-dealer. Everyone has seen heaps of beautiful books, piled up like objectionable rubbish, whereas the ignoramuses who threw them out often did not even trouble themselves to open them and ascertain exactly what they were discarding.

What, then, must an editor-artist feel, knowing and seeing the tragic fate of the true treasures of the home! But here also we shall not be pessimists. Truly, disgraceful testimony exists on the side of readers and of editors. But even at present there are beautiful editions, inexpensive but wonderful, by reason of their simplicity and thoughtful impressiveness. Bibliophiles exist and are also being developed who act with self-sacrifice to collect the best imprint of human ascent.

Just now perhaps, the necessity of co-operation between reader and editor should be especially stressed. The financial crises reflect most of all upon the means and qualities of education. This is sad but true! As though, because of an economic crisis, one would receive indulgence for ignorance and savagery! Just at present the world traverses an unprecedented and deeply-rooted material crisis. A crisis of over-production, a crisis of the lowering of quality.

A crisis in the faith of the possibility of a better and brighter future. It occurs mainly because of the fact that many generations have already been trained to believe that the leading world power is the gold standard. But recalling the entire history of humanity, we know this is not so. Let us not be compelled to repeat again that the true *valuta* is the *valuta* of spiritual treasures, and the sources of these values without a doubt still remain in the books, written in many different languages, but which carry the one language of the spirit. Not *perhaps* but *certainly*, we must now think of the book and must encourage the editors who aspire to Beauty. Even among the crowded conditions of daily life, we must find a worthy place for the real treasures of each home. With the best smile we must greet those who collect the best books and thus refine their own consciousness with the quality of these books. It is necessary without delay to encourage true co-operation in regard to the Book and to accord it again the most important and beautiful corner in our dwellings. How, then, to achieve it, how to appeal to the sterile or besmirched hearts? But, if we think of Culture, it means we also think of Beauty and of the book as a beautiful creation.

In remote Tibetan houses, the wood-cuts for the printing of books are kept in the sacred corner. The host, after having shown you all his jewels, will unfailingly lead you also to this revered corner and will also show you, with merited pride, these revelations of the spirit. He agrees to make prints for you from his wood-cuts, if he sees that you rejoice at his noble collection. I have already written to you that in the East a book is considered to be the most noble gift. Is this not encouraging? If we say to our friends, "Love the book, love the book with your entire heart and revere it as your treasure," we thereby express in this ancient covenant that which is also so urgently needed in our days, when the human mind strives so zealously in the quest for Culture.

Someone, unaware of the real situation, will inquire: "Why are we asked to love and protect the book now when the shelves of our libraries sag under the weight of our annually increasing editions?"

We answer, "We do not speak of the numbers of printed editions, we speak of the love for the book."

Who knows, perhaps this immeasurable flow of printed paper has in turn confused the people's conception of the book as a true value. Not only every librarian but also every sensitive bookseller will tell you that love for the book itself has declined and is erratic. Are the bookshops crowded? As in many other cultural branches, deterioration and a loss of quality has occurred. Everyone who is closely connected with book production will agree with us and will acknowledge that the time has come to think again without delay about the dignity of the book.

I recollect how during our audience at the Elysée Palace, we appreciated how President Doumergue sat against a background of rows of beautiful volumes. What a dignified mosaic blossomed in this precious collection.

The book, as stated in antiquity, is a river of wisdom, quenching the thirst of the world, the Book, whose publication was but recently awaited with a tremor of joy and whose edition was watched with solicitude. The sacred zeal of bibliophiles is not fanaticism nor superstition; no, it expresses one of the most precious strivings of humanity which unites Beauty and Knowledge. It is now the very hour to care for the dignity of the book. No superfluous statement nor dogma, but in an urgent necessity do we reiterate, saying:

"Love the Book!"

Kyelang, Lahul, August 17, 1931.

PLOWLANDS OF CULTURE

I AM very glad to learn of each activity of our Committees of Culture. I believe that everything in behalf of these imperative beginnings is indeed being done without delay. But still I repeat once more how speedily everything must be done, that not a minute may be lost in the interest of the Common Good. Also, that even the smallest donations and signs of cultural help should be treated with the greatest attention. Let every Committee note with the greatest accuracy all these happy manifestations, in order that in the history of our institutions we should know exactly what was brought into the one Chalice of Culture and by whom. Also let none of our Committees belittle their activities by any conventional limitations. The field of Culture is verily unlimited and countless are the useful activities which arise from benevolent discussions. Perhaps that which is inapplicable today, will be most feasible tomorrow, and perhaps what was deferred today may by then be forever lost. Therefore, the discussions in Committee meetings must be so benevolently broad. For it is only the members of the committees who will be the sole sources of suggestions. No, the members of the committees will be the unifying streams of thoughts, which they will gather from their many friends and will summarize from many meetings and experiences. The main thing is to avoid the danger, which so often obstructs the most useful beginnings—this is the pronunciation of the formula "*Impossible.*" How often does the apparently impossible change into the beautiful and accessible, if only the details and outer appearances are slightly modified. Let us not forget that our Institutions attract new masses to the thought of culture. In this are contained happy possibilities, and at the same time a new responsibility, for everything that is admitted into our cultural institutions, should be of really high quality—should correspond to the cultural treasury of mankind.

Of course the Committees will contact many important institutions during their current activities. This co-operation should be based on mutual benefit. Our cultural campaigns, as I have already had occasion to point out, are not merely of financial importance. Their significance is far wider, reaching all possible branches of Culture and inspiring new masses with Culture. Among these masses will also be those who either have never been previously acquainted with the understanding of Culture or who have limited this concept by purely physical understanding. How joyous it is to speak of Culture altogether, to feel that whatever is done for it cannot cover the unlimited field, the ennoblement of the human spirit. In these noble actions, of course, not the slightest possibility should be lost. Not an hour may be lost, when either by action or by an inspiring word, one may speak once more of beautification, of improvement, of elevating human life.

The accuracy of the annals of every committee will be in line with that quality of solicitude which so befits matters concerning Culture.

One may turn to that ever-vital example of the conditions of enlightened educational activity, the words of Paul, the Apostle:

"By the armor of righteousness on the right hand and on the left,

"By honor and dishonor, by evil report and good report, as deceivers and yet true;

"As unknown and yet well-known; as dying, and, behold, we live; as chastened and not killed, "As sorrowful, yet always rejoicing, as poor, yet making many rich; as having nothing, and yet possessing all things."

Himalayas, October 6, 1931.

BE BLESSED

D R. Robert Harshe is not only the Director of the Art
Institute of Chicago, but also a most eminent connoisseur and leader of the artistic life of America. Therefore
his recent letter, in which he definitely states that any
harm inflicted upon our Institutions would be a "national
calamity" is a truly historical document for us. We remember all the letters and addresses written in support of our
Institutions during the invasion of the barbarians, and
it is highly gratifying to see that leaders of artistic and
social movements called our institutions "the Pride of the
Country"; and that so many others asserted that any harm
done to our cultural works would be unworthy of the dignity of America.

Thus, the invasion of the barbarians, which
Dr. Brinton so opportunely recalls, appears as a testing
stone of the achievements of our Institutions. We do not
doubt that each further attempt on the part of the barbarians and all dark forces will call forth similar resistance
and tension on the part of the best energies. Anyone who
has read the touching address of our blind pupil, Leontine
Hirsh Meyers, certainly was aware of the deep sentiments
instilled in the hearts of our students and co-workers by
the cultural aims of our Institutions.

All our co-workers must realize the value of their work,
which could arouse such sincere response at the moment
of a barbaric invasion. The response and letters of wom-
en's organizations with their millions of members, the
letters of Governor Franklin Roosevelt, the written pro-
tests of students, of our pupils, and of many associations

of youth movements, letters of such well-known cultural leaders as Professor Overstreet, Professor Radosavljevich, Professor Patty Hill, Lieutenant-Governor Behman, Malcolm Vaughan, Mrs. Lionel Sutro, Dr. Charles Fleischer, General de Leon, John O'Hara Cosgrave, Harry Elmer Barnes, Ruth St. Denis, Leon Dabo, George Grebentschikov, Hendrik Van Loon and the whole legion of light-bearing warriors of Culture are a most significant historical document of the victorious fight of Light against darkness.

We do not doubt that all these precious testimonials from the friends of Culture are kept on special file in strict order. In the future they will constitute a volume of great historical value. This book should also record, as an instructive fact for future generations, the names of the representatives of dark forces, the names of destructive barbarians, the names of low-minded anti-cultural spirits who tried with all methods of sinister malice to bring disaster upon cultural institutions. Knowing that these dark forces were acting in greed, we would add to this future book all documents of the court procedure, all testimonials and affidavits given by strangers, who were indignant at such criminal secretive, dark intrigue.

Therefore, keep in full order all these precious documents. Perhaps, in accordance with the variety of their contents, they are kept in various departments of our Institutions, but they should be collected into one file, so that not one heroic voice which has sounded in the name of Culture, should be omitted from the memorable records.

We also witnessed a most significant attitude on the part of the press. We saw that only a few organs abstained from actively defending the cause of Culture. The majority of the press, be it said in its honor, has in full dignity and justice exposed all the barbaric perversions and insinuations.

Also we were able to mark some wavering among spiritually weak people, even among our co-workers, who became unbalanced and started to advise various modes of retreat instead of manifesting a persistent faith in the victory of Culture; others, because of their malicious natures, rejoiced at the misfortunes of their neighbors and even tried to intensify the false declarations of the barbarians. Both of these facts should also not be forgotten.

Valor is tested in the fight for a right cause. The true light-bearing warriors are only sustained by difficulties. Every obstacle arouses the tension of the true sacred Fire in them. Thus all historical victories of Culture, which are now the examples of amazement and respect and which comprise the heroic pride of humanity were achieved. One may only regret that the wavering, doubtful, timid people should so erase their names from the annals of Cultural achievements. They turned away from noble deeds and, according to the law of justice, history will turn away from them.

Thus our case, like previous ones, became a public event of extraordinary significance. The case of our cultural Institutions will find an echo, not only in the history of the Culture of America, but also in many other countries. We already see how representatives of many other countries respond. We see how many of them, in the difficult moment of attack, come to our support nobly and even intensify their friendship and co-operation. On the other hand, there are also those who believe that the financial situation of one building outweighs the importance of all cultural ideas. Let us also remember those spiritual paupers who are always ready to retreat and to kiss the bloody sword of the barbarians. Let us remember these cowardly helpers of the dark forces.

The dark forces, who are conscious of their actions, are numerous, but truly innumerable are their unconscious helpers, who so easily bow down before the crude, dark forces. This manifestation is most dangerous, because the gates of the fortress can thus be easily opened by the sycophants of the barbarians. On the gate of Verdun was a most significant inscription addressed to all enemies:

"*Ici on ne passe pas!*"—"They shall not pass here!" The heroic spirit of the defenders sustained the meaning of this command, even at a time when the whole world was reluctantly ready sorrowfully to surrender this stronghold.

There are things in the world which are inadmissible in essence. Every indignity, every concession to the dark forces is already a crime, alike in nature to the actions of the dark, destructive forces themselves. The Realm of Culture represents a light-bearing stronghold, which must not be surrendered under any circumstances. There can be certain strategic moves, but surrender as such is inadmissible and shall not be!

Happily, Culture is not based on *valuta*. Even if many cultural manifestations may be temporarily in difficulty or curtailed, the spiritual treasures of culture cannot be shaken by any world crisis, unless the traitors in the darkness of night will open the gates to the enemies. Therefore, let us be guarded against every kind of treason; let us apply all vigilance; as indefatigable guards, we shall stand on the watch-towers.

Let us find strength to discard all the pettiness of yesterday and to unite in the glory and benefits of Culture. Let us regret all mistakes of yesterday and smile at the radiant possibility of joining hands still more firmly. The great concept of Culture will help us to overcome all petty domestic fatigue which, like the grains of sand in a wheel, can create a harrowing dissonance. We shall display a beautiful experiment of spiritual unity, which limitlessly multiplies forces and sensitizes resourcefulness and watchfulness.

Verily, "may obstacles be blessed—through them we grow." May the names be blessed of all friends of Culture, who were not afraid at a trying hour to give such glorious testimonials of themselves. At the cross-roads of life there arise moments, when no abstract words, but only virile, heroic deeds are needed, only such deeds can be firm steps towards future progress.

What most heartfelt word could be sent to all those

who sincerely care for the future, who understand that only through building up and strengthening the young generations, will the countries succeed? Thus through the power of cultural thought, the "unsolvable problems" will turn into new achievements.

If difficulty reveals true friends, if the trying hour, like the trumpet of valor, summons together all great hearts, then how can one not bless these hours, during which the most beautiful, the most noble, is manifested! Be blessed, all those to whom Culture is not a luxury, not an empty sound, but the one single foundation of Existence.

Blessed, blessed, blessed, be all radiant warriors in the Great Service of Culture!

Agni Yoga, in the book. "Heart," ordains:

"Where is that feeling, where is that substance, with which to fill the Chalice of the Great Service? Let us gather this feeling from the best treasures. Let us find parts of it in religious ecstasy, when the heart trembles before the Highest Light. Let us find parts of it in the realization of the love of the heart, when the tears of self-denial glisten. Let us find parts of it in the attainments of a hero, when might is multiplied in the name of mankind. Let us find it in the patience of the gardener, when he ponders over the mystery of a seed. Let us find it in valor, which transfixes darkness. Let us find it in the smile of the child, when it stretches itself towards the rays of the Sun. Let us find the realization of the Great Service in the flights which soar towards Infinity. It should fill the heart infinitely, inexhaustible forever. The sacred tremor will not become a daily porridge. The highest Teachings turn into a soul-less husk, when deprived of the sacred tremor. Thus in the midst of the battle, ponder over the Chalice of Service, and vow that the sacred tremor shall not depart from you!"

Himalayas, July 12, 1932.

SALUTATIONS TO OUR CULTURAL SOCIETIES

WE send greetings to our Societies! We heartily accept our election as their Protectors. Helena Ivanovna and I shall contribute our best experience and strength to the flourishing of this cultural work.

During the past two years, 45 Societies which are spread throughout 20 countries have been created around our Institutions. Every month, new projects are inaugurated, which emanate not only from places close-by, but from the most distant regions. Thus the decade of our work in America is marked by an entire movement in the name of Culture. In our days of social and governmental unrest, what could be more joyful, more impelling, than the establishment of these manifold hearths of Culture.

As varied as are the manifestations of Culture, so also are our Societies, with their complete fundamental cultural unification. Some are prosperous, some limited in their means, some with numerous members, and some formed with a small circle. Some dream of broad social projects and some seek strength in intimacy. They are as varied, as many-faceted, as life itself. So it should be. It would be most short-sighted to direct the striving of life along a single channel.

Culture, so closely associated with spirituality, is first of all expressed in a subtle creativeness. Because creativeness in its substance, and in concordance with universal laws, is always free, resting only upon a conscious discipline of the Spirit. This consciousness of the Spirit will lead us toward co-operation, also conscious and constructive.

In this way our Societies are primarily constructive in benevolence, creative in Beauty, and strong in the harvests of knowledge.

We already are sufficiently aware that wealth has not created Beauty and Knowledge, but they were created by the human spirit. If you take the roll of universal creators and builders, you will not find fantastic material wealth, but you will find an inexhaustible treasure trove of the creative Spirit.

In my recent address to one of our Societies, I pointed out that no special means are needed for cultural communions; at times not even a cup of tea is needed, because the human heart simmers instead of a tea-pot. They who dream only of having exterior means given to them, would simply have extinguished hearts. The heart also creates means. But no wealth in the world can create a heart, neither trumpets nor drums nor pompous show can surround the strengthening works of culture. Spiritual co-operation will first of all erect those strongholds toward which no darkness can approach. These beacons of warmth and light shall reach not only each other with their rays, but their beneficence shall penetrate even into the dark crevices, where Beauty and Knowledge are only occasional guests.

It is difficult to meet on expanses divided by the depths of the oceans and chains of mountains. It is especially difficult for those hearts to meet that are timid in their search and not always confident in their strength. But it is not difficult for the searching heart to approach the enlightening beacons, the nest of education, or the League of Culture. There they will not meet ridicule, nor will they be rejected; there the stigma of vulgarity will not be demanded. The Societies of Culture must not be impeded with demands and limitations. According to the fire of the heart, and the result of the work, the new milestones of the path are being marked.

Every tree must grow; sufficient time must be allowed so that each root becomes strong. Therefore, the refinement of consciousness also pre-supposes patience, in order that the constructive processes should progress strongly, and the connecting materials be chosen carefully.

If Societies cannot at once have broad manifestations—lectures, courses, concerts, exhibitions—let it be so. If a circle united by the ties of the heart meets for a long time even without tea, for a mutually strengthening talk, let it be so. If there be a co-society seeking new manifestation of its forces, in listening, in their searching, and in exchanging their intimate projects, let it be so.

It would be ill-timed for culture to hear the conventional complaints about absence of means. Travelers are attracted to a fire in the darkness. That means that it is necessary above all to kindle the fire which will attract all that is useful for the spirit. But in one thing all Societies must help each other—a Society is a communion, and every wise communion is co-operation.

The very understanding of Culture obligates us to co-operate and to labor splendidly in sowing the seed. It would not be cultural if, a Society connected with a fundamental ideal, would itself remain divided by borders and nations. The spreading of our Society in many countries gives unusual possibilities and privilege. It gives the possibility of an immediate and direct exchange of ideas, as well as of all the creative material. It is necessary that we should not miss this possibility of Cultural Exchange; remembering that above all of us, there is one Banner of Culture.

This Banner of Culture has at its foundation everything of the best, everything which strives toward light, everything that wishes benevolence. The Banner of Culture is identical with the Banner of Labor: the Banner of infinite perception of the most beautiful. No matter what our daily routine work may be, we leave our workbench, and refreshing ourselves, strive to the festival of Culture. Whether there three or thousands shall gather at this festival, it is still the festival of Culture, a festival of the victory of the human spirit. Our festival will be inspired if a letter from a distant invisible friend arrives at that time; it does not matter if the letter begins with a confession that things are difficult. But for whom are they easy?

A thought about Culture is not a side show, with whistling and drunken destruction. But we know that every letter from this invisible friend will finish with something joyous, in the name of Beauty, Knowledge, and some new victory of Light. And he who wrote the letter knows that the pains of his heart were not listened to with an uncaring attitude, but that the quivering of his search was sympathetically felt, and strengthened in the confidence of his friendly co-workers.

The vocabulary of slander, malice, mutual destruction, at last appears as disgusting. It finally is remembered that the vocabulary of Beauty contains so many attractive, elevated, constructive concepts. Yes, and practical is this vocabulary of the Beautiful because it is vital, and beautiful in life in its living substance.

Besides the letter, besides the call of the heart, we must also exchange professional creations. Among the current ones are some that are not applicable, but that does not mean they cannot be utilized tomorrow.

We all know the meaning of the power of thought projected into space, the power of an arrow of Spirit. But how greatly magnified is this power if it is supported by friendly consciousness; and what can be more useful for Culture if not mutual information, the result of which is active co-operation?

Of course, speaking of Culture, we often find a strange limitation applied to this all-penetrating conception. Erroneously, the idea of something supernatural, almost unattainable in the dusk of daily life is often connected with the concept of Culture. In truth, it is just the contrary. Culture as such will function essentially when it enters into each day of life and becomes the criterion of quality for all our actions. How many calls, words of encouragement, words of fortification, must one must pronounce in the name of Culture! How many aspirations into the future must one proclaim! With the growth of the refinement of consciousness containment will come, and the feeling of responsibility will develop. The difference between the everyday occurrence and daily life will become clear, and thought will turn from yesterday to the luminous tomorrow. In eternal vigilance we shall avoid fatigue and depression. For those who do not know Culture, daily life sometimes seems terrifying, but in it is forged perfection and ascent. A refined consciousness will accept the concept of the ages of labor as a source of infinite creativeness.

The Covenant may be concisely stated, "Be aflame in your heart and create in love." How much benevolence you will bring by initiating those who approach into the world of Beauty. "Together let us progress to where there are no boundaries, nor end, where every benevolent glimmer of light can he turned into the radiant rainbow of bliss for the worlds."

Friends, known and unknown, visible and invisible, I would like to send you not simply a greeting, but the most resounding call for co-operation. We can approach co-operation without delay. Everyone who strives toward Culture has a great reserve of ideas, thoughts and propositions. Out of this treasury of Spirit much can be applied, without delay, and the rest shall find the shortest way of application. Only we must think in unalterable benevolence about Culture, and we must only remember that this unity should be helpful to everyone. No one must be demeaned, because this would not be cultured.

The immeasurable field of culture provides grain for each reaper who knows the meaning of labor. In the name of this resplendent labor, let us turn to each other in mutual co-operation; and let us remember once more that above all of us there is one never-changing Banner of Culture, which guides the resplendent, indestructible future.

Greetings to co-operation!

Himalayas, 1931.

PRAYER FOR PEACE AND CULTURE

CULTURE and Peace—the most sacred goal of humanity! In the days of great unrest, both material and spiritual, the disturbed spirit yearns for these radiant strongholds. But our union in the name of these regenerating concepts should not be an abstract one. In accordance with our abilities, each one in his own field should infuse them into everyday life, as what is most necessary and urgent.

In our Peace Pact of 1929, we proposed a special Banner of Peace for the protection of all cultural treasures. A Committee for promoting the Peace Pact has been elected in New York. An International Union for the Roerich Pact has been established with its central seat in Bruges, where a world Congress for spreading the ideals of Peace through Culture was convened last September. Its results were most significant, indicating how close this aim is to the hearts of all progressive people of the entire world.

New lofty traditions of veneration for the true cultural treasures should ceaselessly thunder the world-wide call from temples, shrines of spirit, from all Light-imparting centers, eliminating the very possibilities of wars, and creating peace for the generations to come. By untiringly unfurling the Banner of Peace everywhere, we thus destroy the very physical field of war. Let us also affirm the World Day of Culture, when simultaneously the world will be reminded of the true treasures of humanity, of creative heroic enthusiasm, of improvement and enhancement of life in all churches, all schools and all educational institutions. For this purpose, we have not only to safeguard our cultural heritage in which the highest achievements of humanity are expressed with all available means, but we must consciously value these treasures, remembering that each contact with them in itself will ennoble the human spirit.

As we have already witnessed, wars cannot be stopped by interdiction, any more than malice or falsehood can be prohibited. But by striving without delay and patiently to the highest treasures of humanity, we may make these products of darkness altogether inadmissible, as the progeny of crass ignorance. Having contacted the Realm of Light, the ennobled, expanded consciousness will naturally enter the path of peaceful constructiveness, discarding, as shameful refuse, all the disparagement of human dignity generated by ignorance.

Already the lists of endorsers of the Banner of Peace are long and glorious. Already the Banner has been consecrated during the Conference in Bruges in the Basilica of the Holy Blood. Thereby we have given our sacred oath to introduce it everywhere with all possible measures. Those from all ends of the world who trusted us and have suffused the space with their most heartfelt wishes, will not look in vain for the Banner above all shrines of real treasures. Each day brings new letters, new responses. The election urn has been filled with precious votes "For Peace." Verily Peace and Culture are at present urgently needed.

It is not so much a new law that is needed, but an imperative wish, a united pan-human desire to safeguard the achievements of mankind, that is so badly needed. Every endeavor, even the most obvious, requires an active start. For Peace and Culture one does not even need a unanimous world-wide vote. The beautiful principles of General Good can be affirmed in every scale, still retaining their vital potentiality. Let us thus greet all co-workers wholeheartedly: "Without delay, proceed victoriously with your full capacities, along this glorious Path!"

Verily, the time is short. Lose neither the day nor the hour! Kindle the flame of the heart to an indomitable enthusiasm. Under the Banner of Peace Let us proceed towards the One Supreme Light, in powerful union as the World League of Culture!

THE BANNER

The Sacred Sign of Peace

RECENTLY we deplored the destruction of paintings of Goya and of the ancient Church treasures in Spain as well as the destruction of the churches in Russia since the revolution; then we heard of the burning of the valuable Shanghai Library and now we read in the newspapers that the President's Palace in Havana was looted by a mob. Thus, besides destruction by war, we notice continuous vandalism. Can one keep silent when knowing of such destruction? Can we permit future generations to believe that we negligently allowed barbarians to destroy that which glorifies the high culture of mankind?

It is our duty to reiterate persistently the imperative need to safeguard the precious treasures from annihilation through crass ignorance. People take little account of the united measures that must be undertaken to avoid these most deplorable new indictments against our present age.

Let us look into the essence of things without being seduced by petty details. Usually these trifles alone hinder the discernment of actual facts. Our Banner, dedicated to the protection of all the true treasures of humanity, is being much discussed at present. There are many new proposals. Some are against open manifestations, lectures and pilgrimages in connection with this idea. Some state that one should only whisper about the destructions which take place, as though we could conceal so public a disgrace. Still others state that not only culture but even civilization is imperiled. And there are voices, which even suggest the immediate construction of a new Noah's Ark. It is possible that civilization itself is already in peril!

Let us hope it is not so.

Many new names are suggested for the Banner, sufficiently long to contain all descriptions. But we know the danger of such long definitions when a short commanding *SOS* should be sounded.

Some suggest that the Banner be sold everywhere to spread it. Still others wish to keep the Banner and all considerations about it, in a hidden vault. Some wish to see the symbol of the Banner in the lapel of every thinking man. Others wish to conceal it and disclose it only during some new extraordinary mishaps. Some consider the wide interest and inquiries about the Banner as a most beneficial sign. But for others, for some inexplicable reason, this is a sign of extreme danger. Some consider that the Banner should be utilized only during war-time and preferably limited to Europe. Others justly affirm that the treasures of Egypt, Persia, India, Japan, China, the Americas and the entire world demand the same immediate protection. Some think that the League of Nations is an organization which makes decisions for the entire world, others point out that its jurisdiction does not cover even half the globe. Such is the diversity of opinions!

Some propose that this Banner should be shown during all international exhibitions that display the flags of all nations. But others believe that it is impossible to have this Banner even in private premises, as it may hinder warfare. To some it appears to be a threatening sign of impotent "pacifism"; to others the Banner appears as a glorious defense of the dignity of mankind. Some regard it as imperative to insist openly on the safeguarding of cultural treasures everywhere. And others, again, desire to postpone all discussion, until after the passage of some law, although they themselves do not know from where they may expect this law—like a *"deus ex machina."*

What is the meaning of all these apparently contradictory but insistent counsels, suggestions and even demands?

They simply signify the great interest in this Banner, which cannot fail to call forth the response of the human heart. We must become accustomed to this diversity of expression of the human mind.

One must know that no world problem was ever decided without the raising of all kinds of symbols. In all processions, an abundance of placards and emblems are carried, these in their inner essence serving the same ideal. Thus, even if someone becomes angered about the Pact and Banner, this is already good. Even though he be excited, in his anger he still thinks of the protection of treasures by which the human race evolves.

It has often been said that an overt enemy is still closer to the truth, than an indifferent fool, who is neither hot nor cold, and who, according to all cosmic laws, will finally disintegrate. But life itself points to the complete urgency to do battle against vandalism. Each daily newspaper, every daily record directly or indirectly indicates the same need. If anyone suggests speaking in subdued tones, we must tell him: "When someone is ill at home, when the heart is torn by grief, would not it be inhuman to demand a tone of icy indifference?"

When something is dear to our hearts we cannot speak of it in frigid terms.

Everyone in this world who has loved someone or something, knows that it is impossible to speak of the beloved with mediocre expressions. The human spirit, during such moments of great tension, always finds a thundering vocabulary of enthusiasm and vigor. No graves, no extinguishers can quench the fire of the heart, if it senses the truth. How, then, were attainments and martyrdoms born, if not from the realization of the great Truth? From where was that invincible daring, that inexhaustible resourcefulness that humanity remembers even from its school books, generated? The lovers of frigid words should forgive the enthusiasm of others who exist by its life-giving, strengthening fire. But let all suggestions be heard, for one cannot undo that which already exists. To those who propose to speak in frigid terms of the most precious concepts, we shall say: "All right, we shall also listen to you. We shall whisper, but it will be so thunderous a whisper as to reach every human heart."

Even silence may be louder than thunder, as is so beautifully related in the Old Testament. But can we forbid the human heart to beat for that which is so vital and dear to it? How can we put an end to earthly and heavenly songs! To annihilate the magnificence of human creative songs would be to embitter and finally to kill the heart. But where is that remarkable individual who boasts that he can always do without the heart?

If in our hearts we call the Banner of Peace the Banner of Beauty this short name will of course resound in the heart but it would be inapplicable in life, because people are ashamed to speak of the beautiful.

Thus also do people act when they come upon the Great Realities. That which they ponder in the quiet of night, appears unrealizable and even shameful to them by day. When we look over everything already published and written about the Pact and Banner, every response that has come from distinguished personalities and from unknown workers, we want to be with these enthusiasts who were not afraid to sign their full names in order to affirm the protection of human treasures. There are before us thousands of letters received from the Americas, from Europe and Asia. One would like so much to enumerate the multitude of names who have become friends through the noble sentiments they express, but this would take many pages.

According to the ancient traditions, an entire city was once spared because of a single righteous man. Then judging by the letters received, and marking upon our map the places of their dispatch, one obtains a remarkable design of the sites where people are thinking of the preservation of the world's treasures, beyond the limitations of nations and creeds. And how many more have not been asked! New friends who have heard about the Banner-Protector by accident have continuously come from far-away. Therefore, let us not prevent any remote and solitary seekers from reaching the One Light. They all, in their own way, strive for constructive good.

In a far-encompassing whisper, let us tell all those who come about love and friendliness; they did not come from egotistic motives, but they came in the name of spiritual treasures, in the name of everything beautiful that is spread in creative labor and knowledge. Whoever wants to cry out, let him do so. Whoever wants to whisper, let him whisper. But let us not impose silence upon any human heart, if it be open to Beauty and Good. If the unique vocabulary of attention and good becomes more voluminous than we thought, then let us only rejoice at this and let us continue to call for the preservation of the true treasures of the world. May our Banner be that sacred symbol of Peace, which by its presence will remind humanity of its evolutionary destiny!

I rejoice that the friends of Peace, Beauty and Knowledge will gather in Washington to affirm the Laws of the Spirit!

If the Red Cross flag protects physical health, then may the Banner of Peace preserve the spiritual health of mankind.

Himalayas, 1933.

FIRES OF THE HEARTH

WHEN Armageddon rages; when countless arrows of hate, division, destruction and decay pierce the space, should we not cherish each spark of friendliness? When, through ignorance, the highest concepts are being defiled, should we not collect all sacred fires around the hearth of the spirit?

When falsehood and superstition attempt to contaminate the most pure in order to widen the abysses of chaos, should we not then search through the best chronicles for the rules of co-operation?

In the most ancient chronicles, as the highest praise to Yaroslav, Prince of Kiev, it is said: "Being a master of books, he read them by day and night and also wrote them, thus sowing the seeds of written wisdom in the hearts of the faithful; and these we now reap, as we imbue ourselves with the wisdom of the books. Books are like rivers, nurturing the entire universe like a spring of wisdom. The most profound veneration is due to books."

In such terms, the ancient chronicles expressed their greatest praises.

Verily, it is one thing to tolerate books and an entirely different matter to love the book in complete striving and devotion to sublime enlightenment.

An incident comes back to me. In the office of a certain president there are two visitors. The walls of the old room are decorated with massive oak bookcases. Through the glass panels, the backs of the books with their rich bindings glow temptingly. Although the bindings are not old, they are heavily gold-leaved. Apparently, here is a lover of books. How splendid that at the head of this undertaking there is a collector who has not spared any money in his tempting bindings!

One of the visitors yields to the temptation of turning the leaves and holding in his hands this treasure of the spirit. The bookcase is apparently unlocked and raising his hand, the book-lover attempts to take one of the volumes. But, oh horror! the entire shelf falls on his head, revealing that these are false bindings without any sign of a book. His most sensitive wish violated, the book-lover with trembling hands replaces upon its shelf this unworthy imitation: "Let us get away from here soon. Can one expect anything decent from such a clown!" The other visitor smiles, "Here one is punished for loving books, because it is a happiness not only to read a good book, but even to hold it in one's hands."

How many such false libraries are spread all over the world! And whom do their owners presume to cheat—their own friends or themselves? In this falsification, an unusually subtle disdain of Knowledge and a refined insult to the book as the witness of human achievement lies hidden. And not only are the contents of the book being violated, but in such falsifications, objective as well as in words, the very significance of the creation of the spirit is being assaulted.

"Tell me who your enemies are and I will tell you who you are," said the ancients. One may say, "Show me your bookcase and I will tell you who you are."

One of the most exhausting tasks is the search for a new apartment. But through this involuntary intrusion into numerous dwellings, you undoubtedly discover observations about the facts of life. You pass through numerous apartments of approximate wealth which are filled with furniture. But where is the bookcase? Where is the writing desk? Why are the rooms sometimes overcrowded with such strange ugly objects, yet these two friends of existence, a writing desk and a bookcase, are lacking? Is there a place to put them? It appears upon examination that a small desk could still be placed somewhere but the walls are all so occupied, that there is no place for a bookcase.

The landlady, noticing your disappointment, points out a small inside closet and with a smile of condescension at indulging your demands says, "If you have so many books you can use this closet instead of using it for other domestic things." Thereby you observe that the tiny measures of the closet, appear to be regal for such a luxury as books.

Observing this regrettable and patronizing attitude toward the book, you recall the priceless libraries which are apparently thrown out on the street-markets. And you once more sorrowfully recall all the stories of how herrings and cucumbers were wrapped in the priceless pages torn from the most rare editions. Then, when you look upon the small bookcase that is being offered to you and you calculate that only with difficulty could even a hundred volumes fit in there, you again hear the worldly sages tell you: "Why, then, keep so many books at home?" And they will only be repeating the words of the famous Muslim conqueror who ordered the most priceless libraries to be destroyed as useless, since it is told that the Koran comprises everything which is necessary for a human being.

The absence of a writing desk is explained quite definitely with the reminder that a writing desk is supposed to stand in an office. Herein is apparent a definite suggestion that outside the office, there should be no mental occupations and evening relaxations are intended for merriment which should not burden the brain. And thus the so-called hours of relaxation, which should be the most priceless hours of accumulation and refinement of consciousness, are dissipated like pearls thrown in the dust of the street.

And thus the book in contemporary usage becomes an object of luxury. The "sane" mind categorizes bibliophiles as extravagant maniacs. The mediocre consciousness altogether unlearns to read, as he even good-naturedly confesses. "I cannot read long books . . . I cannot concentrate . . . I haven't got the time", says a man on his way to a boxing match or to throw balls into the air or simply to busy himself gossiping about his neighbor.

And there is both time and money to possess houses which are a treasury of Knowledge, but the thought about these treasures is not part of our daily habit. By what do people live? Through many objects. But the realization of this as well as the Beauty of the book itself as a creation passes out of life.

So also can one observe the character and the essence of a friend, according to the condition in which they return the books loaned to them. It is very true that you often meet with a most careful, a most honorable attitude towards the book, and then you understand why certain volumes remained intact from the 17th and 15th centuries. But to one's sorrow more often the books are returned irreparably damaged, so that one's soul aches for the desecrated author. To burn a hole in the book, to turn down the leaves, perhaps to tear away the corner, and sometimes even to cut out the illustration which one likes is not considered a sacrilege. Every librarian will tell you about his grievances not only because of lost books but also because of editions mutilated forever.

He who destroys a book reveals the low condition of his consciousness. Truism though this may be, let the reader, whoever he may be, beware of soiling or tearing a book. This already will be useful. In the midst of universal crises, material as well as spiritual, the general attitude towards books will be one of the convincing circumstances. Yes, when we will again learn to love a book disinterestedly, as a pure creation of art, and to sincerely safeguard it, then also some of the most difficult problems of life will solve themselves, without discussions, without evil thoughts and conflicts. And in our dwelling we will also find a place for a bookcase and for a writing desk as well as for the sacred images which by their presence remind us about the Highest, the Beautiful, and the Infinite.

Someone may say, "I knew this long ago, this is not new to me." How good that he says so; maybe on the strength of it, he will read one more book and his attitude towards these true friends of every home will be more solicitous, and in turn, he will say that which is so known to him to others as well. Because it is most often that people say: "I knew it long ago" about that which they have never put into practice, one must say to them again, "The worse for you."

The books of recent editions have become very meager—both in size and in their specific contents. The author is seemingly afraid to bore, because the publisher continually warns him about the peculiar demands of the reader.

And suddenly you discover that most of the books are being read by poor people and the desire for true realities lives in people who earn the bread of tomorrow for themselves with difficulty. Looking over the World Almanac one may follow the statistics of literacy as well as the number of volumes in public libraries of the world with keen interest. How inconsistent with many official reports are the number of books distributed in these National Treasuries! Let us not quote these instructive numbers since the annual World Almanac is accessible to those who desire to become familiar with the consistency of these acquisitions. For many people, the figures will contain great surprises.

Besides that, let us not forget that literacy, although undoubtedly a step towards culture, is of itself not yet a guarantee of reading books or of their sane cultural application. If one could take another census, namely as to how many literate people do not read books, the results would be very instructive. Then also, if from this number, the number of readers of cheap fiction would be subtracted, we would see that the entire number of serious books and editions is supported by a comparatively small number of persons, out of the entire population of the world.

This situation demands a still more respectful attitude not only towards serious editions but also towards those individuals who make out of them a wise and proper application.

Some touching episodes about the loving care for books are not forgotten. Unforgettable is the story of one poor writer who wanted to give his bride, as a wedding present, what to him was the most valuable thing, a Monograph on the creation of an artist who most inspired him. It is also unforgettable when this touching love for books is kindled independently in early youth. A small girl in a home of great wealth carries the Bible illustrated by Doré with difficulty—far too heavy for the strength of a child. She is not permitted to take this book, but she takes advantage of the absence of her elders, not for mischief and play, but in order again to utilize this moment of freedom in communion with the great Images.

Dear to us are these children, the bearers of the best Images, who, directed by their hearts, independently seek the bookcase in their search for this constant friend of true happiness. Edison spontaneously sought the bookcase and from early childhood realized how he could benefit humanity. In the one's attraction to journalism, a heartfelt striving towards the dissemination of what is useful is also expressed.

Let us also remember the great mind, Ruskin, who so touchingly contributed his first efforts and inspirations towards the great Biblical Epos. Let us remember many glorious ones. Long ago, much was already spoken about the power of thought as well as the art of thinking. But every art must be developed and nurtured, and shall the hearth of this sacred art not be near a bookcase?

Let us turn to the bookcase not only as to a comforter and guardian, but also as to a leader and giver of life. Do not the continuously creative minds of great thinkers emanate from it? Does not vitality, and the resistance to all evil and to all the unprecedented obstacles of existence come from it? And does not creative joy emanate from it?

Himalayas, April 19, 1932.

SLANDER

FRIENDS, on several occasions you have communicated to me about fermenting slander. Its forms have become absolutely hideous and false, and can serve only a primitive and low consciousness. I am not entirely astonished at the existence of slander. There are certain species of bipeds which are nourished by fetid decay, cultivated by themselves. The hotbeds of evil and darkness where they dream of injuring culture are especially luxuriant. As we have heard from the ancient alchemists, the dark *homunculi* were generated in dung.

The existence of slander is not new. It is not its existence, but its methods which are peculiar and which must be observed. Despite their many variations, at basis they all manifest their spiritual poverty. After all, as you have already noticed, slander creates inventions which contradict all sane reasoning. As you see, slander does not even concern itself with utilizing facts. It simply invents. And moreover it invents poorly and ineptly.

Only to those who do not know actual circumstances will it appear that inventions of slander are important. However, slander hopes to influence immature minds or those already contaminated by malice. But everyone who strives, either by purity of spirit or with the conscientious Knowledge of reality, at once perceives the coarse and spiritually-impoverished inventions. Incidentally, it is precisely this quality of falsehood that comprises the very usefulness of slander. By its raps, it seemingly beats out an accelerated rhythm, and in the energy of the rhythm a new power of resistance is born. And not only is a new energy born within those who have been slandered, but around them an intense and blissful power in an entire stratum of benevolently honest hearts, is created. You already know of the active bliss of such a tension of energy.

How hindrances create new possibilities is mentioned in the article, "Praise to the Enemies". But now, after a complete series of new observations, one may be amazed, to one's satisfaction, how meager slander is at its very basis. All its pompousness and intricacy are reduced to a most elementary and crude cunning. Slander degrades itself to the point of using the testimony of an employee discharged for incompetency. Slander does not find it difficult to ascribe completely false whereabouts to someone. Slander has no scruples of using unprecedented apparatus. Slander, in its stupidity, tries to confound people with the statement that a writer has never written his works, and a painter never has even touched one of his canvases, and that an inventor, of course, has stolen all his inventions. The existence of the best achievements in no way confuses the slanderer; in essence he is without hope and in his hopelessness, he attempts to lance a negative conjuration into space, intentionally working against what is evident, The worldly sages long since pronounced, "Slander, always slander; something of it will remain." But the Apostle Paul said, far earlier, "Though we seem to ye dead, we live."

Thus, do not be disturbed by slander; on the contrary, study its methods. Such tests beautifully strengthen the living experiment. Slander is ejected and annihilated by the quality of benevolent construction. I remember how many, even of our close friends, could not understand why, in our conversations, we often pronounced the concept of a spiritual battle, the concept of a spiritual armor, of a sword and shield. But the casting out of darkness from benevolent construction is the spiritual battle itself. The partisans of peace need not fear that an aggressive militarism is contained in the conception of a spiritual battle. No, this battle is only the antithesis of evil. And no one would suggest that we should open the doors cordially to each manifestation of evil, decay and slander. Only sorcerers of a low type would arrange a gathering of corpses, or festivals of putrefaction. Such a spectacle would, first, be hideous and as such, anti-evolutionary and anti-cultural.

The slanderers, in essence, are murderers and sorcerers, and if we can confront them with the conception of benevolent construction which confounds them, this will be the most fitting and the coldest shower for these perverted, slanderous hearts. Hence, studying the methods of slander we shall not remain only observers. Pay attention; when you trace a slanderer and ask him about the sources of his information he will never reveal any names. He will not name them, because either he himself is the originator or the closest conspirator in the slander. Certainly, such mentally limited persons who, spreading slander, will insist that they are only repeating rumors may also be found. Their obscured minds cannot understand that at this instant, they themselves become propagators of slander. In other words, they are entirely standing with the slanderers.

I remember how, when my late teacher Kuindji was told of an absurd slander about himself, he shook his head and said, "Strange, I never did anything good to this man." In this sincere remark the teacher, enlightened by life's experience, expressed one more characteristic of the circle of slander. Truly it is multifarious! It is strange to observe how it is at times born purposelessly and from unconscious evil. The folk-wisdom has pointed out special types of simpletons or slanderers, who do not even remember the evil they generated. God preserve us from such simpletons! Frequently, they are not simpletons at all but are, above all, recruits of the dark forces by reason of their ignorance. But ignorance is a crime; this was already stressed in remote antiquity. And each crime, according to the law of justice, will be exposed sooner or later. But a moment of shame is hardly agreeable even to a low and coarse consciousness. Even a dog shuns being shamed. The simpletons of slander are not so numerous after all;

slander is an evident generator of evil; therefore each slanderer belongs, by his very condition and fate, to the dark kingdom. Each advice to disregard slander is not sound advice. One should pay attention to each manifestation; for every poisonous gas, one should have a counter gas. Let us remember that slander is anti-cultural; in every false information, there is slander. And according to the Biblical expression, the slanderer, like a dog, will eat its own filth. The Bible also says, "From time immemorial, the devil was a slanderer." These are the ones who concern themselves with slander.

Finally, slander is the measure of consciousness and the testing stone of the power of achievement.

Himalayas, November 7, 1931.

THE ISLAND OF TEARS

THE ISLAND OF TEARS

PERHAPS the most difficult necessity is the necessity of refusal—refusal to those who come to you with the best possible motives and decisions, who seek help for some excellent purpose that already exists, but one that you are entirely without power to help. And not only that you cannot yourself help, but scanning the entire horizon, you do not even know where to direct those who are in need so that their beautiful desires can be satisfied. A collection of all the messages asking for help becomes the true Island of Tears.

Sometimes you still may assume that some of these people will hold out until new conditions arise; but not seldom, you feel that their call is the last call, and that there is not only no reserve of further physical means, but that the spiritual means are already exhausted, and this is the saddest thing. Besides many personal misfortunes, it is terrible to see that all sorts of educational and cultural institutions are being uprooted. Mankind must be especially cautious of precisely that which is occurring at this present time—the thwarting of the growth of Culture, and that Culture, which by its blossoming, must give a true prosperity, a spiritual prosperity, and a prosperity of every form.

Here before us lies a request concerning a school. If it is not answered, many small children will remain without necessary education. Here, also, a photograph of a great number of children in this group is attached—and what nice, dear faces, notwithstanding their poor clothing! How healthy an element is felt in these little bodies which are ready for spiritual food! And the money asked for this school is not at all large, but there is no source from which to obtain it.

Here is a request for support for a magazine and a very useful publishing house. Everything issued by this publishing house is valuable and absolutely useful. This is not some visionary dream. On the table are lying their most useful books which transmit beautiful, basic and strengthening facts to the new generations. Precisely such magazines and publishing houses, fully constructive, must not only exist but also expand, in the name of the underlying necessity for perfection. And again the requested sum is so small compared to the useful, already-manifested achievements of the publishing house. Nevertheless, this sum is also lacking. And again one has to write: "Let us await better times." These better times will come, but by then the whole tempo of the already organized work will be disrupted. It is very probable that the work will soon cease and you know what it means to reorganize the work anew. So many requests come from publishing houses and magazines, and they come not from one country, nor are they the results of the unhappiness of one people. The variety of nations, places, and all conditions converge in one focus, namely the focus of the fact that the sprouts of Culture are being curtailed.

Here before us, is a completed and meritorious historical institution. The products of its fruitful publishing house and its publications are at hand. The list of co-workers contains in itself a fine number of the most valued scientific names. No one questions the need of such an Institution. The local Government supported it as much as it could. But in order to exist, it still needs a certain sum, also ridiculously small compared to the program of the Institution. But even this sum is lacking. And how many valuable efforts, how much priceless time is being taken from the most necessary scientific researches for fruitless search, in order only that the doors of the Institutions should not be closed altogether! And when they close, where can we go to gather again the necessary combination of strength and conditions? Is it possible that the spirit of mankind has become so profligate as to blindly throw away the most beautiful accumulations and the most necessary researches?

A medical-scientific institution which has already attained definite results and which was hailed by scientific centers is also in the same position; here also a ridiculously small sum is needed, but it is not available. It is just like facing the knife of the guillotine! Here, a very ancient Museum, a national pride, is forced to seek the smallest sums in order to maintain itself. And again the very same knife of the guillotine! Here are requests about the building of a temple so needed when the human spirit is sick. And instead of construction, the knife of the guillotine!

Here are groups of youths of the most valuable Centers of Working Youth who gathered in the name of beautiful constructive beginnings, in the highest visions and understanding which now fight with difficulty for their own existence. And no matter how these seekers of the best spiritual strongholds search, they cannot even find a minimum sum in order to strengthen the existence of their unity. Weakened, they will scatter, driven by want. And when will one be able to unite them again, such valuable ones, who so rejoice the spirit and heart?

Here is a Cultural Society which is striving towards the tasks of Education, Culture, Motherhood, towards the strengthening of all those principles, which, if unrealized shall cause us to suffer a spiritual as well as material depression once again.

They are asking so little in order to exist! They give, as it is, everything that belongs to them, which can be given. But these most beautiful examples of self-sacrifice are being broken by those icy currents, about which the "Transmuting Fire" speaks.

A well-known author, who was widely hailed, cannot even write because he has no means for his livelihood. Does this not express humanity's mad dissipation of its spiritual forces? And not only do all these manifold requests for the support of beautiful foundations remain unanswered because of want, but the universal order of things continues to tread the same destructive directions of sundering the best cultural projects and aspirations of mankind. And the serious thing is that this pertains not only to one country or even to a group of countries; no, this unwelcome news unquestionably comes from all parts of the world. Some one will say: "But the schools continue to exist, the Universities continue to exist, and the Museums also exist." Yes, but let us observe what has been the gradual reduction of the budgets of these Institutions, preserved only for the sake of longevity. Daily we read about the closing of entire scientific departments of Museums, about the interruption of research work, about the ceasing of excavations, about the stopping of construction, about the reduction of the staffs which cause so many needed, irreplaceable young forces to be cut away, forever to be lost in the ruthless ocean of Chaos. "*No*" and "*impossible*" prevail. Denials and dismissals rule, even without the special discussions which are most necessary. Even in the endowed Institutions, we see unprecedented notices about incomplete editions, about the delay of plans and again about the curtailing even of what is most essential.

Of course we must think about the future—of that no one will have another opinion. Even a manufacturer does not produce for yesterday. And now, amidst the same existing ideas about the future, it would seem that the people themselves, in the cruelest way, will begin to cut away everything, even that which is fundamentally necessary for each production.

The world has experienced many crashes and shocks. But is not there some special sign in the spiritual and material misfortune which has now fallen upon mankind? Such a sign exists. And this sign will be terrible, if special attention is not paid to it. This is the sign of universal misfortune. Heretofore, misfortunes were national or local, but now an unprecedented internationalism of misfortune has come. There is not one country, there is not one distant island, which does not repeat its tales of misfortune.

The more in contact you come with the most diverse peoples, the more shocked you are by the universality of misfortune. The small groups of those who lived on incomes which veiled the world for them with an illusory guarantee, have become absolutely insignificant. Any of them who do not suffer as yet, already speak about misfortune. And through these misfortune-carrying affirmations and actions, some destructive invocation of misfortunes emerges. It is as if some invisible sowers of misfortune were passing through all countries and throwing destructive, deadly formulae into the space.

And following them appears a veritable dance of death: "Cut down, arrest, kill, deaden,"—these deadly words in many languages, in various formulae, are being carried over all the world. The phantom of economy has given birth to an army of unemployed and has brought the wages to a standard not answering even the most niggardly needs. Before us are the statistics of various incomes and one must confess that the figures are dreadful.

One thing is clear: If mankind continues to hypnotize itself by invoking misfortune, it shall violate that which is most valuable for its very existence; it shall disrupt Culture; it shall disrupt the progress and accumulation of that which, under different conditions, is irrevocable, or demands many centuries for healing.

The horror of refusal, the horror of killing the living sprouts, cannot continue any longer. It is absolutely necessary to cast aside personal quarrels and personal rivalry to think unitedly about the future generations for whom the foundation of Culture is the only stronghold of the spirit. Instead of calling forth misfortunes, one must sooner or later—and better it should be sooner—begin to invoke the foundations of positive construction; we will thus begin to solve many so-called insoluble problems. Edison lived long, Michelson also lived long, and none of these creators of thought, contemplated suicide. Creative thought is that accumulator of high energies, which feeds all the energies of life. The high energies of creativeness constitute the great elixir of life, eternally sought by men. And this elixir of life proclaims to each one who desires to think, that it is necessary to turn from the destructive invocation of misfortunes to the insistent call of benevolent cultural constructiveness. And if we pronounce the call for the necessity of development of Knowledge and ennoblement all together, this call in itself will be the first stone in the new construction of the positive stronghold of mankind.

We began with the horror and necessity of refusals. Let us finish with heartfelt joy, over the reality of possible construction, even if it be only temporary, even if the malice of destruction and decomposition be put aside only in part. The creation of the thought form is being transmuted into an active one. Therefore one desires so greatly to tell all workers of Culture who have recently received so many refusals and curtailments: "Let us hold out. Let us not separate. Let us cherish even the shreds of friendliness and let us cover the refusals by these seeds of Bliss."

To transform the Island of Tears into a Beautiful Garden, into a Garden of Labor and Knowledge—is not this the first foundation of all positive Teachings of the World!

Himalayas, April 8, 1932.

THE PLUNDERED HEART

IN recent newspapers there were two significant columns; in the left column it told of the tragic suicide of K., the multimillionaire banker. On the same page at the right was a communique about the suicide of the seventy-year-old G. E., another multimillionaire. K. left a significant note: "I am tired." G. E. in his farewell letter says: "Why wait?" These two suicides of multimillionaires who were not financially ruined, but rather spiritually injured, are highly significant.

It would have seemed that K. should have had a great store of vital energy. In only twenty years, he created his universal financial operations. He gave many millions to governments of various countries. Truly, some of his loans were frozen, but this condition could not have been a mortal blow to his spirit because his works were not ruined.

In the case of G. E. many things are still more amazing. It seems that in the vast activity of G. E. nothing was especially congealed. His undertakings even recently were enriched by valuable discoveries and improvements. His broad educational activity and charitable constructions were apparently proceeding enormously. One of his latest charitable undertakings was the construction of a hospital in Italy for Italian children. And suddenly, amidst this expansion, growth and improvement, the chilling voice: "Why wait?"

One also remembers another millionaire who leaped from his airplane, although he left behind him a fortune of millions.

One wonders what force it is that brings one to the

fatal question: "Why wait?" The entire history of these people seems to indicate a tremendous store of vital energy. These were not walking corpses, numb of heart since birth. Much good was always related about K. And really his unusually broad vision, universal in measure, was not satisfied with small decisions. His office in Stockholm soon became decisive in the most diverse and broadest international questions. If we take the list of countries to whom his monetary help has been flowing, we will see the broad thought of K. in the names of these governments. We will notice the creative construction, not only for one of such groups, not for a one-sided political isolation, but for a broadly planned creative work. Friends and acquaintances of K. spoke well of him. One asks where, then, were these friends, when his hand wrote the ominous words, so remote from his person, "I am tired"?

I last saw G. E. in Rochester in 1924. With what unusual animation he showed me the new inventions in his establishment and Institute of Music! It was apparent again that he was not an indifferent philanthropist of his wealth. No, notwithstanding his gray hair, he was a vigorous, vital, creative participant in excellently planned cultural educational institutions. He diligently desired to attract new forces, young and known, that could vitally improve the Institutions. G. E. really loved music. His life, beginning from his early breakfasts to an organ accompaniment, was completely filled with the best music. His was not only an abstract desire to help refine the consciousness of the young generation of America. If we take the lists of all those who passed through his institutions, we see only a broad understanding outside of circles and parties. If, however, we remember all his travels and his untiring personal labor in all his Institutions, it seems impossible to expect from G. E. especially the terrible, joyless exclamation, "Why wait?"

In the famous Japanese methods of wrestling, two repeated strokes are always mentioned, of which the last one seems especially decisive. These two horrible confessions of outstanding multimillionaires and social workers become especially notable in their repetition. Will not these two statements, traversing the world, force many upon many to consider what compelled these really great and outstanding persons to finish the broadest activity with the horrible exclamation of joylessness, because this is not the despair of a pauper who is crushed by the lack of escape, because this is not the last command of a ship's captain, who knows the inevitability of a wreck? In both these cases, a strong will, which has seen the apparition of some reality, cried out to the entire world. Perhaps, in comparison with this dreadful reality, the cries of all friends could not shout above the roar of its killing realism. And one may only call it by the most dreaded word in the entire dictionary—*joylessness.* Not even the stroke of despair, nor the horror of results, but the deadening consciousness of the impossibility of joy. Of course, as has always been said, always and in all things, "Joy is a special Wisdom." The joy of a human is remotely different from the joy of a lamb in the green pasture. But a human being also rejoices at flowers and may be gladdened by them if his heart is not deadened. An incurable, destructive malady may raise the question, "Why wait?" But a heart that is not burdened by age nor by disappointments before the great reality, cannot become exhausted.

Of course, the earthly paths of communion lead to the horror of limitation. I repeat and insist, that if a man does not even know a reason why he speeds around the entire earth in the swiftest airplane, then even the very sun, the very Beauty of space, sooner or later will become for him a leaden oven-door. And in this sorrowful limitation, the man can plunge into the fatal error of the thought of self-destruction. It is quite evident, that he to whom the devastating thought of self-destruction came, never heard of the consequences of such a lawless act against the whole of existence. The voices of science must finally also be added to the commandments of religions, which, in the name of the immutable laws of existence, could pronounce in many ways, how viciously unnatural self-destruction is and what consequences it invariably provokes. Because he who has even once for but a moment realized the Invisible world—for him Infinity ceases to be a round-the-world trip, over the crust of one of the minutest planets. His airplanes would carry not only the accounts of business firms, which at their destination had already lost all their reason of being; his radio would not screech out unnecessary things, but verily those things which would give birth to the joy of the heart. Let us emphasize the joy of the heart, because the forms of life can hardly offer this inexhaustible joy, if the consciousness fails to strive into the future, into that future, where all insoluble problems will be solved by the transmutation of life. All such terrible finalities as "Why wait?" and "I am tired" do not appear as the guilt of one man; they place a responsibility upon the whole of human society. It is credible that a single individual can become tired at seeing, only coldness, greed and treason each day if he unmistakably notices that all his most heartfelt and best strivings are weighed upon alien scales by disgusting and vulgar weights.

No newspapers relate, nor perhaps, will they ever relate, just what situations plundered the hearts of these two great men. Perhaps this tragic exclamation, "I am tired" pertains to those dark slanderers who struck the balance of the heart. Who knows how much treason, how much jealousy, false invention, concealments and selfish perversions surrounded these great social workers? Aspiring to some distant lands, did they not strive to depart from reality, and did they not dream in their nightly solitude of finding those who would understand the truth of their strivings? Let us not forget how one great writer, not long before his death, also sick with a plundered heart, confided to me his suffering, "Maybe there are friends and readers somewhere, but I do not see them, and do not know where they live." The terrible loneliness of great people resounded in this confession which emanated from the last throbs of a burdened heart. Probably this heart felt that his thoughts for mankind were not forgiven him, nor his striving for a world outside of vulgarized conventionality; and a few days later he again said to me, "They are afraid of me, as though I had taken something from them." And he suffered again. Because a small consciousness not only does not strive towards broadening and acquiring true values, but for its pacification, it tries to annihilate that which is not of their measures.

He who spoke of fatigue knew of all these measures; he was not tired of life, but perhaps it seemed unbearably horrible to him to continue fighting against these endless measures of slime. Plunderers of the Heart! When we read fairytales about vampires and werewolves, are they not called the plunderers of the hearts, and perverters of the beautiful existence predestined to all?

Therefore, these two cries of mortal anguish, flying around the world at this time, are not casual. In this repeated confession before death, is contained an address to human society. He, who, amidst tremendous activity asked: "Why wait?" of course, addresses himself in thought to all those who brought the greatest disappointment and in his presence killed that which glowed in this great human heart. The plundering of the heart, so one may call this crime, brings the most horrible consequence—Joylessness.

The abduction of the Heart—is it not also comprised in the kidnapping of children, about which the newspapers are now filled? Perhaps it is not accidental that this news is connected with the name of the national hero of America, Lindbergh. Let the magnitude of this name turn the attention of mankind upon those horrors, which continue to take place and multiply in the world of bipeds. The world has been shaken by this news. Much news and communications pierced the space. The newspapers brought the information that there had been a hasty strengthening of the law against blackmail and threats which condemns the criminal to 20 years in jail and several thousand dollars fine. Of course, it should not be otherwise. The inhumanity of blackmail and threats must be sufficiently guarded against by the government. Protecting the existence of a person, the government thus tries to fight the joyless oppression, the plundering of the heart. If the plunderers of the heart, the despoilers of everything most precious, destroyers and violators, would be driven from human society as foul and unworthy, the tiredness of life would also begin to abate.

In the conviction of the inviolability of the heart, people will begin to rejoice at joys which are expanded and inexhaustible. No one will then ask, with the sigh of anguish, "Why wait?" But he will say, with a renewed understanding, "I await resurrection." And the very Infinity, which those who exist cannot avoid shall not only not frighten him, but shall inspire and call him to a new and endless creativeness. And the suffering heart will breathe with ease, because it will know for what it is waiting, what it hopes for, and what it needs to know. In the name of great Knowledge, in the name of the Beautiful, let us send our best thoughts to those who, with their call of suffering, fearless of reality, have pierced the world with a confessional, about which we all must think, in preparation for the new paths.

Himalayas, March 20, 1932.

RICH POVERTY

"Paupertas, impulit andax,
Ut versum facerem. . . ."

HORACE says: "Poverty impelled me to inspiration." It is astonishing when we recall that as long as St. Francis was a rich, middle-class citizen he did not attract anyone's attention. But as soon as he wedded Signora Poverty and began his spiritual task, he became the world Saint whose name and image kindled and inspired a myriad of hearts towards achievement.

Perusing the pages of the most varied histories of men, we always come to the same unwavering assertion, that wealth is not notable in history as the best means of achievement. Sheik Humayun at the birth of his great son Akbar was so poor that he could not give more than a few grains of musk to his court as the customary gift distributed on such occasions.

The bankers of Babylon were very rich, but history has not preserved their names. Such names are useless in the narrative of human achievement so long as they did not adhere to enlightenment. The chronicle of the movements of humanity remains as something remarkable according to its inner justice for the unprejudiced onlooker.

Contemporaries create many lies and injustices, but time itself makes some significant changes in accordance with the laws of existence. Contrary to these contemporaries, these laws bring into relief all progressive movements and remove into the abyss everything illusory, accidental and transitory. After all, history does not forget and sometimes, perhaps after whole centuries, will accord due justice to a heartfelt human striving towards the common bliss.

The history of humanity after all remains human in the full sense of the word. Thought of gain, self-love, wrath, and cruelty always remain last in some shameful places, and no gold, no porphyry can conceal either ignorance or destruction. At the same time, each creativeness, each true constructive striving do not remain forgotten. Besides, history with poignant attention, often unknown from where it comes, never forgets to stress everything selfless. Although in its own way, everything which strives towards the bliss of humanity is noted. The same history brings us a vast amount of the most unexpected information which, when analyzed, makes an unusual mosaic, out of which much that is instructive for life can be drawn by everyone.

Let us remember the conventional token of human existence—the coin. In this question as well as in many others the history of China affords an unforgettable example. During the movements of our expedition along the remote regions of China we encountered an unusually curious situation in monetary tokens. First of all we were warned by experienced people not to accept silver bars, even though they were marked with governmental seals. For often inside the silver bar, copper was skillfully inserted. We were frequently confused also by the current silver coins which were accepted and evaluated quite differently in various localities. In one city they preferred the coin with a head of Li Hung Chang with six letters; in another, they wanted to have seven letters. Some preferred coins with feminine images and others did not wish to have Chinese moneys and demanded rupees.

To top it all off, we were offered as change some wooden sticks with carvings, with the statement that these signs were the best because they were issued by local gambling houses. Thus, above all the heads of Li Hung Chang, the citizens suddenly placed their trust in the little sticks of the gambling house, finding them of indisputable value. With all the diversity of Chinese monetary symbols, the little sticks of the gambling house nevertheless remained unexcelled in their originality.

Penetrating deeply into the history of China, we may truly find all kinds of curious types of monetary symbols, but after the contemporary little sticks of the gambling house, the most startling perhaps and the most significant form is the money-knives of the Ju Dynasty (715 to 431 B.C.). Among the myriad curious monetary forms corresponding to various aspects of trade, we have not encountered anywhere else the form of a knife. Perhaps in our day of decadence, depression, budgetary failures, the inner meaning of the knife-coin, might be very significant. The debtor would say to the creditor: "Wait a bit, I shall return my debt to you in knives." Or "I have saved quite a number of knives for you." How many misunderstandings would arise by reason of such discussions about knives, at the various councils of the League of Nations. But in the Chinese knife-monies, the traditional Chinese refinement was also maintained. Their form is very beautiful. And the ring on the handle indicates that they could either be tied or strung to something and could be carried about with one. From our judiciary point of view, how many misapprehensions could such money create in the hands of robbers, who would try to convince one that those were pen-knives.

But it is significant that the refined fantasy of the ancients considered it possible to link the conception of a monetary symbol precisely with a knife. For no one has ever yet utilized for a monetary symbol some holy image as such. True, upon later coins there were images of deities, but they were applied as symbols or as guardians of a certain city or country. Who knows, perhaps to some of our contemporary bankers, the image of a knife-coin would be especially attractive and dear to them.

Thus, the history of humanity in some seemingly threatening tokens brings to us the correlation of symbols. The knife, more than any other, is a cruel symbol, a piercing one and crude. But the monetary sign, with all its conventionality is likewise not divine.

History has not forgotten to relate that even Confucius, great in his love of peace and justice, was so persecuted by his contemporaries, that he had to keep a harnessed cart ready and spent a great part of his life in forced migrations. But history has rejected into the abyss the names of these ignorant persecutors. But Confucius not only has remained in memory, not only has he lived through millenniums, but his name has become even more strengthened in the contemporary consciousness.

To speak of persecutions of contemporaries and of the just evaluation which followed would mean, first of all, to expound the history of contemporary religions, the history of all teachings of the world, the history of all creative strivings. Already more than once, we have recalled that there should be issued parallel with the book, "Martyrs of Science," also the book "Martyrs of Art," "Martyrs of Creativeness," "Martyrs of Bliss."

Within recent times we were witness to the fact that Edison, during a session of one of the Academies, was called a charlatan for one of his most astonishing discoveries. The very same term was applied even very recently in the editions of some dignified encyclopedias to some very respected and remarkable names. It is instructive to observe how, in subsequent editions, these denominations were shamefully eradicated. History itself began to set up its indisputable evaluation and the conventional ignorant judgments of contemporaries began to dissolve in shame, giving place to more fitting denominations.

In all manifestations of life we constantly see this crystallization of values, brought about by the cosmic consciousness. For some reason or other, some signs and symbols become obliterated, but others cross through unharmed and remain instructive through all the perturbations and tempests. The wise ancient Chinese for some reason linked the symbol of the monetary sign with the symbol of a knife. And time has brought this symbol to us unblemished. So also, time has brought to us the images of St. Francis and St. Sergius untarnished and vivid, as well as of all those heroes of achievement, mighty in spirit, who, having renounced all the conventionalities of an imperfect earthly life, strove towards true values. And the great poet, Horace, was not only unashamed, but spoke with great dignity of the significance of poverty for his inspiration. And the remarkable painter, Van Gogh, in sending his landlord his amputated ear, seemed to remind him of one who knows how to listen. If people would only understand where the true values are, the values truly needed by them, where that generous poverty lives that is richer than any riches!

Certainly no one would state that trade was not needed. On the contrary, each barter within the limits of culture, should be welcomed. Therefore, in our World League of Culture is included the participation of industrial enterprises; only they should be directed along cultural paths. But one ought always to remark that the cornerstone does not belong to capital and trade, as was so often signified during these days of perturbation. In true co-operation, according to cultural standards, every trade, every industrialization will only serve to enhance the Beautiful Garden.

In his "Nibelungen Ring," Wagner presents many cosmic moments. Unforgettable also remains the significant dialogue of *Wotan* with *Mime* in which *Wotan* permits *Mime* to ask him three questions. *Wotan* replies to all the cunning questions of *Mime*, touching the clouds and the underworld. But, wandering far, *Mime* forgot to ask that which was most necessary for him. *Wotan* said to *Mime*, "Thou hast wandered far, thou hast risen to the clouds and penetrated under the earth, but that which was so needed for thee, thou did not ask. And now thou wilt be mine." Has not humanity, in all its wanderings and vacillations, forgotten to ask about, and to think of that which it so urgently needed?

The book "Fiery World" says: "Thus the dark forces have brought the planet to such a condition that no earthly decision can restore the conventional welfare. No one can believe that the earthly standards of yesterday are applicable today. Thus, humanity is again in need of understanding the meaning of its short presence in an earthly state. Only by a basic definition of its existence in a dense condition and the understanding of the Subtle and Fiery Worlds, can one strengthen one's existence. One 'must not think that a specter of trade can even temporarily afford a secure existence. Life has turned into trade; but which of the Teachers of Life were traders? You know the great symbol of the driving of the money-lenders from out of the temple; but is not earth itself a temple? Is not Maha Meru not the foot of the Summit of Spirit? Thus one can point out the destined peaks to the inhabitants of Earth.

"Let us not forget that each moment must belong to the New World. The World of thought constitutes the living link between the Subtle and Fiery Worlds; it enters as the nearest impetus of the Fiery World. Thought does not exist without Fire, and Fire is being transmuted into creative thought. The manifestation of thought is already realized. Likewise the Great Fire—Om shall be realized."

The same Book reminds us: "People affirm that before a war or calamity, forest fires and other conflagrations take place. It does not matter whether these always occur but it is significant that the people's belief notes the fiery tension before a world catastrophe. The wisdom of the people allots to Fire a remarkable place. God visits the people in Fire. The same fiery element was chosen as the highest Court. The annihilation of evil takes place through Fire. The manifestation of mishaps is followed by burning. Likewise, in the entire trend of people's thinking, one can see fiery paths. People light the oil-lamps and people carry the torches manifested at services. Solemn is the Fiery element in the people's understanding! Thus, let us draw not from superstition but from the people's heart!

"Sincere self-perfecting is not egotism, but has world significance. The thought about improvement does not only pertain to oneself; such thought carries in itself the necessary flame needed for many kindlings of the heart. As fire brought into quarters filled with combustible substance will always ignite, thus the fiery thought pierces the space and will inevitably attract questing hearts to itself."

Himalayas, 1933.

CANIMUS SURDIS

"WE are singing to the deaf!" sorrowfully exclaims the great Italian poet. Again we have an avalanche of news that are concerned with the same things!

A publishing house in Germany has been suspended. There are financial difficulties in the scientific circles of Holland. There is some economic distress in Bulgaria.

Useful publications are being discontinued in Calcutta. There are some terrifying figures of unemployment in America. During the last month in Chicago alone, 38 banks failed. There are difficulties in Sweden. A beautiful project of a children's theater has failed to be realized. Also it has been impossible to commemorate a historical anniversary. H. G. Wells, well known for his foresight urges the necessity of the construction of a new Noah's Ark for the salvation of Culture and civilization. Endless depression! Endless distressful news in letters and newspapers! Everywhere the dark forces are attacking, first of all cultural manifestations. It seems as if Culture hinders them from carrying on their satanic plans to destroy the world.

Among these waves of chaos, one hears isolated voices, dreaming that everything will be restored to the old, by means of a magic wand. Baldwin advises: "Buy wisely and freely!" The *New York Times* has bold head-lines: "Trade revival is essential if unemployment situation is to improve!"—"Urges normal buying!" A leader advises: "Buy motor cars!" What can be better?

May the position of ten millions of unemployed improve! May joyful buying return! But these calls are like the foam of waves against the rocks. From foam perhaps some useful product can be made! Perhaps, but so far the titanic waves of disastrous news rear up, and thunder furiously against Culture.

Even kind-hearted citizens begin to whisper: "Is it the right time to think of Culture?"—"What good is civilization if we have nothing to eat?" Strong forceful men fight the gigantic waves that threaten our crumbling Culture. One has only to read the words of a well-known author, written with the blood of his: "Our personal position is indescribably difficult, yet we fight with our last efforts, keeping up our trust and vigor and love towards sincere friends. The only advantage of our position is the complete absence of the fear for tomorrow, because in any case it cannot be worse than today. But we are exhausted and have become ten years older. Yet in order to stand up under the burden of debts for eight years without the possibility of doing what is most important, one must be of steel and as resistant as an oak. The end of the world is nearing!"

We answer this strong and glorious fighter: On a cross-road, the passers-by were asked with what they were building the future age? One sneered: "With poison gas!" Another hissed, serpent-like: "With submarines!" The third laughed: "By short-selling." The fourth: "With golf." The fifth: "With narcotics." The sixth: "*Après nous, le déluge!*" The seventh: "Through Culture!"

"Is it not a miracle if out of seven passers-by, one still remembered Culture? And not only remembered, but even was not ashamed to pronounce this word, so inconvenient for many. Who knows, perhaps by this one word this passer-by already brought persecution against himself.

"But even so, it sounds miraculous if, at the cross-road, amidst all the turmoil, this sacred, inspiring, uplifting concept was still pronounced. My friend thought that only one passer-by in a hundred would pay respect to the very foundations of life which created the epochs of renaissance, all joy, all prosperity, all daring and all achievements.

"Verily, if this panacea would be granted, without toil, far from the rim of the precipice, away from the cross, and without the danger of a cup of poison, it would not be that precious gem—the very foundation of life. If difficulties are blessed, then verily it is in the name of Culture, which embodies the Light, the Great Service, steadfastness of achievement, all Beauty and all Knowledge.

"If obstacles contain in themselves potential possibilities, then suffering for the cause of Culture will blossom in the precious silver Lotus within one's heart. Only not to lose the entrusted Stone and not to spill the Chalice! Infinity is boundless...not abstractness, but life itself! Nowadays the list of failures is longer than the list of successes because mankind has rejected Culture. Humanity has violated Culture by regarding it as a luxury. Nobody will assert that we are now going through normal times. Even bandits, racketeers selfishly understand the abnormality of conditions, and ingeniously apply their looters' tricks, in order to make the best of this hour of darkness. But there are many young hearts which respond to Light. One must only realize how urgently we must turn to everything cultural, to everything that ennobles the taste and all strivings of life. . . .

"Although conscious fighters for Culture are few, yet greater thanks and honor are due to those who stand as guardians of the true treasures of mankind. As antennae, they transmit throughout the whole world and receive and send calls for nobility, refinement and constructiveness.

"I remember in Mongolia when the expedition miraculously escaped a most dangerous situation, a gray-haired Buriat solemnly raised his hand and exclaimed: 'Light conquers darkness!' This was not something abstract, not a dream! The wise dweller of the desert understood the reality of the Great Light, he understood that darkness was finally doomed to defeat. Thus those who walk with Light will be victorious in the end, but the wavering one will be precipitated into the abyss of darkness."

It is possible that there are so many of the deaf!

Sometimes it seems as if the path of Culture and the conditions of life have separated. But when the lovers of a machine have lost co-ordination, then naturally one cannot expect full speed and one cannot avoid disastrous lapses.

Even the mind of a child understands that enlightenment, education, culture are as fuel to a motor.

The troglodyte threatens: "To hell with Culture, cash first." But by reason of this very fact he is called a troglodyte, and his place is in a cave, not in the Hall of Culture.

Even during disaster the troglodyte finds sufficient gold to secure himself the bloody spectacle of a bullfight, a cock-fight, of races, or to delight himself at the sight of the breaking of cheek bones or the dislocation of limbs or in some carnal pleasures. For such entertainments, money is always plentiful. He will even find some hypocritical excuses, by mumbling something about physical health. But as soon as we approach the urgent questions of the ennoblement of taste, the questions of creativeness and ascension of the spirit, we find ears and eyes are closed. Thus one understands the origin of the old French proverb: "He is especially deaf, who does not want to hear." The Italian poet who exclaimed: "We are singing to the deaf," knew also these deaf ones. At the same time, one also reads news about a new bullet which pierces all armor; of new shields which protect the back in attacks which demand crawling; of new, especially deadly gases and similar "humanitarian" appliances.

On the same pages, some voices rise in indignation against fratricide. But the troglodyte roars with triumphant laughter, because he thinks that he has succeeded in disconnecting the levers of the machine. The saturnine *Alberich* and *Mime* hope that their rule is at hand, when everything connected with Light will be debased and Satan himself, without any trouble, will receive all of his desires.

The apparition of troglodytes is fearful, thus it is not exaggerated. The advertisements in the newspapers of evening gowns, festivals, dinners and races do not hide the misfortunes. Practically one sees news of the curtailing and discontinuation of cultural undertakings in every newspaper.

Thus the troglodytes triumph; they think that their doctrine of gluttony and lust has already triumphed above all circumstances. It seems almost as if special Internationals of light and darkness were being organized. No competitive fanfares will deaden this Armageddon.

Is it not the last hour for all, to whom Culture is not an empty sound, to unite? Is it not the last hour to arrest the strangulation of everything valuable, creative and young?

When you speak of gluttony, lust, speculation, then perhaps your sincerity will not be questioned; but every attempt to turn to Beauty, Knowledge, to the meaning of life, will be followed by mistrust and suspicion of insincerity. Well may you say, that the proverb *"lupus est homo homini"*—one man is a wolf to another,—does not date from yesterday, and that the moon and the sun are still the same.

It is true that long ago another poet exclaimed: "In eternal Beauty shines indifferent nature," and "To good and evil we are shamefully indifferent." But these lines about indifference referred to people, who knew, it would seem, far less than the people of today.

At present even nature is not quite indifferent. Even in remote mountains people speak of unusual earthquakes, volcanic eruptions, of sunspots. And an institute in Nice comments in almost astrological expressions upon the influence of sunspots on human beings, if one is to believe the latest communications of "*Matin.*"

But the present persecution of Culture is not due to sunspots. And the dark spots of irresponsibility upon human conscience are by no means caused by the sun. These spots of irresponsibility are due to darkness, to ignorance.

"Ignorance is the greatest crime", as it was so ordained in the ancient commandments. He who dares to say, "To hell with Culture," is the greatest criminal. He is the seducer of the coming generation, he is the murderer, the sower of darkness, he is suicide.

"We are singing to the deaf", sorrowfully exclaims the poet of Italy. But the poet author of "Beda, the Preacher" answers with cosmic vigor:

> "Silent became the sage, drooping his head.
> "But before he had ceased, the Stones from all the
> world's ends
> "Thundered, in answer: '*Amen!*'."

Himalayas, July 1, 1932.

RIGOR MORTIS

THE Rigor Mortis of the corpse has aroused considerable discussion. The ancient Rosicrucians speak very much to the point about this strange phenomenon, from the point of view of matter. They cite how gradually the deplorable process of Rigor Mortis sets in, not only corporeally with death but, still worse, already during life, inflicting the organs of thought.

Soul-less people are being created under our eyes. One should recognize this process, not as an abstract symbol, but as an evidence of psycho-physical involution. Much is given to man; hence, vaster is the breadth of his instability. But there exist glutinous regions to which the pendulum of spirit may cling for a long time, if not forever.

Much, much effort is needed in order to escape from this Rigor Mortis of thought, in order to re-enter a broad and conscious movement of thought.

A well-known British engineer, an inventor, has recently stated in the press that humanity is not ready morally to accept all our latest inventions and discoveries. This affirmation from a Western scientist is timely and characteristic. It coincides with the ancient as well as the most recent teachings of the East.

In addition to our daily newspaper communications about all manners of anti-cultural terrors, one may find extraordinary indications in the columns of the press, written in a quiet tone as though they entirely corresponded to this twentieth century of our era and to our incalculable age from the beginning of our planetary life.

There have been announcements about the attempts of

some organizations at Broeken to revive black magic. A beautiful young girl and a goat and other attributes of the Black Sabbath were made ready.

In Finland, an entire organization of dark necromancers has been discovered; the desecration of corpses, certain rites in cemeteries and a complete service of the Black Crow was disclosed.

Cases of human sacrifice are mentioned around Bengal Bay. The newspapers state this as a fact, as a reality. The same newspapers announce how a festive crowd in America gathered even from afar to revel in the burning of a Negro.

It was announced that recently a crowd in Berlin decorated banners with the blood of the victims of murder, this, not in the Middle Ages, but now.

In Paris, some individuals attempted to dip their handkerchiefs in the blood of an executed person.

In Spain, the banderillas stained with blood from the bullfights, bring large sums of money.

In our 20th century, the hearts of enemies are still torn out for bloody sacrifices. Verily, humanity is not ready to accept the latest discoveries. On one side, the imminent revelation of the almighty atomic energy—on the other side, the black mass, the cult of Satan, Baphomet and the bloody terraphim.

The human consciousness has become divided. In the general dissolution of the world, the tops and bottoms have separated so widely, that a movement of advancement is hardly conceivable.

In a back issue of a periodical there is the following communication: "We are glad to learn that recently, a society has been organized with the aim of protecting and helping all victims of black magic. If somewhere, someone is the victim of an occult persecution, he may communicate with the editor and all will be done to help the sufferer."

We admit that one rarely reads such a communication. Something must have occurred, in order to admit such a reality to enter life.

After the bloody hecatombs of the unprecedented war, all foundations were shattered. Instead of the expected prosperity, the finances of all countries cracked. The countries have denied all the obligations which they guaranteed and solemnly pronounced. Billions of dollars of their budgets have been imperiled: an army of millions of unemployed has been created. Failures of banks have occurred that would have been inconceivable in former times. The world was set to trembling with great shocks, such as those of the collapse of Krenger and Insull.

Thus, suddenly, like an inexorable karma for the mass murder, there was created a rift of life, a rift of the world. The world has divided sharply along the lines of Culture. How much, then, of conscious, creative good must be poured out, in order to wash away the coagulated blood . And yet, entire organizations go to Broeken for the Witch's Sabbath. "Time" printed a photograph of the goat and the girl, as if it were a vaudeville sketch.

But at the same time under the pretext of the crisis, various cultural institutions are being curtailed. The servitors of darkness scream: "To hell with culture!" This is not fiction. It would be a great happiness to be able to acknowledge that all these ominous threats and actions did not exist.

And the workers of culture weaken upon seeing how their best tasks are being covered with the ashes of darkness. And they seek vainly for something to turn to and a place to gather.

And at the same time, some go to Broeken and some dream of drinking a cup of blood. . . . Nor is it in "occult" novels where one may expect fiction that these horrors take place; but in life, among the starched collars.

Jesting, side-shows, derision, blasphemy have reached their limits. Those who say that evil is equivalent to good must not forget that evil should be regarded as imperfection. Behind good there always stands the origin of creativeness. But now, instead of the invincibly guiding source, verily, the guiding good must retreat to a defensive position, thus losing the initial pronouncement.

Out of shameful physical self-defense, people avoid coming close to Truth, even at the price of spiritual disgrace, but unwilling to lose their conventional stations! One may hear the killing whispers: "Preferable is fossilization, Rigor Mortis is preferable to daring to attack ignorance."

So far, irresponsible consciousnesses calm themselves and succumb to the darkness of Rigor Mortis, but each decay itself does not slumber. It realizes that now, because of human cowardice, it possesses the possibility of initiative. And, verily, the initiative of darkness becomes apparent in the great as in the small.

And darkness uses its usual tactics; it creeps in and crawls about unnoticeably. The servitors of darkness penetrate under various guises; and having once penetrated into the fortress, they scoff in self-content.

The Book, "Fiery World" underlines these dangerous attacks through small actions: "Soul-less beings are known to all. This is not a symbol, but a chemical reality. One may be asked whether these people incarnate in this deplorable state. This question will disclose a lack of awareness of the foundations. No one can incarnate without a store of fiery energy. No one can enter the dense world without the torch of Agni. The dissipation of Agni takes place here among all the wonders of Nature. It is not at all necessary, while scattering Agni, to commit some beastly crimes. From various Teachings we know sufficiently about the successes even of robbers. Usually, the dissipation of Agni is committed in daily life and in the dusk of the spirit. The accumulation of Agni is arrested by picayune actions. One must understand that the bliss of Agni grows naturally, but when darkness encases the process towards perfection, the Fire departs the unfit depository unnoticeably although chemically proven. Beautiful is the law of Eternal Motion whether of evolution or involution. Beautiful is the law which bestows on every incarnated being the eternal Agni like the Light in the Darkness. Beautiful is the law which, even contrary to karma, endows every traveler with Light. Beautiful is the law which does not arrest within one the growth of the fiery garden, even from the age of seven. Even though these first flowers be small; even though they bloom upon tiny thoughts, yet they are a true inception of the future trend of thought. What a multitude of beautiful thoughts are generated in the heart of a seven-year-old, when the dim images of the Subtle World have not as yet left the brain and the heart! Dissipation may also begin then, if the soil of the plant be rotten. In the case of such depletion, one may help, or, as was said long ago, lend Fire. This borrowing occurs also in tiny actions. Thus thrice already I remind you of crumbs. Out of these sparks grow tremendous Fires.

"Do not think of the soul-less people as monsters. In various fields they even attain some unexpected advantages, but the Fire has left them and their works have grown pale.

"Every one is free to choose his own destiny and even up to his final dissolution. But soul-less beings are very infectious and harmful."

Following the catch in tiny nets, come the "civilized savages," a manifestation most dangerous to culture. Then, in order to purify the home from these enemies, tireless in their meanness and vulgarity, one will have to apply and waste the most precious energies, or else the same Rigor Mortis will creep in, resulting in the horrible death of all one's benevolent accumulations.

The crumbs of meanness can creep into the tiniest crevice. This shows how impenetrable the armor of spirit must be! The servitors of darkness can explain each one of their actions, even the journey to Broeken. And they also envelop necromancy with pseudo-scientific explanations. First, pseudo-civilization; then, pseudo-science, pseudo-friendliness, pseudo-dignity, and then, already in the full ugliness of Rigor Mortis, the pseudo-man.

All this is not so far from reality. The banners of

darkness and meanness float not only over "occult actions," they also adorn many festivals, sideshows, bazaars.

People still pray at times about the peace of the world, about the unity of all churches, brotherly love, about great heartfulness. But what peace is conceivable for the grinning skull, when the heart has become silent and the fires are extinguished! And will not pseudo-fraternal love garb itself in the garment of an executioner?

Save us from Rigor Mortis! Safeguard us from all the crumhs of darkness! From all domestic vermin, hairy and infectious.

Light conquers darkness!

Himalayas, November 24, 1932.

IV
SONORITY OF NATIONS

SONORITY OF NATIONS

LONG ago it was said that the souls of the peoples resound not only in their very words but precisely in the sounds of these words. And this is the sonority which truly expresses the essence, because sound is also color and also the entire essence of Be-ness. The comparative phonetics of language provides a beautiful mirror of the souls of peoples. Of course, often the primary sonority has been spoiled through the changes of the ages. Not without reason is it said that every language changes three times during a Century. But if we could hear a language in its purity, spoken by persons born to the language, no doubt the true sonority of the language would also explain much of the character of the nation itself.

In mentioning the word nation we must fearlessly define what nationalism means. If it is a concept identified with hatred for mankind, then it is merely harmful and must be eradicated, as must be each evidence of hatred, wrath, egotism and ignorance. But in the concept of nationalism, there are such precious fundamentals that, conceiving it in the purest sonority of the nations in their highest manifestations, we may envisage one more factor of progress.

Nobody objects to individuality as the expression of an inimitable and most precious composite of feelings and creative abilities. And if there exists an individuality of personality, guarded by all, then in every collective, whether it be a collective of family, state or nation, its own individuality is reflected. This means, that this quality must also be safeguarded. Thus nationalism instead of being impoverished because of its self-ness, will become an essential new sonority in the choir of all earthly peoples.

It is necessary that not only the personal soul but also the great composite soul of the people express that which is best, most precious, highest and most beautiful. If this expression is truly beautiful and exalted, then concepts that are intolerable because of their limitations, such as chauvinism, will find no place in this purified mighty choir of true progress.

Nationalism, impoverished by conventionalities and prejudices, is counterposed by internationalism; but each contraposition often contains in itself the threat of reverse conventionalities. The same has occurred with the contemporary understanding of internationalism. In its striving to find some general formulae, in the effort to eradicate conventional boundaries, internationalism became something destructive, something murky that eludes lofty, distinctive expressions. One fervent internationalist proclaimed that world-balance should destroy each personality and if differences in brain-capacity should impede this task, then by means of some operation, brains ought to be equalized and leveled to some middle scale. Such an absurd obliteration of brains was recommended by a man with a university training. We could overlook his formula of destructive wrath, but we note that in many of his expressions, internationalism, with all its newest superstitions, begins to lean towards an elimination of individuality and an eradication of everything which makes it valuable.

Least of all do we wish to criticize. For as it is, people in their criticism of each other have reached simple slander in such dimensions that to proceed further is already perhaps impossible. But happily, during all tragic moments of human history some precious and all-embracing conception which served to reconcile the horrors of the effacement of personality with the selfhood of an embittered personality has evolved.

Since in all parts of the world, Culture is discussed so steadfastly in various languages, this unique *SOS* of humanity contains the true salvation. Never has so unanimous a choral repetition of the word culture been evident as now. Before us, we have a multitude of books, periodicals and newspaper articles, where this word is precisely pronounced in various redeeming and forewarning concepts.

There, a French academician, discussing true nationalism, speaks of the culture of entire humanity. And you understand that the nationalism of this outstanding historian is not chauvinistic hatred, but precisely the best manifestation of the worthiest essence of a people. No educated man can fail to accept the type of nationalism which has, in its formula, the culture of pan-humanity. Here, from another end of the world, a wonderful philosopher and writer discusses religion and culture. And again, from completely different heartfelt sources, he comes to precisely the same conclusion, the revival of religion through culture and the vital development of human possibilities and responsibilities. From the other end of India, in the *Educational Review* of Madras, a Hindu scientist approaches this urgent theme in an interesting article, "Culture and Nationalism." In beautiful expressions, the author formulates the concept of culture as something living, uplifting, inspiring and adorning. I do not know the author, but because of one and the same law of Existence, we have begun to speak in the same language, resounding with the constant renewal and improvement of human life.

And in other countries, in various combination, this word culture is pronounced, but everywhere, as something that cannot be put off as a true refuge for humanity. Probably this warrior of culture, a Hindu, adopts his national costume; probably the Chinese poet who thinks of culture, does not surrender his Chinese traditions. The scholar of France remains among all those superb historical traditions upon which numerous generations have constructed a highly humane culture. And the followers of Shakespeare and Dante and Goethe and Cervantes understand their romanticism under their own armors. And the newly-elected President of the United States, Roosevelt, knows the complicated composite of American progressive nationalism.

Precisely in the conception of culture, as in a vital daily existence which tends toward success, we all gather and rejoice at each national manifestation. Precisely strengthened by the broad conceptions of culture, we mutually guard the treasures of human genius. The same culture will help us to not only safeguard them as a museum heritage of the past, but it will spiritualize these treasures as the milestones for a luminous future. And nationalism, culture and even a splintered internationalism, all human conceptions, decidedly point out to us that it is impossible to proceed further along the path of hatred for humanity.

The daily newspapers in limitless reproach, assail us with condemnations of inhumanity and ignorance. Despite all its conventional and often stillborn treaties, humanity has reached a horrifying subtlety in crimes of passion. We would wish greatly, that what is said here would be an exaggeration, but not only is it not an exaggeration, but it even represses much for lack of terms to describe it.

All humanity has united in another cry; men clamor about the crisis and under their thresholds try to hide at least a bit of gold in a stocking. But, at the same time, people understand perfectly well that these gold nuggets cannot safeguard their daily bread for long. If humanity would close and dynamite the thresholds of all its houses, then the next day it would probably not go to market and perhaps for a single week it would be willing to remain without socializing. But after that, civilization would again make its demands. Through its mechanical achievements, civilization will never realize what is true nationalism, what is the characteristic sonority of nations, full of creative possibilities. As the next step of civilization, comes the striving and longing for culture. The values of nationalism must be synthesized; for the treasures of creativeness, a background and understanding are needed.

And the voices of the nations ring out with regard to

culture. Each one in his own way has begun to compare this blessed concept with various social tasks. All the embittered and the oppressed have begun to remember that we are gathered here not for mutual annihilation. Each people wishes to develop and to be successful in true self-improvement, in other words, to do that for which we all exist upon earth. And the ignorant concept of selfhood can be transformed into the heroic deed of achievement, if the vital concepts of true nationalism and true culture are understood as the foundations which are inseparably linked with each other.

After the deprivation of the world during the past war, it appears that during this entire decade nothing has improved in human life; on the contrary, everything has become paler, poorer, and still more embittered. As a reaction from the war, people sought unity at the League of Nations, which was begun with the most benevolent intentions; but, as it appears, it does not afford sufficient unity even for half of the world; the League is often a source of all kinds of new misunderstanding. Everyone has heard how more than once, precisely in the League of Nations, States have quarreled which had no common problem either geographically or spiritually.

After the growing disappointment in the League of Nations, new divisions have developed: tariffs, passports, separations, etc. Thinkers and leaders understand very well that we cannot go far in absolute insulation, at the same time, they are afraid of the quickly worn out coins of internationalism. Although next to internationalism stands the scarecrow of nationalism, adorned with all sorts of primordial implements. But this scarecrow is not the soul of the people. This is not the true sonority of all its most precious harmonies. The true treasures must again be fearlessly disclosed. Only a true manifestation of the national soul, not confined by any ignorant prejudices, will indicate the heights of creativeness. In this creativeness, the peoples will strive for world improvement. In other words, they will turn towards the re-creation of their culture.

This beautiful choir of national cultures composed of all the beautifully-toned manifestations of nationalism, will give rise to that creativeness which responds to all heartfelt quests of humanity.

When the human heart has pity and compassion, no one cares whether it be an expression of internationalism or nationalism. If a heart can find compassion more easily in the garments of its own country, let it garb itself in the best raiments, but let it not forget that there is compassion and there is love.

When we speak of the task of culture, let it not be regarded as referring to an apothecary shop with the labels of chemical preparations. Let it be regarded as mutual understanding, as that compassion that can aid in the liberation from the tenseness of a dangerous crisis. The crisis, materially as well as spiritually, is now a raging epidemic.

In horror people scream, "*Impossible, intolerable!*" But have they even stopped thinking about what is really *possible* and what *must* be. Let but the thought of culture of the peoples of all the world, of the souls of the peoples be that living stimulus which will help us emerge from the limits of the threatening crisis, to begin the process of self-perfection again with all the patience of compassion and love to our neighbors.

Let the voice of the peoples resound!

Himalayas, January 1, 1933.

SOULS OF THE PEOPLE

IN the spray of the ocean waves, the inexperienced sea voyager discerns only chaos and mass without any design. But one who is wise in experience clearly perceives the law of the rhythm and the definite design in the rise of the wave. Is it not similar also in the foam of the surging of nations? It would be equally shortsighted not to discern the gigantic waves of evolution. It would be unjust not to perceive the inner Law and the poignant manifestations of a people's soul. In these manifestations the highest immutable justice is reflected.

It is instructive to see how the people's vision and the people's mind turn back to its heroes, in whose many achievements the Soul of the people was expressed. During their constructive achievements, those heroes did not even suspect that they would become the exponents of their countries, the exponents of their country's most valuable, focused psychology. They created benevolence. They followed the immediate call of their heart....they could not have acted otherwise, because then they would not have been the heroes that they were; their memory not only endures but becomes ever deeper in the insight of the people. It may at times appear that the name of the hero, exponent of the people's soul, is clouded, seemingly set aside into a remote depository. But this is not done through indifference. The ocean wave has also its rhythm; rising to a magnificent crest, it seems to dissolve only for the purpose of again rising and asserting its magnificence anew.

America is preparing to celebrate the memory of

Washington. In those preparations the nerve of the entire country is already revealed. Washington is not only a worker to whom the contemporary generations are grateful. No; he is a hero that the soul of a people recognizes. He is a hero who expresses the meaning of America's constructiveness. He is a hero who gave without wavering or deviation, something of which each creative heart inwardly dreams. Hence, the preparations for the celebration of Washington's memory take on the character not only of a national holiday, but of a people's festival.

When you pronounce the names of Washington and Lincoln, you have pronounced the essence of the United States. And no one is more aware of this than the soul of the people. The inspired heart of the nation knows perfectly well where there was creative and self-sacrificing achievement. The nation expresses its immutable values not in hysterical praise, but in a reverent and quivering solicitous attitude towards the names of these heroes of achievement. In the turmoil of life, perhaps those great names shall again remain unmentioned for a time, but no sooner shall the people's soul feel the need for spiritual food, then it will again undoubtedly return to those who led it towards brilliant constructive achievements.

Thus, each country keeps close to its heart the names which led it toward Light. If we turn to France, we will encounter the heroic image of Jeanne d'Arc, at the most poignant moment. Without distinction of tendencies and age, and in the moment of necessity, the nation knows who was its advocate. As firmly as Jeanne d'Arc carried on her heroic action, so steadfastly has the nation preserved her name, and this great consciousness and reverence is expressed in the celebrations to her memory. Nor is this reverence only religious. Even the inexperienced eye sees in the image of the saintly worker, the carrier, the spokesman of the sacred consciousness of the nation. And what a benevolent heroic dream descended upon the shepherdess of lambs, giving her the vision for her guidance over the nation and over an entire beautiful country.

If we pass through Italy, above the heights and strong-holds of spiritual and civic rulers of the world, above the names of all the magnificent Medicis, the same unchanging, eternally vivid and growing image of Saint Francis of Assisi rises. And neither nation, nor crowd can destroy his memory, because he was the exponent of the essence of the country. The restless searching spirit of Italy was transmuted into a beautiful manifestation in Saint Francis. Whatever may happen, wherever the people's path may lead, the spirit of Saint Francis remains alive. In the most remote but, in the midst of labor, the people's heart will smile, in realization that Saint Francis himself shall be its advocate at the universal judgment.

No matter how greatly the Russian heart may ache, no matter where it seeks the solution of truth, the name of Saint Sergius of Radonega remains forever the refuge which sustains the people's soul. Whether this great name be in a Cathedral, in a museum, or in a library, it remains unchanged in the depths of the people's soul. Again far beyond the bounds of ecclesiastic achievement, the constructive and illumined name of Saint Sergius is cherished in all hearts as a priceless Sanctuary of spirit. It is guarded as a haven for the people's consciousness during these difficult moments at the universal cross-roads. In substance, the name of Saint Sergius cannot be obscured nor dimmed by the multitude of other names. The treasury of the people's soul endures from the ancient times to the present. In times of need the people will again turn to him who synthesized their essence.

Among the many glorious names of Egypt, people do not forget the name of the luminous Hatseput, regenerator of traditions, sower of education and constructive builder. Among the changing dynasties of thousands of years, people knew to preserve this name, unquestioned in dignity, and to turn to it when necessary as the all-renewed and strengthened talisman.

The people of India do not confound with other resplendent names: the name of Akbar, the unifier, creator of a happy national life. The people do not forget and will not ascribe one disparaging impulse to the broad thought of the great Unifier of India. Although Akbar was a Moslem, his image stands in the Hindu Temples. Around the head of the Emperor is a halo, which does not appear simply as the distinction of a Ruler. For India, Akbar represents not only the ruler, but the people fully understand him as the exponent of the people's soul. As with other figures equally sacred to memory, he gathered and fought, not because of personal dissatisfaction, but to create a new page of a great history.

If we think of distant Tibet, the organization of the State is linked with the name of the great Fifth Dalai Lama. No matter where the Tibetan consciousness may wander, in substance, it cherishes the name of the creator of the Potala and Tibetan sovereignty, and it cherishes this name as a true foundation of its heart. A whole procession of Dalai Lamas has passed, but the people preserve the name of the builder, the unifier and the creator. In this is expressed the immutable judgment of the people's soul.

Beyond the entire succession of Chinese emperors, do we not judge China by Lao Tze and Confucius?

And not by its trade do we recall the dignity of Greece, the Mother of classic lands; but by Aristotle, Plato, by Phidias and Socrates.

Whatever may befall Germany, she knows confidently who were her great synthesizers: Goethe, Schiller, Durer, Wagner, and all those who will never be deserted by the people's soul, no matter what may happen.

And shall we not judge England by Shakespeare? And would we fail to affirm the significance of Scandinavia with the striving of the Vikings? And among the great seekers and creators, let us not forget that the Mongolian soul always keeps the image of Ghengis at heart. Does not Mongolia, in cherishing the image of the hero, thereby express its power towards ascension?

And does not the great name of King Solomon become

the symbol of an entire profound psychology? Does not the heart of each Jew cherish this invincible, creative and resounding name within? Nor have we mentioned those great names, the highest bearers of Light, which emanated from the secret, sacred cradle of Asia.

It is apparent that one may present endless unquestioned examples, in countries small and great, of the unfailing judgment of the people's soul. In those memories a brilliant procession of exponents of countries, of epochs and of the human spirit are constructed. These spokesmen shall be varied, according to their time and station, according to the circumstances which surrounded them, but some unquestionable contribution to our planet is evinced in the choice of these creative, glorious names and concepts. These names have already emerged beyond the bounds of personalities; they have already become universal concepts of synthesis. They are not so few. And they are the treasury of the planet; the treasury of creative heroic achievement, truly beautiful! The exponents of countries, peoples, with their synthesis, their breadth, are like the snow-clad peaks of the Himalayas; unimpeded by any obstacle they send greetings to one another in rays of light.

In the days of cultural festivity, all these exponents of the finest aspirations of the peoples, who inscribed these aspirations in labor and heroic action, who suffered and did not falter, will thus become the true adornment of the planet; they are the refuge for the people's heart, in its pain and anguish for truth. Will not these exponents of the people help to transmute the anguish and pain of quest into the festivity of heroic action?

In the holiday of culture, among the palaces of Knowledge and Beauty, in the long festival table of the spirit's feast, we shall perceive a resplendent table illumined by light. Whence comes this glow? Where, then, are the guests of this throne? Perhaps they have already descended. Perhaps our obscured eyes do not discern them, being unable to withstand the glow of the supernal Light.

But even the best throne cannot radiate, if it is empty. If it glows, it means They are already there. Without perceiving Them, or comparing Them, one may realize Them in one's heart; because what can the human heart not contain? It is the Light of the heart, that radiates from the resplendent guests of culture.

SEAL OF THE AGE

EVERYONE who has studied the History of Mankind has without a doubt noticed the inexplicable but apparent fact of a definite quality for each age, which has characterized human life on the most remote continents where there could never even have been a possibility of contact or communication. If we take the earliest periods of the Stone Age, are we not struck by the similarity of objects of this period, whether they come from Europe, Egypt, America or Asia? We do not know whether our forefathers spoke one language at that time, but certainly they thought alike, otherwise they would have been unable to create the same forms; nor would they have applied the same technique in all its peculiarities.

When we look back at the Bronze Age, we find the same unifying forms, the same generalization of domestic utensils. For instance, we say "a sword of the Bronze Age," and often do not even pronounce the name of any people, because the object clearly belongs to its Age and the nation is obliterated as of secondary importance. When we analyze all subsequent ages, we again find the same typical quality of the Age, though the way of thinking apparently differs. The Romanesque, the Gothic; each of these Ages has reverberated in the most distant lands. Also the Renaissance: its multicolored forms have soared not only over the West, but also over the East. It is not strange to see the same technique, not only in Russian icons, but also in Italian primitives, in Indian and Persian miniatures, and in Chinese and Tibetan paintings. It is the same seal of the age, the same sign of the human mind, which, without radio or telegraph, dominated the world and its evolution.

But beware lest there be involution, the antipode to evolution! Let us beware lest the mastersingers and artisans even of the Middle Ages should not find cause for pride in comparing the quality of their creations with the characterless forms of our age. There was often no need even for an artist of the Middle Ages to sign his name, because the very quality and the character of the article produced by him, was in itself the best seal. And suppose the seal of the age, this honorable crest of centuries, would turn into a brand of shame in our age! If only it may not occur, as a common sign of all times, that, because of misunderstanding, everything characteristic be obliterated and the human heart become branded by the thorns of standardization!

Some may ask us: "Would it not be presumptuous to predetermine a seal or quality for our age? Those who created human life in the past, did not concern themselves with the seal for their age, but simply did what they considered more fitting and more dignified."

We will reply: "Of course it would be inadmissible conceit for someone to think of establishing a seal for his age, but no conscious human being can help thinking of those lofty examples of sincere human creations, the very existence of which invites our thoughts to comparison."

Indeed, how could we pass by the inner quality of ancient craftsmanship without comparisons and concern? How may one fail to appreciate the care with which a particular piece of wood was chosen for an image of the Madonna? How may one fail to notice the most exquisite application of various shades of amber? How not to admire the most ingenious use in the hands of a Venetian master of the shape of a pearl for the body of a statue? This skillful selection of material fully corresponded with, and even strengthened the technique of the hand of the artist. The brush moved with surety and the chisel boldly followed the creative thought, in its full search for the best expression, without nursing any tempting dream of material gain or similar mercenary ideas.

Those powerful characters which are depicted in the ancient portraits, were not developed casually. They often expressed a strong and guiding thought, that in its radiant flame, all sparks of evil which as hideous reptiles that crept into the human hearth were consumed. The radiance of this glorious flame also reflected on Lorenzo the Magnificent and on many leaders and on all those who, despite their own imperfections, were near to the magnificence of the Beautiful. The title "the Magnificent" came to them through the Beautiful. Eliminate these resplendent sparks of art, and of the indestructible gems of creation, and many countries would perhaps be deprived of the most valuable, which accords them their place of honor in the Pantheon of the World. Without these treasures of creativeness, we would have no right even to think of the Banner of Peace, which in all respects stands as an honorable symbol of spiritual aspiration.

It is not for contemporaries to impose the establishment of a seal or quality for the age, life itself sees to this. But it is no doubt the duty of each thinking being to ponder upon the best quality of every product. In attempting to build a new life, we are facing precisely this vulgar concept of standardization. It is correct that the life of the new era should serve the demands of the wide masses. Verily, life should be adjusted towards an amelioration of human existence, but who can affirm that the characterless form of the product for the masses is the most desirable? And who can inwardly justify the hideous forms of our daily utensils, which lack all character and are manufactured only for the sake of being cheap, as though, in the very hope that due to their poor material they will disintegrate without a trace. Such hope is hideous! Truly, many of our modern books will decompose into formless blocks because of their poor paper. Our poor enamel will break and our metallic alloys, the pride of standardization and cheapness even when deformed by rust, will shock the eye with their ugliness.

The primitives reached us with their brilliant colors, although their creators did not have the conceit to wish to make them examples for the ages. By no means. The ancient artists simply wished to make their creations as excellent as possible in order that the flaming heart itself should feel in its essence that the superlative solicitude had been applied.

The old masters thus believed: "Books are the streams of Wisdom," "Pictorial art is the highest," "Books are the gift of the lofty spirit," "The master of his craft is higher than the knight of the sword." In this sound understanding, fully conscious of responsibility, the art guilds and those of icon-painters and of all manifold creative organizations grew; those bodies of artisans still amaze us with the high quality of their production and the nobility of their striving. It is true, many materials, before they could be applied, took decades for preparation. We know that the oil for painting was stored in monasteries for decades, thus being naturally purified. This was not because of conceit, but because of experience. Why has this Knowledge vanished nowadays? Some may try to explain it by the vanity and rush of contemporary life. Some may even go so far as to state that today mankind has no time to spare for the thought of quality. Such a supposition would be a most malevolent falsehood. The head of a factory of the most prosaic articles once admitted that buyers prefer articles of refined form, and where Beauty of originality is expressed. Quite true! No need to lay the blame for vulgar standardization upon the ignorance of the masses. The most harmful ignoramuses are not among the masses. They, like plague carriers, spread through all classes, sometimes even reaching high social positions. By their negative prominence they bring slander upon the masses. Their perverse imagination imposes vulgar products upon the masses which the masses never have demanded.

Verily, now, materials of high quality should be

prepared for the expression of the human spirit. Now, also, one should prepare the materials for decades ahead, in order that with the achievements of chemistry they may indeed justify their durability and may establish an expedient application of the necessary compounds. But for this, one should, above all, think of the future and of the responsibility of the present generation for the quality of the age. This is not conceit, not pride; on the contrary, it is only a strict discipline over the growth of consciousness and an evidence of care that the ascension of humanity continue in the best steps. In all schools and educational institutions the question of the quality of a product should be discussed from all angles; this refers both to the outer and inner quality. We are establishing a World Day of Culture, when in all schools and public organizations the cultural treasures of humanity may be proclaimed and affirmed simultaneously. Together with the World Day of Culture, an "hour of quality" should also be established. How significant will this hour be for working out the true seal of the age, when young minds, horrified by the possibility of a brand of shame upon their age, will strive towards a meritorious seal, towards a noble sign, which will crown all their creative efforts.

One thing is absolutely clear: At the moment of unheard of tension of world energies, all cultural forces must be united. Verily, at such a significant hour, co-operation in the name of the General Good and realization of the great might of creative thought should be brought into life urgently and victoriously.

Himalayas, November 1, 1931.

MUTATIS MUTANDIS

HISTORY gives us numerous examples of the results of gambling and games of chance during ancient periods. Even the most significant pages of history are filled with stories of how rulers became slaves, having lost, with their gambling, not only their wives and children, but also their entire empires. Many poetic and dramatic works are based upon these demoralizing temptations. Even the cause of the great battle upon that most glorious field of Kurukshetra was a loss in the game of dice.

It would seem as if the conditions of life had long since changed. New codes are laid into the foundation, presupposing a number of acts and consequences. Nevertheless the press brings the strange information that because of the races and the enormous bets made upon them, the birthday celebration of the King has been postponed for another day. If one historian has become convinced, with amazement, at the gigantic extent and consequences of a game of dice, then another historian at some other period might regard with amazement and condemnation such an obvious preference for speculation and games, in place of tribute to the head of an empire. History also notes the ancient benediction of arms before a mortal battle, also in the name of the very same God. Only recently, we witnessed how numerous countries invoked one and the same God to aid them in annihilating their enemies. Time was when we encountered the fact that the heads of empires took their cooks along with them in order to escape poisoning and had a special person for the tasting of the food.

Do not outstanding statesmen now have to recur to the very same means?

One may endlessly bring similar comparisons. They will all arouse one and the same exclamation of astonishment. "But it is the same whether it occurred in hoary antiquity or whether it happens today in somewhat changed aspect and costume! It means we have not advanced any further!" Perhaps in antiquity it even happened more frankly and in a more picturesque way, thus redeeming to a certain extent the inner hypocrisy and wickedness. Besides, in ancient times, there was less written of the hypocritical. The laws of Manu, Hamurabi and those of the first law makers were much briefer, although in many cases their conciseness made them far more impressive.

Since those ancient days, many new empires were born and passed into oblivion. There have been so many changes of rulers that the records of history could hardly encompass all these changes; it is only through the testimonies of artists who, by illustrating a coin, a medal or a stela, bring us records of the new name, and we are given a hint of one more conqueror who has disappeared. But these changes cannot seem amazing when we are faced now with the colossal changes of the entire surface of the planet, when, in addition to the half-legendary but already recognized Atlantis, we have an entire group of historic islands which have disappeared comparatively recently.

Some islands disappear and other shores and peaks emerge. The soil which seems to us so immovable and steadfast, is moving only relatively a little slower than the ocean waves. It would seem as if humanity ought to be accustomed to motion during its long life, and it is exactly this principle of relativity and motion that ought at last to attract the attention of humanity to its own evolution. It was already the enlightened Marcus Aurelius who wrote the wise covenant: "Study the motion of the luminaries as one who partakes of it." But this wise advice has thus far remained entirely without application. If humanity could rise in thoughts to the far-off worlds, what a speedy and brilliant evolution could be consummated.

I know that you will remind me about all the newest discoveries, calling them the crown of evolution. You will speak about isolated, brilliant theories which are read in leisure time. Finally you will speak about the customs of so-called civilized life which now permit what some time ago was only possessed by rulers and supreme priests to the general masses. It is true that our cities, while poisoning the human organism and creating a crippled generation, already provide some possibilities for utilizing the new discoveries. But we do not speak about the sewer systems of civilization. We do not speak of canned vegetables, nor yet about canned music. We speak of that which gives impulse to the best decisions of humanity.

Only recently we lived through a dreadful, meaningless war. We are aware that in this decade the consequences of that war not only have not been erased, but on the contrary, have crystallized and been inflated into real misery. They have become a misery that is well-nigh irreparable, that can only be altered by measures still essentially unknown. How often at our school or university desk we have heard the old advice, "Mutatis Mutandis"—change that which ought to be changed. Since then a multitude of barbaric facts of war and peace have invaded life. Humanity may again be convinced how at the very time when those most sincere were perishing upon the battle fields as victims of world calamities, vile "utilities" were treacherously fattening themselves upon the blood of others. What diabolical inventiveness was expressed by the dark ones, in order to find a thousand ways to achieve personal gain, with full knowledge of how destructively this looting would affect future generations. And if even now a secret ballot were taken as to those who are for war and those who are against it, it is impossible to know what the results of this secret ballot would be. Of course a multitude of women would vote against war, cultured circles would no doubt revolt against this misery, as well as many of the working masses. But let us not think that the number of black ballots would be small. How diversely are the roots of meanness divided! And what miserable and unique reasons would be given as to why we should return once again to the irresponsible times when everything was permitted and everything could be explained by a hypocritical participation in a common task! It is fearful to remember the criminal negotiations which were carried on for rotten and sometimes even non-existing material. It is horrifying for human dignity to look back at the fraudulent documents, criminal recriminations and commands which were the cause of peril to many thousands of people.

"But this has passed," you will say. Since then we have already had such a multitude of facts, conferences and financial agreements! Such and such plan has been fulfilled, but as a result we have an increased destruction; innocent ships have been disarmed and even destroyed in order to be replaced by still more harmful constructions. Even in shops we have taken care to see that the air should be ozonized, but at the same time, the scientific laboratories have utilized their facilities to invent new poisonous gases. Does the scientist in the field of chemistry who has invented the most deadly gas not dream of receiving the peace award? Even now, people dream of such an achievement of science as would, with one fratricidal dispatch, kill entirely populated regions. And perhaps another enlightened scientist dreams about the "successful" poisoning of all waters, in order that everything alive should perish. To this someone may reply that it is not the scientists who are inventing such murderous forces, but that it is the technicians, the engineers. No, dear readers, without scientific knowledge, such murderous brutality could not be invented. And was it not a scientist who discovered the ray of death, and who by the very command of spacial justice, departed to the infernal regions together with his venomous invention?

But things could be simpler, if the scientists would give an oath similar to that of physicians not to permit any dangerous inventions to leave their laboratories. The more so, because perhaps many of these terrible gases and rays could, with the addition of one ingredient, be used for the true benefit of humanity.

Mutatis Mutandis! In the days of extreme calamities one must speedily change that which ought to be changed. And first of all one ought to change that which is harmful into that which is beneficial. Let men not play the roles of fools, as if they did not know what was of benefit. Every human heart knows perfectly well in its depth where the common benefit is, the benefit for the nearest ones and at the same time the benefit for oneself! For nowhere in creativeness is self-destruction demanded. The true common benefit is also the benefit for oneself, because one is a part of the community.

Changing that which was harmful into the beneficial, namely replacing criminal destruction by construction, we accomplish that which is needed for evolution. We accomplish that which is needed, not for evolution-civilization, but for evolution-culture. Someone in a spell of insanity has tried to conceive of a corporation which would undertake the construction of a shaft at the equator to the most incalculable depths. It could be filled with the newest, most terrifying explosives which would split the planet by an unprecedented explosion. The plan is a mad one. But in its very rashness it deserves more concern than the inventions of new deadly gases. And what of the secret protection of narcotics that undermine entire generations and kill entire nations which were glorious in their past? Must not this scourge of humanity, which is more perilous than syphilis, cancer and tuberculosis be exterminated from life? And cannot each one of us name a multitude of other problems which deserve an immediate extermination from life?

The most advanced persons, the enlightened ones must unite without delay to oppose darkness, ignorance, perversion and treason. These advanced ones must unite in all countries, not for the sake of police measures and calls to oppose decisions that are constraining, but rather in the name of Light and education. Feeling the urgent need for the evolution of Culture in one's heart, this luminous League of Culture must unite, casting aside all petty conventionalities, and for the Bliss of humanity must actively change that which needs change.

Mutatis Mutandis!

V
____

LEGENDS

LEGENDS OF ASIA

FROM time to time, absurd rumors have reached me to the effect that during our travels in Asia, I seemed to have discovered an original document dating almost from the time of Christ. I do not know for whom and for what purpose such a version of the story was necessary, but on my part, I should like to confirm my point of view about this remarkable subject which concerns not only the Christian but also the Moslem, Buddhist and Hindu worlds.

Every one who contacts the varied peoples of Asia with sincerity in the moments of their confidence and cordiality hears numerous legends, always benevolent, about the great Issa, about the Divine Being, about the Prophet, about the greatest Sons of Maneach. One, in his own manner, reveals what is closest to his heart. Everyone knows that a wide literature exists that is connected with the name of Christ in Asia, not only from Nestorian sources but also in Moslem and Hindu sources. Much has been written of Christ and of Krishna; much is known of the so-called Christians of Saint Thomas. Long and beautiful are the legends and songs of Kashmir and all of Turkestan about the great Issa. The Moslems attribute the location of the sepulcher of Christ to Srinagar, and the Mazar of the Holy Virgin near Kashgar. Thus, each one in his own manner, speaks of the same thing.

Moslems tell us that they are searching through all ways for compilations of the legends of Christ and that they are willing to pay any price for them. Nor need I quote the numerous books, which have often been written by

Christian ecclesiastics about "Christ in Islam," all the Apocrypha that speak of Christ in Persia and India. In the south of India you can also hear the remarkable words of a Hindu about Christ; and Vivekananda in Bengal found unforgettable expressions about this for himself. In Sindh, Shri Vasvani speaks to his andiences about the Covenants of Jesus, and the Tibetan Lama considers that the Covenants of Christ should lie together with the sacred books in the Suburgan, and the Sard Baksha also glorifies Christ in the deserts. The Prince of Karashar amazes us with his knowledge of these brief legends. In the manifold literature, the article of Sir Lalubai Samaldas and the renowned book of Notovitch are probably composed from various legends. Of course it would be much more valuable if these fragments could be preserved, even though separately, but in their original character. The Archimandrite who wrote the commentaries for the latter book very wisely remarks this also.

In "Altai-Himalaya,", speaking of Kashmir, the Arabian Song, "When Christ was ascending, all who perceived Him were glorified" came to my mind; I cited the Kashmiri legend, "They glorify Christ in the most exalted words. He was higher than the sun or moon." Thus upon a red carpet eight Moslems spontaneously glorified Christ until midnight.

In that book I also state: "There have been distinct glimpses about a second visit of Christ to Egypt. But why is it incredible that after that, He could have been in India? Whoever doubts completely that such legends about Christ's life exist in Asia, probably does not realize what an immense influence the Nestorians have had in all parts of Asia and how many so-called Apocryphal legends they spread in the most ancient times.

"Never may one discover the source of such legends, but even if they originated from ancient Nestorian Apocrypha, at present it is instructive to see the widespread and deep consideration paid to the subject. It is significant to hear a local inhabitant, a Hindu, relate how Issa preached beside a small pool near the bazaar under a great tree, which now no longer exists. In such purely physical indications you may see how seriously this subject is regarded."

Further on I pointed out how the *baksha* of Tourfan, with his *sithara,* upon a chestnut colored horse, glorified Issa:

"As divine Issa went on his wanderings, He saw a great head. On the road lay a dead head of a giant. Issa thought that the great head belonged to a great man, and Issa decided to do good and to resurrect this great head. The head covered itself with skin and the eyes filled themselves. And there grew a great body and the blood flowed. The heart was filled and the mighty giant rose and thanked Issa that He had resurrected him to be useful to humankind."

And in the "Heart of Asia," is mentioned:

"In Srinagar we first encountered the curious legend about Christ's visit to this place. Afterwards we saw how widely spread in India, Ladak and in Central Asia, was the legend of the visit of Christ to these parts during His long absence that was quoted in the Gospel. The Moslems of Srinagar told us that the crucified Christ—or, as they call Him, Issa—did not die on the cross, but only lost consciousness. The disciples took away His Body, hid Him and cured Him. Later, Issa was taken to Srinagar, where He taught the people. And there He died. The tomb of the Teacher is in the basement of a private house. It is said that an inscription exists there stating that the son of Joseph was buried there. Near the tomb, miraculous cures are said to take place and fragrant aromas fill the air. In this way, the people of other religions desire to have Christ among them."

One may then ask what type of mentality concocts, from these remarks, the legends about my discovery of some manuscript of the time of Christ. Instead of our mutual rejoicing at the broad and all-containing penetration of this great understanding of Christ the Redeemer, instead of marvelling in the heart about the immemorable and inexplicable paths by which the name of Christ soared across all deserts, people are anxious only to obscure and to suspect evil motives.

In the latest number of the Hindu magazine, "Dawn" we read: "The Temple of Shri Issa, Puri, became a significant site for Hindu pilgrimages. In Puri there is a sacred temple to which the Hindus throng in multitudes. Not far away play the waves of Bengal Bay. Between the temple and the sea is a beautiful shrine dedicated to Christ. In the center of the garden there is a small "mandir," where, inside, stands a cross! And each evening the *acharya* of the "mandir" reads portions of the Psalms and the New Testament. And during the day, from the neighboring shrines the sadhus come and sit and talk with the members of this small ashram, dedicated to Shri Issa."

I do not know how correctly this description conforms to the reality, but even its suggestion contains the elements of benevolence, about which one may rejoice, if his heart has not withered and been seared in the embers of wrath.

It is illuminating to meet Nestorian cemeteries with crosses over the graves in the most unexpected parts of Asia,. It is interesting to see the coins of the Khans with the images of the cross and to become acquainted with the literature of Prester John. At any rate we must be grateful even to those who invented the tale of my discovery of a manuscript, because, even by the roundabout approach of slander, it provides the opportunity of calling attention to those pearls of the spirit which live through the transmutation of ages.

I have already had occasion to express my belief that no benevolent person would seek to throw a stone at a Moslem singer who sang of Christ in the highest words at his disposal. Nor would he wish to reject a native legend, which gathers listeners who attend with profound, heartfelt interest.

Science does not seek to destroy. The scientist carefully collects all fragments of matter, which at some time, in some hands, may reveal new paths of the history of nations. The road of ignorant negation leads only to destruction. But honest perception is primarily constructive in substance, and in the nobility of its spirit, cannot concern itself with absurd disparagements. We can verify, we can accumulate the fragmentary sparks of the folk-remembrance, which by its evolving legend, provides the true and all-embracing meaning which was not evident at the time.

It would be intolerable through ignorant cowardice to conceal the benevolent legends which open the priceless recesses of the folk-soul and which reunite that which stupidity has separated. With true joy, I recall the opinions regarding this expressed by several Roman and Greek Catholic Priests. Naturally, too, world scientists will find in themselves the justice and conscientiousness to turn to this matter, not with destructive intent, but also with a just impartiality as cordial as that with which the legends of Asia have warmed and stirred countless hearts.

Again I bring thanks to those slanderers who have provided me with the opportunity to express once again these words in the name of what is Good.

Himalayas, 1931.

RISHIS

FROM the steep cliffs, like celestial silvery threads, gleam the waterfalls. The stones with their ancient inscriptions of an Eternal Truth are caressed by the brilliant splashes. The stones are varied, the signs upon them are also varied, but they all concern the one infinite Truth. A Sadhu leaps forward, his lips clinging to the stone, and quaffs the blessed drops of water. Drops of the Himalayas!

A long line of Sadhus and Lamas stretches along the road to Triloknath, the old sanctuary, the site of pilgrimage and prayer. These pilgrims have met here from many different roads. Some, already completing their spiritual journeys, are walking along with a trident; some carry bamboo staffs; others are without anything, even without clothing. And the snow of the Rotang Pass is no impediment for them.

Are all of them righteous? Are all of them highly spiritual? But even a City is sometimes spared for the sake of a single righteous soul! So, be lenient with them; they journey on a good path.

The pilgrims proceed, knowing that the Rishis and the Pandavas dwell here. Here is the Beas or Vyas; here is Vyasakund, the place of the fulfillment of all wishes. Here, Vyasa Rishi compiled the Mahabharata.

The Rishis lived here, not in legend alone, but in reality. Their presence breathes life into the cliffs which are crowned with glaciers, into the emerald pastures where the yaks graze and into the caves, and the roaring torrents. From here, those spiritual calls that humanity has heard through all ages were sent forth. These calls are taught in schools; they have been translated into many languages, and this crystal of acquisitions has been deposited on the cliffs of the Himalayas.

"Where can one find words with which to praise the Creator, after seeing the incomparable Beauty of the Himalayas?" sings the Hindu. Along the paths of the Guru, along the peaks of the Rishi, along the mountain paths of the pilgrims of the spirit, lies that treasure, which no torrents of rain can wear away, nor any lightning turn to ashes. He who walks towards the Good, is blessed on all paths. How touching are all the narratives which tell of the meeting of the righteous ones of various nations. The tops of the deodars in the forest touch each other in the wind. Thus, everything that is of the highest meets without injury and harm. There was a time when quarrels were settled by single combat and decisions were reached by a conference of chiefs. So do the deodars discuss matters among themselves. What a meaningful word: deodar—the gift of God. And this significant name is not without reason, for the resin of the deodar has healing powers. Deodar, musk, valerian, roses and other similar substances comprise the beneficent medicines of the Rishis. Some have wanted to do away with these medicines by substituting an invasion of new discoveries; however, humanity again reverts to the foundations.

Is the story of the miraculous Stone a fairytale? But it is well known that it is true. It is known how the Stone comes. Is the unicorn of heraldry a fairytale? But it is known that in Nepal there is a single-horned antelope. Is the Rishi a fairytale? A hero of the spirit need not be imaginative; this also is known.

Here is a photograph of a man who walks through fire without harming himself. This is not fiction, but an authentic photograph taken by the Chief of Police of Pondicherry. Witnesses will tell you of the same trials by fire in Madras, Lucknow, Benares. And not only does the Sadhu walk harmlessly on the flaming coals, but he leads behind him those who desire to follow him and hold on to him.

In Benares, a Sadhu sits in sacred posture upon the water of the Ganges. His crossed legs are covered by the top of the water. The people flock to the banks, amazed at the sight of the Holy man. Another Sadhu lies on the points of iron spikes, as though on a soft bed, and his face shows not a trace of suffering or discomfort.

Still another Sadhu has been buried alive for many days; another swallows various poisons without any harm. Here is a Lama, who can levitate himself; another Lama by means of "to-mo" can generate his own heat, thus protecting himself against snow and mountain glaciers. There is a Lama who can give the death stroke with his "deadly eye" to a mad dog. A venerated Lama from Bhutan relates how, during his stay in the Tzang district in Tibet, a Lama asked the ferryman to take him across the Tzam-po free of charge, but the cunning man replied, "I will gladly take you over, if you can prove that you are a great Lama. A mad dog is running about here doing great harm—kill it." The Lama said nothing; but looking at the dog, he raised his hand and said a few words, and the dog fell dead! The Bhutanese Lama saw this himself. One hears frequently in Tibet and in India of the same "deadly eye" and the "eye of Kapila." And on a map of the 17th century printed in Antwerp by the authority of the Catholic clergy, the name of the country, Shambhala is mentioned .

Parts of the same great Knowledge are scattered everywhere, as on the map printed in Antwerp, on the photograph of the Chief of Police in Pondicherry, and in other testimonials of Lamas,

If one can walk through fire, and another can sit on water, and a third remain suspended in the air, a fourth repose on nails, a fifth swallow poison, a sixth kill with a glance, and a seventh lie buried without harm, then one may collect all these grains of Knowledge in himself. And thus the obstacles of lower matter can be transmuted! Not in a remote imaginary age, but now, right here, where Millikan's cosmic rays are also being studied.

But all these are not yet Rishis. Of the Rishis, the great Spirits, Shri Vasvani speaks more remarkably. This enlightened spiritual leader and Evangelist of the Good, whose words are accorded great veneration, comments as follows:

"Blessed is the nation whose leaders follow thinkers, sages, seers. Blessed is the nation that receives its inspiration from its Rishis. And they are men who will bow to Truth alone, not to custom, conventions, popularity. The Rishis are the great rebels of humanity. They tear up our comforting cults. They are the great nonconformists of History. Not consistency, but Truth is their watchword. We need this rebel-spirit in all spheres of life today—in religion, in politics, in education, in social life." (*Dawn*, June, 1932.)

Remarkable words! Not all Rishis walked on fire, nor did all of them submit to being buried alive; but each of them contributed an entire spiritual realm for the Good of the World. Each of them, like a Boddhisatva possessing mastery, strengthened the new achievements of progress!

Each of them pronounced the sacred oath for the construction of a renewed, refined and beautified world in his own language!

For the sake of a single righteous being, a whole City was saved. As beacons, lightning rods and citadels of Good, stood the Rishis of various nations, creeds, of various ages, yet one in the Spirit of salvation and ascension for all!

Whether the Rishi came upon fire, whether he arrived home upon a stone, whether he came upon the whirlwind, he always hastened for the general Good. Whether he prayed on mountain summits, or on a steep riverbank, or in a hidden cave, he always sent out his prayers for the unknown, for the stranger, for the laborers, for the sick and the crippled!

Whether the Rishi sent out white horses to save the unknown voyagers or whether he blessed unknown seafarers, or guarded a city by night, he always stood as a pillar of Light for all, without condemnation and without extinguishing the flame.

Without condemnation, without mutual suspicion, without weakening each other, the Rishis ascended ever upwards to the eternal Mount Meru.

Before us is the road to Kailas. There rises one of the fifteen wonders described in Tibetan books: The Mount of the Bell! Along sharp ridges one climbs to its summit. It stands higher than the last junipers, higher than the last yellow and white mountain ranges. There Padma Sambhava once walked. This is recorded in the ancient monastery Gando-La. It is exactly here that the caves of Milarepa are situated. And not one but many have been sanctified with the name of the hermit, who hearkened to the voices of the devas before dawn. Here, also, are the spiritual strongholds of Gautama Rishi. Not far away are also legends which surround Pahari Baba. Many Rishis walked there. And he who gave the mountain its enticing name, "Mount of the Bell," also thought of the call of the Bell for all, of helping all, of the Universal Good!

Here Rishis lived for Universal Good!

When Rishis meet on the mountain paths they do not ask each other: "From where do you come?" Is it from the East, or West, or South or North? This is quite apparent: they come from the Good and go to the Good. An exalted, refined, flaming heart knows where is the Good and in what it can be found.

Some of the travelers in our caravan were once arguing and discussing the qualities of the various Rishis. But a gray-haired pilgrim, pointing to snowy peaks, sparkling in their complete beauty, said:

"Are we to judge the qualities of these Summits? We can but bow in admiration before their unattainable splendor!"

"Satyam, Shivam, Sundaram!"

Kyelang, Himalayas, August 11, 1932.

THE SWORD OF GESAR KHAN

WATER is served around in a tin cup. This little cup still exists; it has traversed all of Tibet, China, and Mongolia. And here is a Yagtan which was made some time ago in Kashmir. The old thing outlived the whole of Asia, endured all methods of transportation. It should be well taken care of, it knows so much. And here is the banner of the former expedition, "Maitreya in Glory." Since then we have met under various aspects of this growing concept. Far away is the Tibetan painter who painted this Banner. Lama Malanov who decorated the Banner with Chinese silks is no longer alive. The Banner witnessed much. It won over the wild goloks to our side. It astonished and softened the Tibetan governor; it smote the forehead of the Amban of Khotan. And during the construction of the Suburgan at Sharagolchi, it glowed with its vivid colors. Now it is in the Himalayan Institute which is a fruit of the Expedition. May it guard over all the curative herbs of the Himalayas which hold so many of the best potentialities.

Every object which crossed Asia with us has become unusually dear and unforgettable. The very difficulties of the path have been transmuted into unusual joys, because they are surrounded by a spaciousness which absorbed so much of the wondrous past.

The little bells of the caravan mules are again ringing. Again steep ascents of the mountain paths. Again, we encounter travelers, each carrying his own secret of life. Again tales about local spiritual treasures, about memorable places. Again the heroic sword of Gesar Khan is left in the rock. And again caves and peaks of the sacred pilgrimages are before us. The eternal travelers pass us with their packs upon their backs. Not faith alone, but an unconquerable attraction to this strange life entices them along the difficult mountain paths.

We are going to Lahul. It is again a continuation of the expedition. One feels just as before, save that then there was no mail; no informations of the world reached us during many months. But here we are still on the rim of the last mail runners, and the world's turmoil can knock at our door weekly. Beyond the Rotang Pass the dry Tibetan air blows up; the same curative and inspiring air which healed all those in quest of spiritual ascent. At night in the clear sky covered with its countless stars, with the Milky Way and with its newborn and dying luminaries, glowed strange flashes of light. These are not from simple heat lightning, but the remarkable Himalayan radiations of which literature has spoken more than once.

After having crossed Tibet and Ladak, one can appreciate Lahul. The snowy peaks, colorful shrubs, fragrant Juniper, bright-tinted wild roses are not inferior to those of the most fertile plains of Tibet. Many of the sanctuaries, stupas, caves of hermits, are not poorer than in Ladak. On the rocks are the same ritual figures of archers pursuing the sharp-horned mountain rams with their arrows. The ancient ibex was the symbol of light. Here are the same burial rites, in sepulchres lined with stones and in stone burial vaults. Above Kyelang rises the majestic mountain of "spiritual tranquility" with its sacred three-peaked summit, similar to Narbu-Rinpoche. How many medical books and writings are kept there by the Lamas! The famous local Lama doctor is already working for us with a coolie boy and, like Panteleimon the Healer, he fills the basket slung over his back, with herbs and roots. It is good that George knows the Tibetan language so well. It is good that Lama Mingyur, who knows so much of Tibetan literature is with us. The first few days, some books were brought to us which as yet had never been translated. Among them are also medical writings and a poetic description of the local sanctuaries. The environs are filled with famous names; here are the caves of Milarepa who hearkened at dawn to the voices of the devas; here also lived Padma Sambhava and Djava Guzampa. All the great Apostles of the teachings were in need of the irreplaceable radiation of the Himalayas. Not far from here is the waterfall, Palden Lhamo. Upon the rocks, nature itself has designed the figure of the austere goddess riding on her favorite mule: "See how the mule has raised its head and its right leg. Look how distinctly the head of the goddess is seen!" We see, we see! And we hear the continuous song of the mountain stream. We pass caves and the rocks of the Nagis. These are inhabited by remarkable snakes. We are amazed at the ancient palace of the Takhur of Gundla. We are amazed to see how some of the gabled roofs and balconies remind us again of Norway. It is instructive to observe the flat roofs, which are an unmistakable heritage of ancient Asia, and these sharp and unexpected gables which remind one of the North.

We do not forget the reception arranged for us at Kyelang, the capital of Lahul. We entered Kyeland, decorated with garlands of flowers, preceded by trumpets and drums.

As we approached Kyelang, an unexpected and touching spectacle awaited us. On the roofs stood Lamas in high purple tiaras, with gigantic trumpets. From the flat roofs, the yellow and red petals of wild roses were showered at us. The crowd thronged in festive attire. The school children, standing in rows, shouted greetings to us at a signal from the Wazir. And on the arches and houses were colorful signs with touching inscriptions. Approaching our summer headquarters of the Himalayan Research Institute with an ever-growing procession we were again met by Lamas with trumpets, and the daughter of our neighbor, Anu, wearing a high turquoise headdress, presented us with the sacred milk of a yak. Thus Kyelang, lost amidst the snow peaks, wanted to express its cordiality.

We were overwhelmed, not only by new discoveries, but

we succeeded in seeing the rare Lamaistic mystery: "The Breaking of the Stone." A group of nomadic Lamas from Spiti, presented this unusual mystery that was never written about in our yard. George gives a complete translation of it in the Journal of the Institute.

It began when the Lamas dragged a huge stone, which was more than a yard and a half long from our hill: Two people could hardly carry it. A temporary altar was set up and a long row of ritual dancers with chants and prayers, depicted the destruction of the evil forces. There was also an exhibition of the piercing of their cheeks with needles. There was a remarkable dance with swords including jumping on the blades of the swords. One must admit that this procedure truly demanded great skill, otherwise the two swords pressing the stomach could very easily have pierced the intestines. Amidst these dramatic episodes, as is to be expected, a semi-humorous interlude was also introduced. The ruler of a wild country appeared disguised as a shepherd; he was greeted with the laughter of the spectators, provoked by a dialogue concerning the secret treasures of this ruler. But towards the end of the mystery, all humorous interpolations ceased and one noticed a more concentrated inner preparation. These conjurations and preparations ended as follows: One of the Lamas lay down on the ground and two others with great effort lifted the huge stone prepared for him and placed it on his stomach. At the same time, the old Lama, who had pierced his cheeks and thrust himself upon the swords, lifting the round stone that was the size of about two human heads high above his head, threw it with all his force on the stone which was lying on the stomach of the Lama. He repeated this same action with similar force. Upon the second blow, to the amazement of all present, the long stone split loudly into two parts, thereby liberating the Lama who was lying on the ground. Thus, the heavy material world was conquered! The evil forces were conquered and the mystery play ended with a joyous choir and the dancing of the Lamas to the accompaniment of a Tibetan painted balalaika. Esther Lichtmann succeeded in photographing the scene before the throwing of the stone but it is natural that at the moment of the breaking of the stone on the Lama's stomach, all present forgot photography and gasped deeply. Of course the forms of this unusual mystery with its victory over the low material world are heavy, but no less heavy are also the actual material forms of common life. Let us also not forget that upon the broken stone was an image of a man drawn with charcoal and chalk whose physical substance the lamas pierced with the magic daggers, *furpa*, in a previous ritual dance.

A Lama from Kyelang comes to us. George and Lama Mingyur are writing down the local chants and Esther Lichtmann will take down the melodies. We are going to look at the ancient images on the stones. Once more we are convinced that the Chortens, added to the old images of hunters and mountain sheep are the latest additions. As before, we think that these sharp-horned sacred sheep, the symbols of light and their searchers, the tireless archers, are symbols of far more ancient Cults. Here again we are touching upon the still inexplicable Solar Cults which recall the remote concepts of Druidism.

Again we pay visits to the monasteries. There are interesting books about hermits. From the flat roofs we again admire the vast glaciers, snow peaks, and deep ravines with thundering torrents. Here is the mountain of spiritual tranquility, here is Peak M. and here are also the tempting roads to Ladak and to sacred Kailas.

Here are the dances of the Lamas. Those who are unfamiliar with them call them "devil dances."

"Ignore this foolish name. The dances of the Lamas have a deep symbolic meaning."

"And what about the horns?"

"The protectors of the animal kingdom and the rulers of the elements have this symbol, but have nothing in common with the devils. Soon you shall mistake the rays of Moses also for horns. Oh, what ignorance!"

After a long ritual full of age-old gestures, the dance

ends with the mystery in honor of the black-headed Lama who defeated the impure king Landarma, the cruel persecutor of the faith.

Karga, an ancient plot of land. The remnants of an ancient fortress. Chortens, mendangs, covered with stones bearing the inscriptions of prayers. People say that there are also ancient graves here, but we could not excavate in order to avoid any controversies with the archaeological department. Our attention is mainly attracted to the numerous carvings on the rocks. Again, sheep and archers. Very ancient ones. Lama Mingyur beckons to us with pride to look at a stone upon which is an image of a sword. This is why the painting, "The Sword of Gesar Khan" was conceived. Where did we see these characteristic forms of the sword-dagger? We saw them in Minussinsk, we saw them in Caucasia, we saw them on many Sarmatic and Celtic antiquities. This sword points to the very same theory of the transmigrations of people which is so distinctly carved on this ancient, brownish purple surface of stone, polished by the ages. Is this a sign of a battle, is this a sign of a courageous crossing?

Here is also the legend about the warriors of Gesar Khan, who came from afar and settled here. They also brought the first apricot pit. Of course they do not mean the Mongols who reached Lahul in the 17th century. The folk memory preserves something far more ancient and significant.

And opposite, beyond the river, high on the rock, rises the most ancient monastery of this region, Gando-La, founded by Padma Sambhava himself. An antiquity of the 7th-8th century. Old alluring sites.

And here is old Pinzog, the troubadour, narrator of the saga of Gesar Khan. Calmly sitting on the floor of my studio, he narrates his tale and chants in recitative, the verses of the great hero of Ladak, Tibet, China. Does not this chant date from the 6th century, and are not the significant gestures of the singer also from that period? Judging from the worn-out exterior of Pinzog, no one would surmise these rhythmically plastic gestures and subtle variations in the improvisations of the refrain. Everything is pointed out: how the hero prepares to meet his enemies; how, before his march, he takes the wise counsel of his father's sister; how he prepares his arms. . . . Pinzog examines the armor and tightens the bow, and seems to glimpse the enemy in the mountains. . . . "And do you know that here in Kham there are rooms of Gesar Khan where, instead of beams, there are numerous swords belonging to the hosts of Gesar Khan?"

"Not only in Kham but also in Zanga, there is such a monument of the warriors of Gesar Khan," adds the heretofore silent Lama.

In one time, the singer cannot narrate all the achievements of Gesar Khan. One must also tell about Bruguma, the wise wife of the hero. One must not forget the heroes, and all the victories of the invincible defender of truth. What may one not hear in the mountains of Tibet and India! The newspapers just now have told of a man who swam the river Djumna holding on to a tiger's tail. And this is not a fairy tale.

The Hindu doctor writes to us that cancer, this increasing scourge of humanity, is absolutely unknown on the Himalayan heights.

The Tibetan Lama doctor from Tashi-Lhumpo brings Tibetan medicines; among them are also remedies for cancer. We also recollect the official statements of a successful cancer cure, by the deceased Buryat doctor, Badmaev. Lama Mingyur informs us of the edible roots which are found in the woods of Sikim; he promises to obtain them for us. From our friend the colonel, we receive news that the workmen of Captain B. were terrified during the whole night by a giant who appeared, frightening them to such an extent that they abandoned the work and ran away. To this the Lama added that in Sikim cases are also known of the similar apparitions of giants, messengers of Dharma Pala, who are sent with forewarnings or to divert wrathful actions. Thus, life is multi-varied.

Here is the house of the Thakur from Kyelang, of Pratap Chand, or in Tibetan, Sange Dava. The old building is in the style of the Tibetan fortified courtyards. The host and hostess meet us at the entrance. The servants are adorned with silver and Chinese brocade. The trumpets of the Lamas thunder. First of all, we are invited to the solemn service in the house chapel. There are many family relics. There are many excellent tankas, on which we find Shambhala and Rigden-Jyepo and Milarepa, and many other heroes of achievement. The service proceeds in Bhutanese fashion. After this we are shown not only the jewels, but also the books and woodblocks for printing. This is not a simple household; the Thakur is the ruler of the region, and the family has many possessions. It of course ends with Tibetan tea and Zampa. Here also negotiations begin for the construction of a house on the Thakur's ground.

And again the conversation concerns the images on the rocks, the undecipherable inscriptions, stone graves, and secret sacred books. Besides the places in Kulu Valley one place is mentioned near Trilokanat where, according to tradition, books were hidden during the persecutions of the fierce Landarma. On the mountains there are also ruins of some ancient dwellings. They say that when the warriors of Gesar Khan came, the Tchud fled underground in Altai from the white king, and the old Lahulis and the other citizens of Lahul departed for the summits. From a historical and archeological point of view this region has been studied very little.

The paintings, "Menhirs in the Himalayas," will recall the menhir-like stones recognized in the mountain passes from the most ancient times to our day. This custom, no doubt, has some connection with the ancient menhirs of Tibet which we discovered during our expedition in 1929, similar to the menhirs of Carnac.

The painting, "The Three Glaives," depicts the ancient design on the stone near Kyelang, capital of Lahul. Lahul, in a distorted pronunciation, signifies Southern Tibet. The local designs on the rocks and stones merit study.

Ladak, Dardistan, Baltistan, Lahul, Trans-Himalayas, parts of Persia, Southern Siberia (Irtysh, Minussinsk) abound with various images of similar technique and which spontaneously remind one of the rocks of Boguslan and the images of the Ostrogoths and of other great migrators.

The designs of Ladak, Lahul and all the Himalayan mountains are divided into two main classifications: The Buddhist, which comes to us in the form of a Swastika (this is true of the Buddhist as well as of the inverted Bon-po, the Lion of the Steeds of Gesar Khan, reminoz inscriptions, chortens and other characteristics of the cult).

The other type of design which has come down to us from more ancient times is linked with the pre-Buddhist Bon-po and other cults of fire and is still more fascinating because of its mysterious character, its original Druidism, which is so interesting a study in connection with the great migrations.

The chief subject of these designs (which have been partly reproduced in the works of Dr. Franke, 1923) is the Mountain Goat which is the symbol of fire. In the technique of these designs one may distinguish a series of stratifications from the most ancient (resembling the Swedish halristningar) to the most recent which give the evidence of the inner existence of some cult.

In addition to the mountain goats in all possible variations, one may observe the designs of the sun, hands, dances of ritual figures and other signs of ancient folklore. This type of design, suggesting the most ancient traditions, offers a unique study.

To the other designs we were able to add two more not previously observed. On the site of Karga and near Kyelang itself (Lahul), we found a sword design. The significance of these designs is puzzling, but it is especially interesting that their shape coincides entirely with the shape of the bronze swords and daggers of the Minussinsk

Siberian type, which was so characteristic of the earliest migrators. Without making any hypotheses, or, even less, conclusions, let us record this instructive detail as one more guiding milestone.

Let us not forget that the old Catholic missionary related to that the site of Lhasa was called Gota.

The ruins of the ancient Temples of Kashmir remind us amazingly of the foundations of the Alan structures which flourish so greatly in the form of the "Romanesque style." De la Vallee Poussin gives the information about foreigners who built Temples in Kashmir. In addition, Sten Konov points out that Irila belongs to the tribe of Gata, which according to his deductions signified Gota. All such signs are highly useful in the great transmigrations of the peoples.

A telegram from Leh. The expedition of the Institute arrived safely. The caravan encountered neither sickness nor losses. The collections are excellent. We thought so; we thought that Ladak would not disappoint our collector. Instructive experiments are again ahead. And who would not be kindled by the wonders of the Himalayas?

Whence, then, comes this unusual lure of the Asiatic paths? The mountains do not stand as giant barricades, but as enticing milestones. From behind the peaks, glows the radiation of the Himalayan snowy kingdom. The local people, those who have heard of something sacred, point to this radiation. For it radiates from beyond, from the very tower of the great Rigden-Jyepo, who labors untiringly for the welfare of humanity.

Kyelang, 1931.

MAITREYA

ON a piece of palm bark, with a sharp stylus, a friendly Bhiku is writing in Singalese. Does he molest anyone? Is he writing an appeal? No. With a smile he is sending a greeting to the far-off lands beyond the seas. A greeting to the good, benevolent people. And he does not expect a reply. It is simply a benevolent arrow into space.

In Kandy, in the ancient capital of Lanka-Ceylon, we are guided along the old traces of the past: The Temple of the Holy Tooth, the Temple of Para-Nirvana, the wondrous treasury of sacred books in their hammered-silver binding-boards. "And what is there in the small closed temple?" . . . "That is the Temple of Maitreya, the Lord of the Future." . . . "May one enter?"

The Guide smiles and shakes his head beningly. "In this Temple none may enter save the chief priest."

Thus, the luminous future must not be contaminated! We know it lives. We know its symbol is Maitreya, Metteya, Maitri,—Love, Compassion. Upon this luminous sign of all-understanding, all embracingness, the great future is being built. It is pronounced with the most reverent solemnity. It must not be defiled or blasphemed by light-mindedness, curiosity, levity and doubt. The Vishnu Puranas, and all other Puranas, that is, all the ancient covenants, speak in their highest expressions of the luminous future which humanity serves, each individual in his own way.

Messiah, Maitreya, Muntazar, and the entire glorious succession of names, which in such diversity has expressed this very same sacred and heartfelt striving of humanity.

With special exultation, the prophets speak of the future. Read all the pages of the Bible, where the best hopes of the people are expressed. Read the Covenant of Buddha about Maitreya. See how gloriously the Moslems speak of the Prophet of the Future.

How beautifully India speaks of the end of the Black Age of Kali Yuga and the glorious beginning of the White Age of Satya Yuga. How majestic is the image of the Kalki Avatar upon the white steed! With equal warm-heartedness, the far-off Oirots await the White Burkhan. Our Old Believers who heroically go in quest of the "White Waters" in the Himalayas, make this difficult journey only in the name of the future. In the very same name of the luminous future, the Lama, with tears, tells us of the treasures and the might of the great Rigden Jyepo, who will annihilate evil and re-establish justice. Towards the future lead the conquests of Gesar Khan. Each New Year, the Chinese man lights his candles and prays to the Lord of the Future. And in lsfahan, the white steed is kept saddled for the Great Coming. If you want to contact the best chords of humanity, speak with the people of the future, of that to which the human mind aspires even in the far-off deserts. Some special sincerity and solemnity pervades these strivings toward the transfiguration of the World.

In these darkest times, in the suffocating void of thought, with especially evocative force, resounds the encouraging voice about the Great Advent, about the New Era, about the time when humanity will be able, with wisdom and inspiration, to utilize all its predestined possibilities. Each person interprets this Radiant Age in his own way, but in one thing all are alike: precisely that they interpret it, with the language of the heart. This is not a casual eclecticism. On the contrary, it is just the opposite: from all directions to the one because in every human heart, in the entire human kingdom, exists one and the same striving to Bliss. And all are laboring to reunite in their substance these scattered little spheres of Mercury, if they are not too heavy with oil and not too fluffy with dust.

What an example there is in such a simple act as the outer soiling of the spherule of Mercury! One may still glimpse the trembling of the inner substance, but the surface is already besmirched. It has become grimy through outside depravity and has thus become isolated from the universal consciousness. The path to the universal body of all-unity is already intercepted. But if the surface is not yet soiled, with what impetuous striving these scattered drops fuse again with their primary source! And you cannot identify them any longer, nor will you distinguish the small particle that was assimilated by the whole. But it lives, it lives in all, it lives in the Great. The force of all-unity joined it and forged it to the universal concept. All teachings know this universal body under various names.

In the most unexpected manifestations we meet with these all-unifying signs. In the posthumous writings of the Elders of the desert unexpected indications were sometimes found about the Himalayas. These writings, mandalas and other extraordinary signs arouse one's amazement and astonishment. But the Lama from the far-off mountain monastery, when asked about it, smiles and says: "Above all divisions, there exists one great unity, accessible only to a few."

Thus the trends of thought of the most seemingly distant individualities are merged. Denial and condemnation, most hideous aspects that obscure the light of the heart, are being erased in these highest signs. Often in our present day, we invent special expressions for the ancient understanding. We say pensively: "He understands psychology." This means in essence that he does not deny and does not condone his ignorance. We say: "He is practical and knows life," which means in essence that he does not condemn and thus does not set obstacles for himself. We say: "He knows the sources," which means he does not disparage because he knows how harmful each disparagement is.

In "The Resurrection in the Flesh," N. O. Lossky cites: "A worker who counters his striving against the strivings of all other workers is in a state of isolation from them and dooms himself to utilize only his own creative force; hence, he is capable of producing only the most elementary actions, such as repulsion. The release from such impoverishment of life is reached by way of evolution which creates higher and higher steps of concrete One-ness.

"The members of the Heavenly Kingdom, not entering into a state of resistance, do not commit any acts of repulsion in space. Consequently they do not have a material body; their transfigured body consists only of manifestations which are luminous, sonorous, warm, etc., but which do not exclude each other, that are egotistically isolated, but that are capable of mutual interpenetration. Having attained a concrete One-beness, which means having absorbed the strivings of each other and the tasks of Divine Wisdom, they collectively create the Kingdom of perfect Beauty and the manifestation of only Good. And they so create their bodies that, being mutually interpenetrating, they are not in possession of one personality, but serve all, complementing each other, and forming individual omni-entities, which are organs of the all-embracing wholeness of the Heavenly Kingdom. The free and loving unanimity of the members of the Heavenly Kingdom is so great that all united, one may say, 'one body and one spirit.'

"Concerning the super-spaciousness, its significance is well expressed in the creations of the Father of the Church the Holy Gregori Nisky. 'The soul is not confined to spacial limitation,' he says, 'therefore, for the spiritual essence, no great difficulty is involved in pervading each of the elements, with which at some time it has come into union, during integration, since it is not divided into parts by the unruliness of the elements; the spiritual and dimensionless essence is not affected by the consequence of distance. The friendly connection and acquaintance with the former parts of the body is forever retained in the soul.' "

To whom, then, will the words of our famous contemporary philosopher be especially clear and close? Certainly a high Lama will express heartfelt response as well as benevolent understanding of them. Moreover in his realistic metaphysics he will find a corresponding substantiation for them, and with elation he will join the discussion about the spirit; in other words, this constitutes his striving. The Lama will recognize the universal body as Darmakaya. He will call the highest communion of the representative of the spirit, Dorjepundok. And chiefly he will do so, not in the spirit of discord or in dispute, but in that benevolent communion by which all harmful boundaries are so easily erased.

In the East they also understand Metalnikov's idea of the immortality of the cell-unit. The idea of unity, indivisibility, indestructibility, is appreciated. The one who understands Dharma, can also speak of immortality. With equal benevolence, they understand de Broglie, Millikan, Raman, and Einstein. The main thing is that there should be a language of approach. For mutual understanding one must know the inner and outer languages. One must know not only the outer hieroglyph; one must know the derivation of the sign, the evolution of the symbol, in order that an incomprehensible exterior should not become a new barrier.

Is it then so difficult to unite in Bliss? One person may consider the sacredness of the Ganges as superstition; but a true scholar will give its due to the wisdom of the people. It is truly beautiful to contact the facts and foundations of the people's wisdom. The waters of the Ganges are revered as sacred. And it is astounding that with the countless multitudes of swarming, people do not contaminate each other in the waters of the sacred river in Benares. But in addition to faith and to psychic protection, nature adds one more precious factor: Only recently it was discovered that special bacteria exist in the water of the Ganges which destroy other nests of contamination. The old Knowledge also manifests its firm foundation here.

All signs of unity are touching. The Buddhists see the icon of Saint Josav, the Hindu Prince, and wish to have a copy of it. The Lamas see a fresco of Nardo di Cione in the cemetery in Pisa and begin to explain its contents and the significance of the painted symbols. And when you read to them about Saint Josav from The Golden Legend they smile cordially. And in this smile is that same benevolence and containment which made room for Aristotle on the portals of the Cathedral of Chartres together with the Saints and Prophets. And also the images of the Greek Philosopher upon the frescoes of the churches of Bukovina. The image of the Mohammedan Akbar is in a Hindu Temple. Lao Tze and Confucius are in an aureole of Catholic Saints. All the black Madonnas and Rockamadura are from Negro soil! And King Solomon is in the Greek Orthodox Church of Abyssinia. If only one does not close one's eyes intentionally, a multitude of benevolent facts will flow in. Verily, following the covenant of Origen, "We see with the eyes of the heart."

And not only do ancient Chartres and Bukovina revere the great Philosophers upon their portals. The newspapers of New York thus communicate the news about the Riverside Church: "Confucius, Buddha and Mohammed, together with Christ are modeled on the portals of the Baptist church. The new era of religious tolerance is expressively symbolized in the images, where great scientists and philosophers, many of whom in their time were condemned for heresy, occupy a place together with saints, angels and leaders of religions. . . . Moses is modeled shoulder to shoulder with Confucius; after Buddha and Mohammed follow Origen, St. Francis of Assisi, Dante, Pythagoras, Plato, Socrates, Aristotle, St. Thomas Aquinas, Spinoza and Archimedes. . . . Together with Dr. Fosdick who gave this testimony of his broad thinking, another representative of free thought, Dr. Holmes, has announced in a sermon that the Temples of the future will represent the synthesis of all great religions of the world."

Similar are the sermons of Dr. Guthrie who speaks in

one of the oldest churches of New York, St. Marks-in-the-Bouwerie. All remember his Buddha Day and other days devoted to other leaders of religious thought. The new temple of the Episcopalian Church on Park Avenue,, under the leadership of the eminent minister Dr. Norwood, strives towards the same blissful synthesis.

If a venerable Moslem affirms that the Tomb of Christ is in Srinagar, and begins in the most devout manner to enumerate all the traditions and cures which have taken place near this Tomb, one cannot reprove him severely; for he speaks with the most benevolent intentions. Likewise, you will not interject objections when in Kashgar they speak with conviction about the tomb of the Holy Virgin being in Miriam Mazar. Neither will you protest when they speak to you of Elijah the Prophet in the upper Indus, for, first of all, you feel their benevolence, and secondly, in substance, there is nothing to contradict this. Let us altogether regard all these benevolent signs of unification with care.

Or will you in wrath speak against the throne of King Solomon in Srinagar? On the contrary, you will rejoice that these thrones are many in Asia and, according to the words of blessing, the wise King Solomon in his all-unifying force, flies even now above the vistas of Asia in his wondrous flying carpet. You will rejoice and remember the Amos Society in New York and its broad and benevolent aims.

There is special joy when you hear the great names of Messiah, Maitreya, Muntazar united and pronounced in the same place with the same benevolent reverence and unifying signs.

Let us remember the touching Tibetan legend about the origin of many sanctuaries, and let us especially remember this now when these benevolent signs do not bind us with the fetters of the past, but exultingly impel us towards the future.

And what is the invocation of the wise Apostle Paul when he writes to all ends of the world, to the Romans, the Hebrews, the Corinthians, the Ephesians, and to the Galatians: "Purge out therefore the old leaven, that you may be a new lump."—"Therefore let us keep the feast not with the old leaven."—" Let he who is weak in the faith receive ye, but not those who are filled with doubt and discord."—"For one believeth that he may eat all things; another, who is weak eateth herbs."

"Let us therefore follow after the things which make for peace and things where with one may edify another."

"Everyman's work shall be revealed; for the day shall declare it. It shall be revealed by fire, and the fire shall try every man's work, no matter what it is."

"When they shall say "Peace and Safety,' then sudden destruction cometh upon them."

"Quench not the Spirit."

"Let us therefore cast off the works of darkness, and let us put on the armor of light."

"Achieve love, be protective of spiritual gifts."

"It is not grievous for me to repeat the same things in writing to you, but for you it is useful."

What is the command and prayer of spiritual reunion? For the future, the armor of light is needed.

Isaiah also, not only deploring the past, but with enthusiasm for the future, gave his forewarning with the ominous words: "Maller—Shelal—Ash—Baz."

Akbar planted the young trees along the roads of India not for the past, but for the future traveler.

What can be worse than to remove something and to leave "the site empty?" says Zlatoust, "And when the soul diverts from love, then its mental gaze is clouded."

Verily the unifying signs are very precious! We do not forget the word of Vivekenanda about Christ, "If I would have met Christ during my life, I would have washed His feet with the blood of my heart." Are there many Christians who have in their hearts the same vital and uplifted feeling? And can one forget the words of the same Vivekenanda, who asked the Chicago Congress of

Religions: "If you consider your teaching so supreme, why then do you not follow its Covenants?"

Can one forget the fact that once when a Christian church was in an impoverished condition and was threatened with being sold at an auction, Jews voluntarily and spontaneously bought the Christian sanctuary and returned it to the Metropolitan Diocese. The Metropolite E. will affirm this.

Is it not in the name of bliss that the Rabbi Kabbalist tells you: "You are also Israel if you search for Light." And will you not smile benevolently at the Namtar of the Central Asiatic Bakshi with regard to the miracles of the great Issa-Christ? And will you not listen after midnight in Kashmir to the glorification of Christ from the lips of the Moslem choir, accompanied by the zithers and fantastic drums? Also I recollect all the reverential and deeply touching words of the Moslems of Sinkiang about Issa the Great and the Best.

Or if we take a book of the Reverend James Robson, "Christ in Islam," then instead of hostile signs whispered by ignorance, we will see innumerable examples of sincere understanding and benevolence. The Old Believer sings the verses about Buddha. The New Testament is also placed among the sacred books in the suburgans. The Dravidian reads Thomas à Kempis' "Imitation of Christ." The Moslem in Central Asia speaks of the Holy bells beyond the mountain which are heard at dawn by the Holy Ones. Why does the Moslem need bells? It is simply a need for the call of benevolence. The Siberian Old Believers are carrying out pilgrimages to the universal "White Waters".

Let us remember all the sayings of all ages and people about the Holy People.

The narrator does not even know about whom he speaks, whether they be Christians, Buddhists, Moslems or Confucists. He knows only of the benevolence of the achievements of these Holy People. They, these Holy Ones, radiate an unearthly light; they fly; they hear at a distance of six months' journey; they heal, they self-sacrificingly share their last possession, they dispel darkness and untiringly create bliss upon their paths. The Old Believers and Mongols and Moslems and Jews and Persians and Hindus . . . they all speak in a similar way. The Saints become pan-human, they belong to the whole world as steps of the true evolution of humanity. Everything contains light. The chalice of grail is above all, bliss. The divine Sophia, the All-Mightiest Wisdom, soars above the whole world.

The curse leads only to darkness. Not by wrath, not by succumbing, but upon the blessed milestones one can cross the most tempestuous ocean.

Here are the words from the Koran:

"O peoples of the earth, throw off all ties whatsoever, if you desire to reach the Encampment prepared for you by God.

"Maybe then it will be possible to force the people to run away from a condition of apathy, in which their soul exists, towards the Nest of Unity and Knowledge; it will force them to drink the water of eternal Guidance." . . . "That is the Holy and eternal lot, the heritage of pure souls at the Divine Table."

Here is from the great Shambatyon from the Kabbala:

"Eldad Ha-Dani describes the river Shambatyon which united the children of Moses, as a stronghold of spiritual unification. The Moslem writers, lbn-Fakich and Kasvini relate how once the Prophet asked the Archangel Gabriel to carry him over into the site of the 'Children of Moses, (Banu Muza), into the land of the righteous ones. "Gelilot Herets Israel", identifies Shambatyon with the sacred river of India, which has healing properties." Healing unifications!

Let us not imagine that these ideas about all-understanding, about unity, are close only to innovators who shock the dogmas.

The Orthodox Catholic and Roman Catholic churches constantly pray for the "reunion of the churches, for the time of peace." This hope for the most spiritual, most heart-felt unification, is not a dogma; it is the most life-creating, benevolent principle. And after this external reunion they hope for an era of peace. From the church pulpits we are carried into endless conferences for Peace which also, each in turn, with more or less success, express the dream of peaceful times. Upon this spirit, the inner hope of all mankind unites. Both the ones who are most remiss and the others who are most eager and regenerated are dreaming of the days of peace and of the most splendid reunion. In the depths of the heart we understand that persecution, revilement, and curses, only lead to horror, divisiveness, and to pettiness. They lead us to subtle falsehood and vile hypocrisy.

The Messiah will come over the bridge. The Kabbalists know of this unifying symbol. The Great Rider comes upon a white horse and the comet is as a sword of Light in His hand. A distinguished Abyssinian says: "We have an ancient legend that when the Savior of the World shall come He will pass over a stone bridge. And seven know of His coming. And when they see the Light, they will fall down to earth and will bow before It."

Is it accidental that the coming of the Messiah takes place over a bridge? What symbol is closer to the thought of unity, of reunion? Already Maitreya is seated not in Eastern posture but in Western, with lowered feet, ready for the advent. . . . "Verily never has the time been as short as ours." . . . "The time is intense." . . . "The time is short." . . . "The time is close," the people exclaim in varied tongues, trembling with expectancy, gathering the best symbols around their hopes.

With wordless expression, by their glances they will reveal the striving of their spirits towards the Most Exalted which has the premonition of all suffering, of all the fires and the whispers of the misunderstood heart. They are inwardly awed by the very thought of revealing the most superb dream to the spirit of the people. And there is no obscurity which could intercept this path to the future, where prayers will be ameliorated, where peace will prevail and the spirit will exult in a joy not of today but in the exultation of the luminous tomorrow.

Why are these times of peace so necessary to mankind? Every heart knows, that an epoch of peace is necessary for knowledge and construction. Hostile periods have brought on the material and spiritual crash. The human heart knows this as well. Periods of hostility have created the unrest of unemployment, through which the most worthy striving towards the improvement of quality has been lost. Periods of hostility have resulted in numerous conventionalities and in those atrocities which come from the absence of quality, in other words, from a spirit of savagery.

Very often conferences for peace evoke a pitying smile because of the hypocrisy of the people who gather to do away with methods of destruction inconvenient for them, in order to replace them with more subtle and modern methods.

But even among those who gather, there are always some to whom the creative principle of peace is close. And these (not the bestial ones) will still strive towards luminous unification, towards the great universal body like the spherules of pure Mercury. These striving ones can always find the means of accord because by day and night their hearts pray for unification. If this voice prevails, one is able to also realize that indestructible ennobling of the spirit which is imparted through the realization of culture, because each aspiring spirit in search of culture, also knows the great sense of union and the time of peace in his heart. He needs this sense of union, this time of peace, in order to open the gates of light. "Do not stand in the way." . . . "Do not obscure the sun," said Diogenes, not because he desired to be a sluggard. He asked that light not be obscured, lest it give way to darkness.

Truly, the future does not tolerate do-nothings. All has become dense. In the pressure of energies each moment of conscious labor is significant. Each banishment of egoism is significant. And the affirmation of co-operation is luminous.

The age of Maitreya was always indicated as the age of true co-operation. Natalie Rokotov, in her remarkable book on Buddhism that has been based on the sources, thus characterizes the Age of Maitreya: "The future Buddha Maitreya, as His name indicates, is the Buddha of Compassion and Love. This Bodhisattva, because of the power of his qualities, is often named Ajita the Invincible.

"It is interesting to note that the reverence of many Bodhisattvas was accepted and developed only in the school of Mahayana. Nevertheless, the reverence of the one Bodhisattva Maitreya, as a Successor chosen by Buddha Himself, is accepted also in Hinayana. Thus, the one Bodhisattva Maitreya embraces the complete scope, becoming the personification of all aspirations of Buddhism.

"What qualities must Bodhisattvas possess? In the Teaching of Gotama Buddha and in the Teaching of Bodhisattva Maitreya, given by Him to Asanga according to the tradition in the 4th century (Mahayana-Sutralamkara), the maximum development of energy, courage, patience, constant striving and fearlessness was first of all emphasized. Energy is the basis of everything, as it alone contains all possibilities.

"Buddhas are eternally in action; immovability is unknown to them; like the eternal motion in space, the actions of the Sons of Conquerors manifest themselves in the worlds.

"Mighty, valiant, firm in His step, not rejecting the burden of an achievement for the General Good.

"There are three joys of Bodhisattvas; the joy of giving, the joy of helping and the joy of eternal perception. Patience always, in all and everywhere. The Sons of Buddhas, the Sons of Conquerors, Bodhisattvas, in their active compassion are the Mothers to the All-Existing (Mahayana Sutra)."

In giving the covenant of Shambhala, does not the

East speak about the very same Light, which is heartily awaited with benevolence and unity? . . . "The Universal Eye of Shambhala carries benevolence to mankind. The Universal Eye of Shambhala is like the Light upon mankind's path. The Universal Eye of Shambhala is that Star, which has directed all seekers.

"For some, Shambhala is the truth; for others Shambhala is a Utopia. For some, the Lord of Shambhala is a venerable sage; for others the Lord of Shambhala is the manifestation of abundance. For some, the Lord of Shambhala is an adorned idol; for others the Lord of Shambhala is the Guide of all planetary spirits. But We shall say the Lord of Shambhala is a Fiery Mover of Life and of the Fire of the Mother of the World. His Breath glows with flame and His Heart burns with the fire of the Silvery Lotus. The Lord of Shambhala lives and breathes in the heart of the Sun!

"The Lord of Shambhala is the calling one and the called! The Lord of Shambhala is the transmitter of the arrow and the one who accepts all arrows! The Lord of Shambhala breathes the truth and affirms the truth. The Lord of Shambhala is invincible and transforms destruction into construction! The Lord of Shambhala is the peak of the banner and the summit of light.

"Accept the Lord of Shambhala as the sign of life. I shall say three times—of life, because Shambhala is the pledge of mankind's strivings. Our manifestation is the pledge of mankind's perfection. Our manifestation is the affirmed path to Infinity.

'The Lord of Shambhala manifests three ordinances to humanity: The teaching manifested by Maitreya calls the human spirit into our creative world. The teaching of Maitreya points out Infinity in Cosmos, in life, in achievements of the spirit! The teaching of Maitreya holds the Knowledge of the Cosmic Fire, as the opening of the heart, which contains the manifestation of the Universe.

"The ancient legend, affirming that the manifestation of Maitreya will evoke a resurrection of the spirit, is correct. We will add that the resurrection of the spirit can precede the manifestation of the Coming, as the conscious acceptance of the Teaching of Lord Maitreya is truly resurrection!"

Does not the East evoke the same spiritual strength, affirming the just necessity of the Hierarchy of Light?

"In the reconstruction of the world, one may be sustained only by the affirmation of the New World. The establishment of a manifested decision can enter life only through the great understanding of the universal regeneration, by the path of the great law of Hierarchy. Therefore those who seek the New World must strive towards the affirmation of the law of Hierarchy, which leads by the affirmed Hierarchy. Thus one may only establish balance in the world. Only a flaming, guiding Heart shall manifest salvation. Thus the world is in need of the affirmation of the law of Hierarchy.

"Therefore, according to the Law, Hierarchy is being affirmed in the shifting of countries and by the substitution by fire of everything that is departing. Therefore, it is so necessary to accept the Law of Hierarchy, because without the chain, one cannot build the great ladder of ascent. Thus it is necessary to ardently accept the affirmation of the grandeur of the Law of Hierarchy.

"It is necessary to reiterate about Hierarchy. It is correct, that the hierarchy of slavery has ended, nevertheless, the manifestation of a conscious Hierarchy is accomplished by the suffering of humanity. There is too much slavery in the world and each flame of consciousness is oppressed too greatly. Slavery and conscious Hierarchy, are as day and night. Therefore do not hesitate to repeat—conscious Hierarchy, the Hierarchy of Freedom, the Hierarchy of Knowledge, the Hierarchy of Light. Let those who do not know the concept of the New World ridicule because each understanding of the New World is terrifying to them. Is not Infinity horrible to them? Is not Hierarchy burdensome to them? Because, themselves being ignorant despots, they do not understand the creativeness of Hierarchy. Being themselves cowards, they are terrified before Hierarchy. Thus, let us place in the balance the most needed understanding of the approaching Great Age—Infinity and Hierarchy.

"One must accept Hierarchy as an evolutionary system. For those spirits who have not outlived slavery, one may repeat that Hierarchy absolutely differs from despotism."

"What path then is the most affirming one? The most real way is heroic self-sacrifice. The most wondrous fire is the flame of the heart, imbued with love to Hierarchy. The heroic action of such a heart is affirmed by service to the highest Hierarchy; therefore the self-sacrifice of a subtle heart is wondrous. The spirit-creativeness and independent activity of a sensitive servant imbues the space with fire. Thus verily harmonize the visible and invisible; the present and the future, and the predestined shall be fulfilled. Thus the self-sacrifice of a subtle heart imbues the world with flame.

"According to the construction of strata, the evolutionary spiral is being extended and the involutionary is being contracted. One may observe this same fact not only with individuals but also with ideas. It is very instructive to discover how ideas are born and how they accomplish their cycle; often they seem to disappear completely. But if they are evolutionary, they reappear in a broader way. One may study the spiral of the roots of ideas for evolutionary thinking. The task of gradual containment of an idea can facilitate the progression towards the highest understanding.

"Labor, create benevolence, revere the Hierarchy of Light—this, Our Covenant may be inscribed upon the hand even of a new-born child. Thus simple is the cause which leads to Light. In order to accept it, it is necessary only to have a pure heart.

"Hierarchy is planned co-operation. If any one tries to explain it by the conventional understanding, he will only prove that his brain is as yet not ready for co-operation." Thus it is said.

Upon what, then, can we agree? On what basis may we forgive? Upon what shall we base our understanding? Upon what may we broaden ourselves? Upon what shall we avoid offense? Upon what may we move forward? Encircling all the spheres of Dante, we come to co-operation. Co-operation, compassion, are love itself. Ordained by all the hieroglyphs of the heart, love is the Mother of the World. Inexhaustible is creative love, which has conceived the Tribe of Holy people, who know neither earth nor nation—who hasten upon wings of spirit to give succor, compassion, co-operation, who hasten in the name of bliss, who carry the drops of all-understanding, all-embracing bliss.

The world is hastening towards reconstruction. Human hearts are tired of wrath. In tumultuous labors they remember again about culture and the signs of Light, and they whisper to each other: "The future exists, that is why we have come here. Not for defamation, nor for terror, but we pass here for mutual labor, for knowledge, for enlightenment. Let us then take hold of this Universal Light; let us achieve the transfiguration of the world, the pre-ordained, the pre-destined."

All peoples know that the site of the Holy men is on the mountains, up upon the peaks. Revelation comes from the peaks. The Rishis lived in caves and up on the summits, there where the rivers find their sources, where the eternal ice has preserved the purity of whirlwinds, where the dust of meteorites carries a purifying armor from the distant worlds, there is the rising glow. Thither is directed the striving of the human spirit. The mountain paths attract one with their very difficulty. There the unexpected occurs. There the people's thought moves towards the Ultimate. There each pass promises an unprecedented novelty, gives promise of the viewing of new facets of the great outlines.

Upon the difficult paths, upon the dangerous mountain passes stand the images of Lord Maitreya of the resplendent future. Who made the effort to place them there?

Whose was the labor? But many they stand: gigantic, as if not humanly created. Every traveler adds a little stone to the growing mendang. Does one's heart ridicule this stone offered to the steps of the future? No. The difficult and dangerous path opens one's heart. One does not ridicule; but, in smiling benevolence, one adds his stone also to the laying of the step of the all-Containing Light.

Long before dawn, under the stars, the entire neighboring mountain beyond the river is studded with tremendous roseate fires. They glide along, gathering into garlands, breaking into fragments; they flash out and disappear, or they are moving back and forth or unite into one powerful flame. In the cold November air, we admire this Himalayan marvel, which is familiar to all local inhabitants. In the morning you can ask the Guru about it and he, with sparkling eyes, speaks about the fire s of Devita; another whispers about the resplendent legion of the Maitreya .

There are the fires of earth . But here is the heavenly glow. Tibet knows "De-me" the fire of the deity and "Nam bumpa," a fiery glow.

Over the snowy peaks of the Himalayas burns a bright glow, brighter than the stars, and fantastic flashes of lightning. Who has kindled those pillars of light that march across the heavens? The polar and midnight regions are not near. The northern lights cannot glimmer in the Himalayas. These pillars of light are not from the Northern scintillations. They come from Shambhala: from the Tower of the Great Coming One.

"Maitreya Comes."

To Him they pay reverence. And reining back their steeds in the vastness of the purple Gobi, they exclaim solemnly:

"Aldar!"

Kyelang, Himalayas, August 24, 1931.

VI
GREETINGS

DECADE

TEN years have elapsed since we laid the first stone of our institutions in America. It is but natural that we should have begun them with the Master Institute of United Arts in order to immediately emphasize, in full measure, the thought of unity. In this way our thoughts, which had already found their acceptance in other countries, were transported and became enrooted also in the soil of America. For ten years a vast literature has been assembled through all departments of our cultural center. I do not now attempt to write a history of these collections. On this day of greeting we need not become chroniclers, but we shall express what seems to us to be most unquestionable in the growth of cultural beginnings.

Dear co-workers, nor do I attempt simply to praise you, because is it possible to praise a man who is completely devoted to the idea of culture? Is it possible to praise a man for honesty? Can one give praise for spirituality? Or for inspiration through Beauty? Because all these are human foundations, outside of the tenets of which no one can be considered a cultural worker. Praise is always relative. But fact is absolute. And so now on this memorable day, marking a decade of arduous labor in the name of Culture, I wish to measure that which is undeniable.

Glancing back upon all labors, upon all our battles with ignorance, it becomes apparent that the creative work proceeds incessantly. This is not praise. This is only a manifestation of fact, of true spiritual valor. Can we recall even one year spent in rest or self-indulgence? Can we name even one month out of these one hundred and twenty months when that which was done was not strengthened, and when thoughts did not direct themselves toward new regions in the cultural field?

And so here, placing our hands upon our hearts, we may say that there has never been a year, or month, or even a week when thought and labor did not mold new possibilities. There was never a day when endless obstacles were not turned into opportunities. This realization of ceaseless striving, of perpetual creative labor, must verily be the sign of today. We may be questioned about the order of our plan. According to individual judgment, someone may suggest a substitution in the order of our work, but no one may say that energy was not devoted towards the Good.

There is nothing astonishing about the fact that for ten years the Institutions have developed prodigiously. In the incessant flow energy is comprised a great magnifier, a great current that vests the workers with a strong armor.

I regret greatly that on this significant day I cannot be with you and cannot vitalize the thoughts which I send to you with words. But in the name of that ardent and constant work of which I speak. I feel that the organization of the Himalayan Institute completely justifies my physical absence from America today. It is now more than three years ago since we brought into our departments of art, also the province of science, because Culture, in its origin of synthesis, does not permit boundaries or distinguishing separations. We see that all conventionalities, so harmful to progress, are born only through ignorance. Yet each one of us may state that in his activities he found the essence of the national spirit far stronger than the attacks of ignorance. Dealing with the people, striving in the heart towards Knowledge and Beauty, we may remain optimists. Let us today not recall the difficulties. The memory of difficulties may attach our ship to the wharf. Recalling our difficulties, we involuntarily begin to think of a merited rest; in other words, we begin to permit ourselves the most harmful thoughts. Because where is rest amidst the limitlessness of creativeness? Remaining unshakable optimists, we only strive to re-enforce our ship with new sails.

"Strange people," someone has said of us, but our friend answered: "Verily, unusual people. They meet even all difficulties with a smile."

Whence is this smile born? Only in the realization of the extent to which the work in the name of Culture is always needed and perhaps, especially now. And so let us begin the new decade with the same unrestrained striving, with the same clarion call about Culture and with the same indefatigability.

Let us pay homage to all who helped the growth of these Institutions and let us pity those whose names have become identified with darkness.

I have so often said, Culture is the reverence of Light. Even the grass and the plants strive towards light. How must people then strive with inspiration and exaltation to one Light if they consider themselves to be higher than the vegetable kingdom!

This very night, above the chain of the Central Himalayas, an extraordinary illumination is glowing. It is not lightning; the sky is clear. It is the luminous glow noted very recently over the Himalayas by scientists. In the name of Light, in the name of Light borne by the human heart, let us work and create and study.

This greeting will reach you, friends, almost at the date of the decade of our institutions. Do not forget in what manifold ways public opinion has responded to our constructiveness. Each one in his own way has expressed his interest: one has sent a congratulatory thought and another one his praise. One has helped and co-operated. And finally, those within whom no good thought dwells, have sent their slander, and in this form, they have also expressed their concern. Slander, as monstrous as it is, is a form of recognition. And one must collect these typical signs, as unavoidable expressions of a language foreign to us.

Among the manifold dialects, there are many

unexpected consonants and by one letter, it is difficult to determine what a sign, sometimes outwardly euphonious, may carry within. Often in life an intent to malicious slander is utilized. The main thing is not to turn one's eyes from this intention. Hence, remembering the good signs, let us also remember the typical caresses of slander. Without it, the earthly repast would be incomplete. But, precisely at this full repast, I want again to welcome all friends and co-workers who walk in friendship so as to help the needs of Cultural Life.

If we can help these very vital needs of human existence—it is already beautiful. And if at the day of the decade we can direct our thoughts towards vigilant constructive works, it means that we are already on the right path. The realization of the correct path will give us that exhilaration, perspicacity and resourcefulness necessary, tirelessly and faithfully to help the construction of a luminous life.

Greetings!

Ten years ago we planned the beginning and development of our Cultural Institutions. We must say that, following the basic program, we have succeeded in many points beyond the aims originally set. Now entering a new decade, let us look into the future and indicate new mileposts, along which the development is to proceed. I underline "development," for one may develop oneself or be destroyed, but one may not stop at the same point. These words should be pronounced at a moment of the greatest material world crisis, at an hour in the world when much is cut away, forgotten and discarded, like the load of a ship in danger during a raging storm. But when a ship is in danger, every man on board contributes all his experience in order to combat the difficult situation victoriously. Humanity knows no panacea higher than Culture, and will never know one, because Culture is the total of all achievements of the fiery creativeness. Our ship also has difficulties in the storm of the world's ocean. And of course, all our material estimates, which were fully correct for a normal condition of things, have quite naturally been shaken under the pressure of the coming ninth gross output. We begin the new decade with an appeal to the masses for co-operation. We started our Cultural Institutions for the people and now the masses of the people should manifest their might in the understanding and appreciation of cultural activities.

During all periods of history, spiritual power has created possibilities of existence. A reasonable economy on one hand and a fiery creativeness on the other, build a firm foundation. Even in the most difficult hour the builder has no right to think only of economy, which due to the worthlessness of the poor material used, may be the cause of explosion and destruction. We must look into the future constructively!

First of all, let me speak of our central Institution. The Museum is not a dead storage depot, nor a miser's treasure; the Museum is inseparable from the concept of a Center of Culture. The Museum is already the Abode of the League of Culture. In the broad plans of Culture, it is impossible to decide beforehand about unavoidable restrictions, or about secret, exclusive possessions. It is just as difficult to foretell every beginning of constructiveness. Sometimes the term "one-man museum" has resounded in space, and I must admit that such a definition has always been against my liking. Not because I am against the expression of individuality; individuality and character create the style, and style is the seal of the age and the rhythm of Eternity. I did not like the term "one-man museum," because to my mind it sounded like something limited, whereas no concept of limitation enters into our program. Already in 1923, I proposed the Section of American Art, for which the collecting was already then begun. I understand that this Section cannot as yet be exhibited because it is in the process of formation, and parts of it are being sent on exhibition around the States, acquainting wide masses with the art of their country. In 1929, on returning after a long absence on our Expedition, we began the planning for a whole series of Sections. The Eastern Section was actually begun. The foundation for a Russian Section was laid, under the care of our Siberian Society. The artistic material which was brought back from the expedition into Mongolia and Tibet, had become the foundation of the Eastern Section, and the collection of icons became the nucleus for a possible future development of the Russian Section. Rooms dedicated to the names of St. Sergius, St. Francis, to the Thinker Spinoza, to the Great Teacher Origen, the Maha-Bodhi Room have all laid the beginning of a mighty future construction of the Museum of Religions. In 1929 and 1930 we also planned the Section of Italian Art, appealing to the large Italian colony in America, and it is not our fault, if our fellow citizens of Italian descent have not as yet responded to our desire to show the best representation of great Italian Art. But what has been postponed, is not yet lost. We shall continue as previously to fill space with our calls in the name of unity of all cultural forces. At that time the thought of French, Spanish, Swedish and Finnish Sections, and of a whole series of manifestations of South America had crystallized. Of course on such a wide front, and especially at such a difficult time, one cannot proceed as quickly as one would wish. But we have always before us the initial plan which we had when constructing the building, which is that, in due time, this building should serve the multiformity of Sections of human creativeness in a continuously adapted, changing form, thereby becoming a Living Cultural Center for public use. It is precisely the strengthening and development of this plan that is before us, as the immediate task of the New Decade. We shall be happy to welcome Sections dedicated to individuals, thus imprinting on the minds of the young generation the fruits of entire activities, reminding and inspiring them about the synthesis of building the future life. To affect the growth of all these diverse manifestations, we have to appeal not only to various communities and classes of society, but also to other different countries, which must understand that precisely in America, where so many different nationalities have united, each effort towards synthesis is especially appropriate; chauvinism does not befit America.

But again, let us not limit ourselves by setting premeditated programs of what should be done in the first instance. Let life itself show us where and in what is the greatest vitality and flexibility. The history of growth will show best, which elements prove to be most widely accepted and constructive.

Of course in our program the fundamental quality should never be overlooked, for I am sure that nations and fellow citizens will of course wish to be represented in the best and strongest way. Luckily the position of rooms in our Building is such, that they can easily be turned into Beautiful units, arranged and gradually connected one with the other.

Let us remember the beautiful interiors of Cluny, Chantilly and other remarkable museums in castles and previous private residences, which even helped to give the greatest overview and persuasiveness to the exhibits. Our various cultural societies are indeed the natural curators of the proposed Sections.

During the current year, the Museum of our Himalayan Institute Urusvati, was also founded, which gives one more important note of synthesis, and by its new aspect appeals to the fertile creative mind of the young generation. And how closely the life of the Museum with our Master Institute of United Arts, and with the exhibitions of our International Art Center and Theater, is connected. As in Nature, the vegetable kingdom mutually sustains itself, so also all these branches do not burden the stem nor do they exhaust the roots, but on the contrary, give new vitality to the whole tree.

A great number of new branches may be added quite naturally to the Master Institute of United Arts and I need not enumerate the desirable classes of applied arts once again, which I have repeatedly mentioned before, and which would give the most useful and enlightened artisans to the State. Our task is to select the best teachers, and with all our forces, create the best possibilities for our students, surrounding them with a highly-cultured, thoughtful atmosphere, concentrated in such a United Center, generating real creativeness; creativeness, not limited by narrow prejudices and other products of ignorance. The exhibitions of our International Art Center should also be developed in the same direction. In close co-operation with individual creative forces, with artistic societies and Governments, these exhibitions should attract the best creations of countries and, in blessed multiformity, they will affirm mutual understanding and friendliness between nations. Let us remember that the path of Beauty is the path of mutual admiration and understanding.

Our Press should continue to strive towards the radiant Future by means of the same expanding channels that unify and manifest true cultural information both about the past and the future, without any restrictive limitations. In the short period of its existence, the Press has issued a series of books, the Bulletin of the Museum, and has already pronounced in space the word "Oriflamma," the Art Journal. Public opinion enthusiastically welcomed the launching of the first issue of the Journal Urusvati of our Himalayan Institute. Projects about a newspaper have started. Already many publishing houses and Institutions have come with inquiries about co-operation. May our educational Press flourish and develop along the same enlightened cultural lines.

Neither can we refrain from rejoicing and foreseeing a quick growth of Urusvati, our Himalayan Institute. Before us, the walls of the biochemical laboratory with a cancer research department are being erected. Each month brings the need for new containers to store botanical, zoological, archeological and ethnographical collections. The expeditions to Ladak and Lahul have just been successfully completed and a series of publications has been planned. Every new find proves once more how correctly the location was chosen and how accurately the plan develops.

Our Societies are growing, creating an extraordinarily useful unity among the cultural forces of all nations. Proposals are constantly being received about the organization of new societies.

The co-operation and affiliation with a number of educational, artistic and scientific Institutions has taken place. Let these channels of activities also become broadened, for what can be more precious and attractive than co-operation, in which the gathering of the experience of accumulated possibilities and useful beginnings mutually strengthen one another and eliminate the detestable concepts of decomposition and disunity from daily life. Thus under the Banner of Peace in the name of Beauty and Knowledge, advance onto the New Path! No obstacles can stop the striving of the Spirit.

The service to Culture is a noble achievement of humanity. And it is the duty of everyone who is thinking of the General Good, to bring his share of co-operation into the Chalice of Evolution.

Credo!

Himalayas, October 24, 1931.

URUSVATI AND CORONA MUNDI

I. Urusvati

*Address of the President-Founder on the Third
Anniversary of the Foundation of the
Himalayan Research Institute*

ON JULY 24th, 1928, the foundation of the Himalayan Research Institute was laid. Let us cast a retrospective glance at these three years and see where we stand. The Institute already has quarters in Naggar, in the choicest valley of the Punjab. The foundations of the Institute's Museum are being laid in Naggar as well as in New York. The third anniversary finds us constructing the walls of the biochemical laboratory with a department for research into the cure of cancer. A recent statement in the press by Dr. Hofmann gives statistics indicating that in America alone, 120,000 people perished from cancer, so that it is plain to see how opportune is this beginning at the Institute. As we read the articles of leading scientists regarding the need to investigate medical substances in their local habitat before they are altered by alcoholic tinctures, we are able to perceive how greatly needed and fitting it is that the location of the Institute be amidst the richest region of the Himalayas. We should not forget that the Kulu Valley, which has focused in itself all the majestic names of humanity, starting with Mann, Buddha, Arjuna, all the heroic Pandavas, Vyasas, Gesar Khan, is an exceptional locality of which the scientific significance only now begins to make itself felt in the richest of material. This is true in its historic, archeological and philological aspects, as well as in its botanical, geological and physical character; the Institute, as is now apparent, has before itself, the most fruitful work.

Let us not forget that out of the thirty-six months of its existence, more than eight months were spent in sad and absolutely unnecessary friction which caused deep financial as well as moral injury. But, as is our custom, in pursuing only the positive milestones of life, we shall not pause at negative manifestations! Let us be grateful to all those who aided a cultural undertaking and let us forget those, who through ignorance, tried to impede the scientific work. But even while deducting the above-mentioned period of time, we have a succession of outstanding, practical results. Under the guidance of the botanist of the Institute, five expeditions were organized by the Institute in Kulu Valley itself., There were five expeditions in Lahul, Beshar, Kangra, and Lahor, and, at present, an expedition is proceeding in Ladak and Zanskar which, we hope, will give the same rich results as those gathered from the above-mentioned sites. During this period, the expeditions mentioned gathered rich botanical collections which enhanced not only the Museums of the Institute, but were also sent as gifts to the University of Michigan, the Botanical Gardens in New York and the Museum of Natural History in Paris. Dr. Merrill, head of the Botanical Gardens in New York as well as Professor Mangin, director of the Museum of Natural History in Paris, noted the great significance of the collections gathered, among which are complete collections of new species which at present are being studied by these outstanding scientists.

Together with the botanical collections, the Institute compiled numerous ornithological and zoological collections, which are preserved in the Museums of the Institute, and about 400 specimens were sent to the Museum of Harvard University in Cambridge.

Besides research in the natural sciences, a series of works is being undertaken under the guidance of the Director of the Institute, George N. Roerich, in the local study of dialects, history and archeology. During our stay in Pondicherry in French India, an excavation of local pre-Buddhist burials in urns and sarcophagi was made with the aid of the corresponding member of the Institute, member of the Catholic Mission, Father Fouchet. The director of the Institute completed two scientific works, one published by the Yale University Press on our Central Asiatic Expedition and the other, "Animal Style," published by Seminarium Kondakovianum in Prague. At present the director of the Institute, in cooperation with the well-known connoisseur of Tibetan Literature, Lama Mingyur, is busy with a study and translation of the books on Tibetan medicine, as well as with the preparation of the Grammar of the language of Lahul and other surveys of Tibetan Literature, which will be published shortly.

Close to the time of the third anniversary of the Institute's, its first "Annual Report" for 1930 was also published. Those participating were the President of the Archeological Institute of America, Dr. Magoffin, the famed French archeologist, Count de Huisson, the biochemist of Harvard University, Dr. Pertzoff, and the director of the Institute. This issue of the Annual Report is devoted to the leading Sanscritologist, Professor Lanman, Honorary Advisor of our Museum in the Department of Science. One should record that for the last three years, the body of the Honorary Advisors in the Department of Science has become strengthened by the greatest scientific names, such as Professor Millikan, Professor Raman, Professor Metalnikov, Dr. Sven Hedin, Professor Einstein, Sir Jagadis Bose, Dr. Merrill. In addition to Dr. Magoffin, Dr. Hewett is also included in the Department of Archeology,

There are Corresponding Members of the Institute in America, Europe, Africa and Asia and many Universities and scientific institutions have expressed the desire to co-operate with the exchange of collections as well as with publications. The Carnegie Foundation has given a generous donation to the Library of the Institute. Several publishers have expressed interest in the exchange of publications.

Sincere appreciation should be expressed to the Committee which met under the Chairmanship of Mrs. Ittelson, and as a result of the work of this Committee, several donations were received and possibilities were opened for further developments.

Entering the new triennial, we must again stress the special fitness of the place chosen for the Himalayan Research Institute, because the scourge of humanity, cancer, is almost unknown here in the Himalayas, and in addition, Tibetan medicine, from time immemorial, has in its keeping remedies against cancer and tuberculosis which have been used with success. Of course such remedies must be investigated in the most careful and impartial way.

The soil of the Himalayan valleys is distinguished by an unusual fertility, which permits a great variety of vegetation all the way from Alpine flora to almost tropical vegetation. As was shown by our early collections of local vegetation, there are many new species.

Before us is the task of setting up an electrical plant and the equipment for a biochemical laboratory with a department for cancer research. Where is there a better place to study cancer than in a locality where it is altogether unknown as it is here in the Himalayas? We know that new means will be required, but we do not doubt that they will come, because public opinion is in keeping with the measure of the cultural mission. There exists such a beautiful concept as that of a spacial justice and when the beginning is proved sound, the destined help appears; this prevents us from diminishing the scale of the project and from stifling the cultural structures, so necessary to humanity.

And thus we enter the new triennial filled with the consciousness that our work is urgently needed, that the field of our activity is correctly chosen, and that the sympathy of friends and broad cultural classes promise a powerful development of the generally useful foundations. Where there is common usefulness we shall not retreat but will preserve our enthusiasm, which transforms all obstacles into resplendent possibilities.

Kyelang, 1931

URUSVATI AND CORONA MUNDI

II. Corona Mundi

MONHEGAN. The White Foam of the Atlantic Waves. The Gray Rocks. The Huts of Fishermen. A half-shattered Harbor. The small steamer—the *Governor Douglas.* That true friend Charles Pepper, during my exhibition in Boston recommends, "Visit Monhegan, one can work there." And Theophile Schneider and other friends of the Boston Club add similar counsel. Summer 1922. I am painting the Ocean Series on Monhegan. The Indian Significance of the Name of this island is told to us. Upon the mossy rocks, the fragrant, wild strawberry has suddenly reddened. During the foggy days, the horns of the lighthouses moan and it seems as though you are somewhere far away. We are reading articles on Art; the significance of creative work in life and in the Culture of the peoples is discussed. From the "Paths of Blessing," we mark the motto for the International Art Center, where the communion of nations in peaceful creativeness should take place. The name Corona Mundi—the Crown of the World; not that this center is the crown of the world, as some ignoramus has said, but the crown is all-uniting Art, which elevates creative work, the resplendent heroic deed of the spirit. Humanity has always yearned for this panacea and it will be still further in need of it. Days of still greater disturbance and darkness will come, and the human spirit will find no other haven, save the invincible stronghold of beauty. A beautiful remembrance. If only each country could possess such citizens as our friend Louis L. Horch, and more such open hearts as dear Nettie S. Horch. Do financiers in many countries understand so broadly the past as well as the future significance of

Art? Would not many smile derisively if they were told of exhibitions in prisons or hospitals or artistic activities in villages? And suddenly here are people, who would have seemed to be enclosed within city limits, who would have seemed to be fettered by the tyranny of Wall Street, who understand so broadly the tasks of Art, the tasks of creativeness, as if from early childhood they had been prepared for these elevating domains. Because no matter how much one speaks of Art, about Beauty, without inner subtlety of consciousness, if the heart be dead, none of its noble rhythms and harmonies can resuscitate the inanimate corpses. At best the dead hearts shriek "Intolerable dreams." And why intolerable? Is it not because they disturb the sleep of ignorance? And why dreams, when the history of mankind confirms that only through the treasures of Culture, mankind received the right of existence. Only through the thoughts of the beautiful, mankind can move ahead and hope for a better future. Imagine for a moment an entire country of such citizens with hearts open towards Knowledge and towards the Beautiful. Even if by a single heroic action of the spirit, countries can advance, then what a golden age would await the energies of co-workers, who are burning with Culture? The walls of Jericho fell before the blasts of trumpets, could not, then the strongholds of darkness be shattered by harmony of ardent, cultural hearts? Would not the problems of life be decided, then, easily and freely? And what balance of spirit and body could come to mankind, ridding it of bodily and spiritual ailment! Humanity should be grateful to its fellow citizens, who, despite all difficulties created by darkness, are carrying the torch of broad understanding, the torch of benevolence and unceasing labor. They know that they will never see the many sprouts of their heroic deeds, but they also know, with their whole heart, with their whole being, that what they are doing is imperative and no derision of ignorance can divert them from their resplendent labors for the good of the future generations. Only the malevolent and ignorant could say that they want to build monuments for themselves. But he who thinks of benevolence has no time to think of monuments. Besides he knows how perishable are the materials of construction. But it is in human hearts and in the spirit, not with hands, that monuments are being built. These monuments are indestructible and imperishable. The history of mankind reveals how a supreme justice records the heroic deeds achieved for the good of the World. What good can there be without Beauty and Knowledge, without a constant, untiring and resplendent labor? This is our motto of Corona Mundi. "Humanity is facing the coming events of Cosmic greatness. Humanity already realizes that all occurrences are not accidental. The time for the construction of future culture is at hand. Before our eyes the re-evaluation of values is being witnessed. Amidst ruins of valueless bank-notes, mankind has found the real value of the world's significance. The values of great art are victoriously traversing all storms of earthly commotions. Even the "earthly" people already understand the vital importance of vital Beauty. And when we proclaim: Love, Beauty and Action, we know truly that we pronounce the formula of the international language. And this formula, which now belongs to the Museum and Stage must enter everyday life. The sign of Beauty and Action will open all sacred gates. We walk joyfully beneath the sign of Beauty. With Beauty and Action we conquer. Through Beauty we pray. In Beauty we are united. And now we affirm these words, not on the snowy heights, but amidst the turmoil of the city. And realizing the path of true reality, we greet with a happy smile the future."

Already a tenth part of a Century has passed. Much has already been accomplished. So many splendid people have approached, and immeasurable are the plans for the future. It must succeed in helping nations, and governments to exchange the best products of national creativeness. Lecturers, benevolent messengers are traveling through countries, affirming how greatly Culture is needed. The young generations are approaching and before them is the need to regard the flame of knowledge striving towards the Beautiful as the only solution of the problems of life. Life does not reject that which is vital. We already see that there are not enough hands to fill all the chalices which are outstretched. There are also enemies, but these mostly because of misunderstanding. And even unfriendly manifestations are turned only into new possibilities where the task itself is correct.

I send a glowing greeting to all our co-workers, to all who have approached and to those who are approaching. The all-uniting Banner of Culture has already appeared as a visible symbol. This Banner of Benevolence shall still further help those young ones, resplendent in their desire to approach and in harmony to construct the steps to the future.

Greetings from the mountains. And honor to all who are thinking of Culture.

TO THE MAHA BODHI SOCIETY

A BEAUTIFUL commandment is given in the Sutras: "The Teaching is like a flame of the torch which kindles numerous fires; these may be used to prepare food or to dispel darkness. But the flame of the torch remains unchangingly aglow" (Sutra 42).

And during the sermon the words are pronounced: "Let the Light be firm as adamant; victorious as the banner of the Teacher; powerful as an eagle, and let it endure eternally."

Verily this is a beautiful Commandment of steadfastness, readiness, devotion and noble actions.

* * *

Great is the Joy of Construction! Noble is the deed of Creation! Beautiful is each endeavor in the name of Spiritual Culture! For all Buddhists and for all devotees of lofty Culture, this day is truly a memorable one. The great concept has risen again from the ashes. The great attainment is reinvoked in the minds of all thinking humanity, showing that the Truth is "like a flame of the torch, which remains unchangingly aglow." Every faithful pilgrim, who has visited the old sanctuaries of Sarnath has been aware, in his innermost heart, that it is not without great reason that this historical place has remained concealed like a hidden treasure. Precisely at the predestined time it will rise in all its spiritual glory, that glory which inspired those who beautified this great place, creating such unforgettable monuments, as the celebrated Image of the Blessed One. The reproduction of this Image, inimitable in its grandeur and Beauty, is cherished now in all parts of the world. Under the most unexpected circumstances we had occasion to witness the reverence paid to this glorious monument of Eternity. People from the most diverse stations and creeds were united in admiration of this benevolent Image of mercy. Beautiful is your thought to make of Sarnath a Center of Buddhism. Indeed, what other site could equal Sarnath, when you consider its inimitable historical glory and its geographical location! We know that each tree requires time for growth. Thus the Center at Sarnath will also follow the natural law and will develop gradually and steadily through the untiring efforts of its devotees. Patience, devotion, unity and love will bring to this Center its glorious predestined Future! In our days, when mutual understanding is so needed, when the world collapses beneath wrath and destruction, each human heart must aspire towards spiritual unity and creative construction. In the name of these noble deeds, I am sending to you, devoted Builders, my sincerest thoughts and heartfelt wishes for ever increasing success!

* * *

On memorable days one must think of these matters which should not be forgotten. During these difficult days of material world-crisis, let us look back on the causes which created such a wide-spread calamity. One would have expected that the discoveries and inventions of the most recent years would have given humanity new, unusual possibilities. The means of communications, submarines and ships, underground and overground railways and all aircraft offer their services for speedy interactions, and it would seem, for unprecedentedly intense activity.

But, instead of expected benefits, we find disaster and misfortune everywhere. In the countries apparently most prosperous, terrifyingly great armies are forming of many millions of unemployed. What joy could the afore-mentioned diverse ways of communication bring to humanity?

Let us mentally weigh the transported goods: is there

amongst the merchandise a sufficient and dignified place allotted to true spiritual values? It has been said and repeated again and again: "Man cannot live by bread alone!" And if such unusual facilities of transportation and communication have been granted humanity, they should first of all convey spiritual treasures, those treasures, by which the most powerful countries were formed. Those treasures, which created the beautiful epochs of renaissance, the rebirth of the most lofty Culture, before which, at present our hearts enthusiastically quiver.

If we could have recourse to those great treasures of the spirit, what bottomless darkness would be our goal! But let us not forget that difficulties in themselves always contain great possibilities, that the most difficult material hardships always give an impulse towards true spiritual seeking and achievements. Then the constructive solutions of seemingly insoluble problems will descend upon mankind like a beautiful, light-bearing Messenger.

The Teachings also foresee difficulties, but following them, a radiant era is always predicted. May this change not remain abstract, but may it saturate the creative thinking of humanity, lifting it upwards towards a positive constructiveness.

When we recall the remains at Sarnath, Nalanda, Kapilavastu and other memorable sites in India, Ceylon, Nepal and Indo-China that are still partly covered, the thought occurs to us as to why these historical places should be in ruins. Could they not, like many other monuments, still be standing to inspire human minds?

But near these ancient sites we already see new structure s and we know how much is predestined; verily each year brings new relics and revelations. "Peace to all beings", these relics thus ordain.

May this Command not remain nebulous and abstract; may it blossom like a flame, with silvery lotus petals, innumerable, as the number of striving hearts.

"Peace to all beings!"

* * *

Friendliness!

"Does an Arhat rest? You already know that a change of labor is rest; but the true rest of an Arhat is his thought about the Beautiful. Among various labors, the thought of the Beautiful is already the bridge and the power and the stream of friendliness. Let us estimate the thought of malice and the thought of bliss and we will become convinced that a beautiful thought is more powerful. Let us organically analyze various thoughts and we will see that a beautiful thought is a treasure trove of health. With beautiful thinking, an Arhat perceives the ladder of ascent. Such active thinking comprises the Arhat's rest. In what, then, could we find another source of friendliness? Thus one may remember this in moments of particular oppression. When the blinds of selfishness are being drawn everywhere; when the fires are being extinguished in the darkness, is it not time to think about the beautiful? Let us not defile or disparage this path! Only therein shall we attract that which seems so wondrous. And as for miracles, is it not the unbreakable contact with Hierarchy? In this contact lies the whole of physics, mechanics and chemistry and the panacea of all things. It seems that by only a little striving one may remove all obstacles; the entirety of this circumstance is immeasurably difficult for people! Why have they clipped the wings of Beauty?" Thus speaks the book, "Fiery World."

"Is everyone here? Is everyone ready?" Thus do the sentries call to each other upon the walls of the strongholds. From the towers comes the answer: "Ever ready. We are vigilant in the name of bliss." Verily it is necessary for all who think of bliss, to call out to each other in the present dark hour. Across all mountains and oceans, it is necessary for all hearts of truth to hold together in union.

In a solemn hour, how can we fail to unite and send to all friends, known or unknown, a word about friendliness. Such friendliness is not an evidence of weakness, or indifference. Within it is inherent the striving towards truth. Linked with it is the desire for the best success and unprejudiced Knowledge. Perhaps never before has the world been so greatly in need of the foundation of friendlliness.

"Peace to all living." But the path to such peace is through the friendliness with which our hearts must he filled, always, at all times of day or night, at each encounter because, nowhere has the command: "In him whom you meet, seek an enemy" been given, Quite the contrary, friendliness appears as the creative beginning which constructs a rejuvenated, transformed life.

Was it necessary that so many ages of our earthly life had to flow by so that, amidst the anguish of destruction and repression, we now remember once again about the armor of light, about the armor of friendliness. Perhaps this is superfluous, perhaps earthly life is flowing by in an adequate spiritual and physical well-being? Perhaps it is not necessary for us in this hour before dawn to agonize our hearts with the miseries of men?

But it is impossible to close our eyes to the daily news of spiritual tumult, of assassinations of body and spirit, of horrible specters of lies and mutual slander. Humanity has reached the boundaries of disintegration. It is necessary to construct, to dedicate oneself, without delay, to the resplendent construction, which is implied in the elevated concept of Culture. Where, then, are the vocabularies of benevolence; where, then, are these lofty concepts which can bathe the festered ulcers of the world with benevolence, ulcers which have been so hideously uncovered in our present days.

These miseries are not mirage-like. Each one of us has gathered an unlimited amount of information regarding all kinds of disintegrating horrors, both in private and public life. The good, as such, itself begins to appear to many as something ephemeral, beyond reach, so remote that to strive towards it is seemingly outside of human possibility.

But there can be no doubt of this omniscient Bliss,

when every human heart knows what friendliness is. Notwithstanding, all defilement, obscenity, ignorance, slander, treason, every person—even one who is spiritually destitute—each biped, nevertheless knows the meaning of a smile, not a derisive smile, but a benevolent smile of friendliness. How may we then approach discussions and decisions, if we do not disarm ourselves through true friendliness?

We must not think that this is natural only for the chosen few. The great Teacher came to all. All the commandments speak of that which belongs to all. From the simplest principles, the covenant of friendliness has been ordered to all, all, all. In the ardor of the heart, this friendliness will also be transmuted into love, into that very life-creating, love that works wonders, which, upon the entire armor of Bliss, says: "Let all who live have life."

If a heart cannot as yet contain this all-embracing commandment, there still remains for him the simplest, daily path of friendliness. Beginning with the family, the race, from those who are near to one, the path of friendliness ascends by the great spiral to the highest abodes.

We speak much about the heart, but without fundamental friendliness what manner of heart may it be! Even wild beasts feel the concept of friendliness deeply. By what, primarily, can a man resist even the most brutal attack? The eye of friendliness, the benevolent glance, will arrest the most beastly claws.

The illumination of exalted hearts, their glow of light kindled by love, has sometimes originated from such daily friendliness. This great power had its inception at that single bonfire, around which the travelers of the desert gather. And are we not travelers? Did we not make all the deserts of the spirit waterless? It is terrifying to remain in the darkness, unarmed, when out of the black mist are borne the shouts of hate and mutual strangulation.

Light is needed. The sacred light is needed. Needed are the weapons of light, which by their resplendence will disperse the legions of decay and decomposition. The first armor of light, about which the commandments of all covenants have spoken so beautifully, will be pan-human friendliness. The first quality of that friendliness will be incessant creativeness, constructive labor, which, instead of being the burdensome fetters of daily existence, will be transformed into the glory of a creative festival.

It is this creative love, this general friendliness, which the sentries guard as they call to each other upon the walls of the strongholds in the hour of solemnity,. "Is everyone here?" "Is everyone ready?"

Mettasuta sends his wise call of friendliness with the words:

"Just as the mother, risking her life, watches her only child, so let each one cultivate a friendly thought towards everything that exists. Let him cultivate within himself benevolence towards the entire world, as well as friendliness, above and below and everywhere, without limits, without hate, without hostility! (Mettasuta, 7.8)"

Himalayas.

BEAUTIFUL GARDENS

GREETINGS: Your General Assembly of March 24th, in the name of Culture and Peace, in the name of Knowledge and Beauty, is one of those historical milestones of humanity which will infuse new courage and triumph into future generations. To the one who will come, it will be deeply significant to know and to feel in the heart that the travelers who passed before him not only thought inwardly about the values of Knowledge and Beauty, about the true values of Spirit, but expressed them also in their lives. Let those who come, realize how these testimonies of the Beautiful took place even amidst the most difficult times.

Let us not hide from ourselves that the present times are verily the most difficult. It would seem that the material and spiritual crises have reached their apogee. But where is the apogee in Infinity? In other words, will the deepening and accumulation of the crises cease unless people—all who think of bliss—unite in trust and full consciousness, to sustain the constructive foundations? Each abstraction must be cognized as a reality, because in the real world there are no foggy abstractions, there is only one great Reality.

You are gathered together not in the name of small, domestic works, but in the name of the Great Reality. Instead of meaningless dissipation of time for self-gratification, you are trying by united efforts to strengthen the consciousness of the masses in the name of the Real and Beautiful. You have understood that the true idealism is the great Realism. You have understood that leisure is the same joyous work, in the name of the same spiritual values. The joyous use of time means joy to the spirit, and thus each joy, highly ennobled, represents not a feast in the hour of plague, but joy of the Spirit clad in the beautiful armor of courage. Some fossilized being may say: "Is it timely in the days of material unrest, to speak of education?" May shame be upon such a petrified heart, if in petrification the concept of shame is altogether possible.

Yes, our beloved ones, you know that just in the time of unrest, the most strained striving towards education is necessary. Let us turn to the pages of history and we shall see that the times of florescence were created by the power of Spirit. This is not a truism; this is an affirmation which we must repeat to each other. The monster of doubt approaches with its temptation by day and by night. And wherever it finds even the smallest cell open to contamination, it immediately sows the most evil seed. Primarily, how did the heart, which revolts against education, fossilize? Fossilization began with the smallest doubt based on ignorance. The greatest miseries derive from the smallest doubt and he who doubts will neither cross the abyss nor the mountain stream. And now, not only is Armageddon thundering, but there have seemingly opened entire gaping abysses, which menace Cultural Communion. We are positivists and optimists and therefore we speak not from pessimism nor despair, but we speak also purely about reality. It would be timid of us to attempt to be silent about reality. The example of the ostrich who buries his head in the sand believing that he is already saved because he himself does not see the danger, is inadmissible in human existence. No....one must direct one's eyes with special expansiveness and vigilance in order to find all the destructive and decaying causes. If doubt comes from ignorance, then wrath, lies and treason also emanate from the same source. Hence education, the discipline of mind and spirit, are that panacea which saves from all destruction. Let them not indict us for repeating truths which are supported by dozens of millenniums; but the contemporary condition of the world, so evidently shaken, forces us to repeat this and to gather together to testify with our hearts how much we desire constructive Bliss. Shall we attire ourselves in mourning clothes, because of the cause of all unrest? This would again be something of the old trend of thought. He who strives toward Reality is far from mourning and despair. He is filled with tension. He knows that, when strengthened by invoked and gathered energies, he becomes indestructible if his heart is striving to bliss. This joyous builder knows what the fire of the heart is, and he knows that if this mighty talisman is radiating, then the blackest darkness will be pierced and dispersed under the rays of Light.

In the name of Light you have gathered tonight; in the name of the joy of the Spirit, you wish to know each other and mutually to strengthen each other. Under the Banner of Culture and of everything Beautiful, you proceed joyously upon the mountain path and you even bless the sharp stones because you could not attain the heights along the smooth surface. If there would be no turmoil, if Armageddon did not thunder, perhaps your friends would not unite. Daily well-being is not a sower of achievement and heroism; without miseries we would not have the many beautiful examples of history. If obstacles would not temper the swords and shields of the heroes, humanity would now be deprived of many benevolent attainments.

Airplanes are ready for flight; marine and submarine communication is open. A hundred-thousand tonnage is at your disposal and the radio shrieks through the entire world, and perhaps far beyond its boundaries. It means that a detail of the achievement is already at hand. We have only to agree about the type of load for the air and marine iron-birds, and what to put upon the lips of the radio. Education, Education, Education, Knowledge, Peace, Beauty! Whatever they, who fear every great idea, may say, whatever the decaying destroyers may whisper; you who have gathered in the name of the Beautiful, will not fear any whispers and ill-speech.

The flame of the bonfire illumined the achievement of Holy Jeanne d'Arc and the thorns of the lofty and enlightened path of Saint Sergius; these stand as glowing memorials of human achievement calling and proving that everything is possible, even the highest, here in our earthly life. And here, within the boundaries of earth and beyond earth, let us meet together in the firm conviction of mutual work for Education. Each in his own way, each in his own garden shall plant the best tree, and shall water his seedlings daily so that these will not wither due to drought. And in everyday life, let there be the same great joy that brings us together today. And there where the great Magnet of the Heart radiates, there our forces are multiplying, for Bliss is conquered by efforts. The same benevolent efforts are transmuted into a Festival where many fires are needed in order to dispel the depth of darkness. Thus let us kindle these fires of joy. Let us leave to the beasts all quarrels and disputes, but let us strive to Bliss in the glory of inspiring labor.

Be together, be united and raise your beautiful gardens!

Urusvati, Himalayas, March, 1932.

TO THE WOMAN'S HEART

IT IS truly precious to greet each activity in the name of Culture. I cannot but express my best feelings for all your present activities, which are so needed when everything pertaining to Culture, to the realm of Art and Knowledge, is subject to cruel reprisals.

When morals become debased, some people sometimes even go as far as to use such heretical exclamations as, "To hell with Culture, I want cash!" Such brutes are unwilling to acknowledge that even money, namely prosperity, comes only from the source of Culture. If for a moment we try to imagine the world without all its discoveries, all the wise and beautiful creative achievements, then the world would inevitably submerge into the darkness of misery in the fullest sense of the word.

We shall never tire of repeating that the epochs that flourished, the epochs of renaissance, the epochs of prosperity, all emanated from the benevolent source of Culture. To try to separate the so-called materialistic life from all the beautiful attainments of Culture, would mean to try to imagine a living man without a heart.

It is not necessary for me to repeat this to you, as you all are of course in full agreement with it, otherwise you would not be so active in the cause of Culture. But with every opportunity, it is our duty to saturate space with the imperative call, with a heart-felt prayer for Culture, because in this way we fill the very source of emanation which nurtures the highest human energy.

Once a certain woman of the press, having read my address "To Womanhood"—to Woman as the Bearer of the

Covenants of Culture—accused me of flattery. But there is not the least bit of flattery or exaggeration when we assert that, after all, it is just women who, from the hearth to the Government, sow the seeds of Culture. What flattery is there in the statement that the child hears the first word of Culture, in one form or another, from its mother. And is it an exaggeration, if we do not forget that it is just woman who began most self-sacrificially, without personal motive, to introduce the cultural formulations, not only within her own small family but also in the great family of nations.

To state a reality is not an exaggeration; it is only the noting of past steps in order that the steps of the future may be attained more easily and more consciously. There is a wise saying: "The world without woman is like a rock devoid of flowers." This general canon contains neither flattery nor exaggeration. The more so as it is well-known that "to deprive the earth of its flowers would mean to lose two-thirds of its vitality."

Therefore, let us take reality as it is. The same reality in our daily news indicates that, in spite of the tremendous achievements of Culture already attained by humanity, many of these achievements remain unassimilated in numerous circles. If a literate person, pretending to be of civilized standing, can condemn Culture to hell, it means that he has not yet even reached the stage of civilization.

Each of us in his own field unfortunately meets with similar statements in a more or less vulgar form. Some people dream of the renewal of depressed trade, unwilling to remember that without broad cultural considerations there can be no flourishing of an international interrelationship, either intellectual or economic. It is impossible to consider trade, finance and all material questions without consideration of general cultural principles.

All those who regard Cultural activities as a luxury, are either out of date or fossilized, because even the oldest writings remind us how highly and vitally the questions of true education and expansion of horizons were esteemed.

Often we are ready in words to unite, to shake hands mentally in friendship and co-operation, but as soon as it comes to deeds, there seems to appear out of nowhere some peculiar, malicious unsteadiness and people are again filled with infectiously destructive paroxysms. Thus seeing your active striving in the name of Culture, I want to greet them as most necessary, as a panacea against all the present depression created by the murder of Culture.

The same widely diffused depression in all activities inevitably also reflects on the outlook of the young generations; therefore, each action in the name of Culture now becomes especially imperative, as the one life boat during a disastrous storm.

Again without exaggeration, we may say that everyone speaks nowadays of the current crisis. Therefore it is not an exaggeration again to turn to the sources of history, which reveal quite definitely how great nations avoided the approaching crisis, turning towards blissful streams of Culture.

I know that you all are in accord with these thoughts. I know that despite difficulties and opposition, you fight for the panacea of Culture in your homes and in all your educational fields. It is true that "difficulties in themselves contain new possibilities," if only this ancient wisdom is realized and utilized in life.

In the name of Culture, I hail you, and send you my most heartfelt greetings for your noble fight and for co-operation!

Himalayas, June 20, 1932.

THE CITROEN EXPEDITION

THE second expedition arranged by Citroen has returned. We have received the newspapers with the first information about the results. We have seen the first photographs of the objects brought by the second expedition. We deeply regret the loss to the expedition with the premature death of its chief, Hard, but we were delighted that the remaining participants of this expedition, in the persons of Louis Odouan-Dubreuil, J. Haken, O. Teilhard de Chardin, and others returned safely and brought new scientific reports. We were delighted to hear about the splendid new drawings of Yacovlev. From personal experience we are aware of how difficult such trails are and how necessary it is to value each success among these achievements of valor.

After this second expedition arranged by Citroen, one cannot but make a complete conclusion and mark the uniqueness of these undertakings. We did not see the first exhibition, the results of the African Expedition; however, we know the reports about it and the excellent edition of the field works of Yacovlev, who expressed the unrepeatable character of the countries through which they passed.

Both expeditions, the African as well as the Asiatic, evoked definite attention, so needed in the contemporary movements of culture. Looking over the staff of the expedition one may delight at the unusually successful and varied assembling of co-workers from all specialties. Every branch has been represented by one of its most vital and best qualified workers. And yet this does not happen often and everyone knows that such a diverse accord is not easy to select.

We know of many expeditions which not only failed to reach their goal, but fell apart on the way because of the inexcusable mutual human antagonisms. But in the case of Citroen's expedition we see not only the conquering of difficulties, but also a vital, convincing, multiform result.

In this case, we are reminded that the automobile, as one of the most powerful methods of communication, became a unifying force in scientific, artistic, and cultural researches. In this sense, the introduction of an industrial factor, as a unifying and connecting link, appears to be uniquely valuable.

The tasks of Culture, about which so much is spoken at present, also demand contemporary expressions. Culture as such excludes each jealous, antagonistic separation. If the heights of civilization and the highest dominions of Culture appear primarily to be a synthesis of all the conquests of human genius, the methods for the fulfillment of these broadened tasks must also be truly contemporary. In other words, the broad horizons of Culture, as the elevation of the general trend of thought, impel us towards all contemporary discoveries and improvements.

Motors, the radio, television, all submarine and subterranean communications, must lead towards mutual understanding and unity. It is precisely these collective expeditionary tasks which were expressed with particular vividness in the expeditions of Citroen, and which recall to us the duties of co-operation not based upon nebulous abstractions but upon present-day discoveries. Visitors to the Citroen exhibitions, and readers of the reports of these expeditions, are grateful for their collective unity, which not only transports them vividly into other lands, but which, by its multiformity, actually broadens their consciousness.

Some time ago, as was remarkably defined by Anatole France, people were afraid of each synthesis, of each generalization, and thereby forced an inevitable, insignificant and fierce disunity upon themselves. The entire culture of our most recent times, in its industrial aspects as well as in its spiritual aspirations, strives towards an expression of true co-operation. Mankind is strenuously seeking formulae which would make it possible to come together for peaceful and creative work. All new Conferences, new Societies, Institutions, in one or another measure, have within themselves this task of cultural unification and mutual understanding.

If it formerly seemed that cultural unification could be expressed primarily in some cultural and artistic domains, it now becomes especially clear, that such unification is much broader than individual branches. It is expressed in a generally elevated trend of thought, in the sense of universal creativeness in all paths of life.

Thus, in the name of Culture, from the League of Culture, one wishes to thank all undertakings similar to the enlightened tasks of the Citroen expedition. In other words, one wishes to thank the inspirers, the builders and co-workers of all such undertakings, who, by their self-sacrificing labors, are stimulating human thought, and of course, elevating it to a new level. Without these courageous discoveries, mankind would again stoop to the routine of daily vulgarity. We know all the difficulties of transportation upon mountain paths and upon the sands of Taklamakan and upon the glacial slopes.

Upon the path we have encountered many benevolent local stories about the remarkable explorer, Sven Hedin, as well as reminiscences of Prezhevalsky and the mission of Pelliot and many others, who brought from the depths of the desert new considerations and new impulses for human thought.

Let us not regret that the romantic camel caravan gives way to the motor, airplane, railroads. Let us not regret that the "long ear" of Asia yields its possibilities to the telegraph and the radio. But let us believe that these improvements will live not only with civilization, but that they will enter benevolently into Culture, not lessening the worth of spiritual values.

The more that jealously-guarded science will be spread, the more it will bring bliss. Folk legends and traditions, thousands of years old, if correctly interpreted in the new light of research, will but give brilliant new possibilities, and in true co-operation, there cannot be anything hostile, anything that impedes or demeans. Everything destructive and decomposing will remain within the limits of ignorance. But every step of co-operation and unification will mean movement towards true enlightenment.

These considerations appear when we see before us the collected works of the last expeditions. One wants to thank the directors and participants for that vigor of thinking, which they are undoubtedly bringing into the human consciousness, at present so agitated and so oppressed, because the new step of progress will verily be predicated on the condition that the latest improvements will give their assistance to science and art.

This collective creativeness imparts that vigor of the spirit, of which the new generation is so much in need.

Sincere greetings!

Kyelang, Himalayas, August 20, 1932.

WREATH TO ROBERT NORWOOD

WHEN the Rev. Dr. Robert Norwood came to say good-bye to me before my departure in 1930, his last words were: "We shall meet again!" Who knows when this meeting will take place! But I know one thing, that it will take place under the same sign of rejoicing of hearts, under which our earthly meetings took place.

Are there many such enlightened spirits, who stand guard in defense of Religion? Are there many such people who bring into everyday life the elevated feeling of realization of the Godly? Are there many servants of the Church who can express the Eternally Beautiful with such unshakable enthusiasm? Are there many amongst us who can understand both the web of everyday life and the radiance of great achievement? And are there many amongst us who have carried the light of their friendliness and well-wishing through all torrents of our earthly existence?

Ask any Old-Believer on the remote Altai mountains, whether there exist many such good people. He will answer: "They are as few as the ears of wheat after a raging hail-storm."

If you ask a Tibetan Lama, if there are many such good people in our world? He will say: "Also of the high snowy peaks there are but few".

If you ask the Bikhu of Ceylon if there are many such good people in our world? He will point at the working elephants and will say: "Even of these good elephants there have remained but a few."

So they say in the East.

If you ask anybody in the West: "Are there many of

such good people?, they will answer: "You know yourself how rare they are; and by the way, the number of high radio aerials is also very small, but even these few unite the world."

These passages come to my memory from one of our talks with Dr. Norwood. "Well, well," he added, "if even such good people are rare, the easier it is for them to be united. It is not quantity, but quality that matters." And now when Dr. Norwood is in the invisible Abode, I remember his words and the above passages from our conversation.

Without eulogizing, let us say that indeed such people as the Rev. Dr. Norwood are rare. It is they, who, as high aerials, unify the whole world in everything that is best in mankind. Especially now, when the world, as after a hailstorm, is so sharply divided along the line of Light and darkness, when the forces of darkness try to inflict a fatal harm upon Culture, then such Guardians of the Good and of Bliss, as Dr. Norwood, do appear.

He was born in Nova Scotia. This place is surrounded by many wonderful legends, and an elevated spiritual quality is known in such regions. The Wonderful has also touched Dr. Norwood with Its radiant wing. I recollect how upliftingly he described one of his blissful visions to me. You could feel that indeed only a person who had actually contacted the higher spheres, could speak in such elevated terms. "I believed," he concluded, "that it lasted but a moment, but the watch showed that three hours had elapsed."

Dr. Norwood expressed the same highest inspirations in his sermons. It is no surprise that his congregation was so numerous. It is not surprising that his followers loved him so deeply. And when he spoke, the listeners were also so uplifted that they never thought of the time. It is so precious that in our days of restlessness there exist in our midst such uplifting guiding spirits. We shall never forget how beautifully he blessed our Banner of Peace.

Verily, Dr. Norwood knew what friendliness is, and

what Love is. He was generous, giving away widely his gifts of true love and compassion. When he spoke of the decoration of his beloved St. Bartholomew's Church, he, in realization of highest concepts, inspired the andience to action. He was not abstract. He was an active plowman, who consciously labored in the field of Culture. He knew the full Beauty of daily, untiring labor. He knew the lofty art of creating servants of Light. He was loved here and will be loved there.

In electing Dr. Norwood now as a Member in Perpetuity of our Society, we also do not act abstractly. For us he lives and we know that we shall meet him with the same warm-heartedness as we did in previous meetings.

Let Peace and Light lead his ascent!

Himalayas, October, 1932.

ANNIVERSARY OF YERMAK

TO, the glorious anniversary of Yermak! To all Siberian friends! To all sons of Siberia, heartfelt greetings!

When we last sailed upon the rapids of Irtysh, a diamond cutter said to us, "Here drowned our Yermak Timofeevitch. Or rather, he did not drown, but his armor was too heavy for him, and it dragged our valiant knight down." In the eyes of a Siberian, Yermak did not drown. A valiant knight could not drown!

And not only is the glory of Yermak alive, but he himself lives in the consciousness of Siberia. In Kirlyk, on the road to Ouimon, a Shaman spoke to us about benevolent Oirot, Messenger of the White Burkhan. Oirot appears upon a white horse and proclaims, "Sain galabyn sudur!"—A sign of the good era!—But the old man, an Old Believer smiled. "But this is not Oirot at all, but Yermak Timofeevitch who animates our land. It is he who guards over the Stone!

The Stone! And the entire country is a great Stone, a precious adamant! Will it be Tigeretz? Or Kotanda? Or Ak-kem? Or Karagai? Or Studenetz? Just the same it is *The Stone.*

And the ancient wisdom carried over the tradition of the precious mountains—Sumir, Subur, Sumhir, Sumeru—to Siberia. There, "the blacksmith forges the destiny of humanity upon the silvery mountains!" White is the snow and white is the silver of Belukha, the Mother Herself. And the multi-colored grass is much taller than the horseman. And everything resounds with Belovodye. Verily, Zvenigorod. So it shall be!

"Between Irtysh and Argun. Through the Gobi, through the salt lakes. Through Kokoushi. Through Bogogorshe. Over the Ergor itself rides a rider."

The Siberian paths are not small. Great is their dream. Great is that which is predestined to them. The land of the White Burkhan, the land of the good Oirot. The land of Sambatyon. The land of the Subterranean Wonder. The land of the blacksmiths from Kurumchi, who shoed the horses of all great travelers from the East to the West.

Can one recall Yermak Timofeevitch, without remembering Siberia itself? According to the sweep of the Siberian paths also is measured the path of Yermak, who transformed legend into life.

And the banner of Yermak in the Cathedral of Omsk of course carries upon it the image of St. George. Upon the same white horse in an immortal armor the Holy Warrior guided Yermak through many rapids, making the hopeless possible.

It would be strange to speak about the universal significance of Siberia. It is familiar to every school child. Strangers, looking over the map of Siberia, only ask, "Are the dimensions correct?" This infiniteness of Siberia mystifies one! Need we still speak about its semi-precious stones and mines, discovered and undiscovered, already written about or still undescribed? Or speak about forests, cattle-breeding, gold-mines, or the soil? Need we cite vast quantities and dimensions, which even then do not equal the reality?

Today it is permissible not to calculate nor to rationalize, not to dissect with earthly measures, but commandingly to celebrate the anniversary of Yermak, putting aside all divisions and coming together in memory of the great spirit, who did not fear, who did not become petty, but who gave us a great and constructively sounding call.

Just as the bells of Zvenigorod, as the Holy sites of Kitej, call us and purify us and command us to march towards progress, so also let this day witness the oath of benevolent constructiveness.

We cannot but mention today also the Holy Guardian of all strongholds of Kitej, of all the monasteries of the Spirit, of the Blessed St. Sergius. The very infinitude of Siberia brings all the warriors of heroic achievement, enlightenment and unbreakable valor close today.

Let us celebrate the day of Yermak. Let us remember with joy, that through all Siberian spaces, this name as a banner, resounds with untiring vigor. Joy is not often predestined. Many things try to obscure the predestined spaces. Not every armor fitted the powerful shoulders of Yermak. But he found for himself a sword, a banner and a spear because he desired to find them. Yermak's heart pointed out the path to him, because the heart knows the defined paths .

Is it accidental that the dates recall to us the name of Yermak? Does that name not provide us with one more measure for constructiveness and for all achievements, searches for Bliss because, for spiritual fortifications, signs are being sent to us which are invisible only to the blind?

If today we would become illumined by the bliss of co-operation, would that not be a veritable festival? And could one not rejoice, with streams of tears, at a heroic deed?

It is not to discover Yermak, not to discover Siberia. One cannot discover that which has been discovered, but it is for a festival that we have gathered today. Let this powerful festival suffuse all the young hearts with the tremor of heroic deed, with the passion for constructiveness and the pledge of co-operation. At least on memorable festive days let us remember about friendliness, about mutual labor.

At present, when the universal difficulties are first of all thrust against culture, against all educational possibilities, let us find in our heart the strength to be together, to be friendly and to think of the great and of the glorious. The measure of divisions has overflowed; the Siberian spaces recall the virginity of labor. When shall we remember about labor that has been untouched if not during a festival which gives us advice for constructiveness?

My late uncle, Mr. Korkunov of the University of Tomsk, called me constantly to Altai, already in my childhood. "Better come sooner," he wrote, "Anyhow you will be in Altai." Verily it is so!

Then in 1919 rumors had me buried me in Siberia and a mass was given for me in the Cathedral of Irkutsk. The Great Siberia draws one even in such an unusual way.

I would wish to have been with you today. I would wish to talk of the banner of Yermak, of Belovodye, of Belukha, of Ergor itself. But from Asia I am sending to all you, my friends, my best greetings. The snows of the Himalayas bear witness to the snowy peaks of Belukha. The cuckoos count the dates. The woodpecker repeats about indefatigability. And Saphet, the white horse, recalls the horses of Oirot, and Yermak and St. Egorius Himself. We celebrate this day with you all and beg for co-operation. Great was the salutation of Yermak with the gift of Siberia. Great was the pledge. Great also the heroic deed. A festival, a glorious festival this is!

Himalayas, 1932.

SPINOZA

"Watchman, what of the night? Watchman, what of the night?"
"The watchman said, 'The morning cometh, and also the night!' "

THROUGHOUT the night of human consciousness, up to the very dawn, the ever-vigilant thought-creation of Spinoza stood its guard on the dikes of Holland.

It called out to the darkness: "Why is matter to be regarded as unworthy of divine nature?"

The very disintegration of the substance of matter, let us say, even that which protects Holland, would threaten with peril an entire country, because the "chaos" of ocean rises higher than the level of the lawfully manifest. How then can we underestimate the meaning of matter, which has been manifested by the great creativeness of spirit? Where is the law which bids us to disparage and reject?

"The stone which the builders have rejected shall become the keystone."

This article is no pretense at a revelation of Spinoza. How is it possible to reveal that which has been discovered long ago and which has already penetrated the best minds? But at a significant hour, it is joyful to recall a wise one, a carrier of the treasure of thought, who opened one more channel to the beautiful synthesis.

Is it by accident that time itself reminds us of the glorious achievement of thought? Amidst the tremors, errors, disillusion of the weak spirit, the reality of this great, self-sacrificing personality astonishes one, like a sudden meteor from the far-off worlds, affording us, by its example, lessons in the understanding of life, which are nurtured and felt in one's heart.

The austere image of Spain, fatherland of Spinoza's family, the arduous destiny of the compatriots of the Moranos, the legend of Sabatai Zevi, the flash of Uriel da Costa, the tragic death of his first teacher, his acquaintance with Bacon, Descartes, Hobbes, Giordano Bruno, DeWitt, these seekers of truth, who undertook for themselves the burden of surrounding ignorance; all these make up the keynote of the life of the Thinker.

More than once, attempts were made against his life; in The Hague, where a statue of Spinoza now stands. The Thinker was arrested as a French spy; indignant over the murder of his friend, DeWitt, Spinoza wished to mark the site of the murder by the inscription *"Ultimi Barbarorum."* In this cry of his soul, he poured out the deep pain of the heart.

Tragedy is the unfailing fellow-traveler of the seekers and finders of the Treasure, of those who have touched mystery. But it carries in itself that magnetic conviction which brings together the guiding and summoning legend of truth. The name of Spinoza is surrounded by this heroic legend, which forcibly affirms the depths, the reality, of the conclusions of his trend of thought.

The uniqueness of the life of the Thinker himself, his triumph over human weaknesses and conventionalities, all these milestones, these beacon fires and torches of that sorrowfully stern march, illumine the image of Spinoza with a light which is kindled only by the power of thought and the reverberation of the heart. The wise one knows that the morning will not come swiftly, but he does not fear to set out upon the path by night, even if the night be starless and if through its pall, he can hear the ominous roar of the ocean.

"Think more broadly! Think better! Do not permit your thought to lack the precious essence. Dare not to disparage that which great thought has evoked from out of the unmanifested chaos."

While humanity stands appalled before the selfcreated economic and spiritual crises, the hours of destiny throb out the dates that recall the great figures, who by their vital example affixed the impression of their achievements. At the very moment when humanity is so greatly appalled at the wavering of its ephemeral illusory standards, there come reminders of one who could not be held back by any dams; who ascended along the luminous arch from Amstel to the Valhalla of Highest Matter. When the fragments from our earthly crashes seemingly bar the paths, there appear the messengers of the transmutation of thought into matter and matter into thought, who ascertain even the weight of thought.

The opponents of Spinoza speak of details, discuss his words, without desiring to see the basic trend of his thought. There is nothing baser than to tear from a multitude of successive signs, separate details, and to brandish those in an attempt to confound or to violate the current of thought. Out of the most precious tablets, one may construct very strange designs.

Whoever has affirmed another great value has thereby already enriched the possibility of evolution; he has thus already become a glorious guest of honor at the feast of culture. Dessication and decay or affirmation and unfoldment; there is no middle way.

The thought of Spinoza is destined to flower. It is not in vain that so many young hearts are attracted to it. The young hearts leap, not to the abstract, but to the real; they feel the direction of life.

Spinoza asserts that "Science has one destiny, to which all its branches are striving, namely, the highest perfecting of humanity." . . . "Those who deny that men can attain virtue and truth deprive themselves of these, by this very denial." . . .

"True cognizance generates only through the essence of things or through their Knowledge: Proximate Cause."

Let us not forget that Spinoza strives to "such a finding and possession as will give constant and highest joy in eternity," to those "pure and clear thoughts, where passion ceases to be passion." Thus Ethics ceases to be an abstraction and becomes the guiding star of joy in true vital application.

These reminders explain why the name of Spinoza attracts youth. Not only the gray-haired sympathize and help, but the young hearts also co-operate and quiver at hearing of the eternal joy.

In the orbit of the same happy guests revolve many glorious names almost contemporary to Spinoza: Kepler, Galileo, Leibnitz call to the far-off worlds. Along the same shores of Amstel at the same hour crosses another magi of light—Rembrandt, accomplishing "the highest joy in eternity" in his own way

Speaking of the flourishing of Spinoza's thought, one cannot fail to remember our Spinoza Center in New York, that young group which gives joy, which gathers in the name of a great Thinker. Remembering this century of youth striving to bliss, to the purification of life by means of thought, one always feels a heartfelt tremor, desiring to send youth a greeting for the success of its communions. They also do not have it easy; thus it was not easy for the Thinker himself, nor is it easy for any enlightened ones. But for the transmutation of thought a great fire and a mighty effort are needed. It is difficult to melt graphite which records thought, but nevertheless, under a mighty fire, it produces a diamond.

Spinoza could rejoice in his observation of the Rings of Saturn, as he turned to the far-off worlds. But he also studied the earthly laws, as the equilibrium of the foundations.

The Rabbi Gamaliel says: "The study of the law is a noble deed, if united with some art. Our occupation with them diverts us from sin. But each occupation unaccompanied by artistry leads to nothing." And the Rabbi Yehudi adds: "He who does not teach his son an art prepares him to be a highwayman." Spinoza, knowing his art of grinding delicate telescopic lenses and having attained considerable perfection in drawing, verily answered the covenant of the harmonization and ennobling of the spirit.

More than once Spinoza received offers in money in exchange for only a few concessions in his views, but he stoically rejected them.

More than once he was threatened with murder or with the looting of his possessions. But could the ignorance of malice stop the torrent of thought? In order not to inflict danger upon his landlord, he offered voluntarily to face his assailants when they came to murder him. Does not the refusal of Socrates to escape from prison resound with the same nobility of spirit? Or the story of the dungeon of Origen Adamantius? And does it not remind us of other great examples? Spinoza asked a friend not to translate all parts of his tracts into the Dutch language in order to avoid interdiction of his thoughts. And does this not call forth various great parallels, ancient and contemporary, when the words of bliss were proclaimed by ignorance as "dangerous poison."

As tokens for the human spirit rise, so do the milestones of courage and of cognizance of an unrestrainable nobility, and at the destined hour, among the underbrush of the weeds of ignorance, the spiritual human eyes, aroused, will see with unearthly fires and will exclaim: "One more pillar of the commands of King Ashoka has been found." . . . "A new stela of the laws of Hammurabi." Kings—high priests, proto-sages, proto-evangels! Kings of spirit, your stela, surrounded by a spectrum of tears of salt and joy, is being guarded invincibly for a new understanding.

At his tri-centennial anniversary, people will turn with new benevolent attention to the renewed and penetrating image of Spinoza, and once again, they will rejoice over his evolved consciousness, because the enchantments of thoughts never wither. Of course, true values find a place for themselves with difficulty. The standard depositories are not containers for them. It is painful to open an eye full of dust and especially when not a speck of dust but a beam of wood, impedes.

One recollects the following truly "historical" episode:

When the mummy of Pharoah Rameses the Great was found, it was packed in the pages of the newspaper *Le Temps* and brought to Cairo in a wagon. The custom official weighed it on the scale and "Not finding a corresponding custom levy in the list of tariffs, applied the ruling in regard to salt codfish to it."

To us, the Holy relics of the ancients are in the category of salt codfish!

This is not a tale of the Middle Ages but our very recent past which finds a parallel between the reverence of relics and salt codfish. And can we ascribe such ignorance only to our past? Up to now, a skeleton is imported under the tariff of second-hand things.

And even now, are not the foundations of culture being destroyed? Do we not attempt again to deprive matter, the great Materia Matrix, of Her Divine origin? Do not the ignorant try to place all scientific raptures into the coffin of dead symbols?

Verily not by accident have so many books of wisdom been revealed now forewarning and preventing the possibility of new deplorable errors. Verily not by accident does time itself, by its dates, remind us of knights and heroes of thought, who, like the heroes of antiquity, have quaffed the poison of the world!

How will we then celebrate the tri-centenary of Spinoza? With what will the friends of his thought celebrate? Best of all, with that which would be closest to the Thinker himself, the creating of eternal joys. So let us try and find herein creativeness of luminous benevolence and renewed co-operation! ... "Joy is a special wisdom!"

Concerning the wise, one does not have to conclude with an exclamation. Perhaps the closest of all to us will be the words recorded by Plato, those epically clear words of Socrates, confirmed by his own life, when he drank poison, as the redeeming chalice of the world:

"He who during his entire life has renounced pleasure and the adornment of his body as things external and leading to evil; he who striving to the pleasures of Knowledge has adorned his soul with the befitting adornments: temperance, justice, power, liberty and truth, he can be assured in a happy destiny of his soul; he can calmly await the hour of his departure into another world for he is ready to depart whenever fate summons him."

Urusvati, Himalayas, 1931.

GOETHE

Wär nicht das Auge sonnenhaft,
Die Sonne könnt' es nie erblicken.

Alles könne man verlieren
Wenn man bleibe was man ist.[*]

THIS likeness to the sun, this might of the personality, these banners of the significance of Goethe were
expressed by himself. Again in time, perturbed humanity
is reminded of the invincibly beautiful image in which
the entire substance of time is expressed. No adjectives are
needed for the expression, "time of Goethe" or rather the
"epoch of Goethe." The name of Goethe became an honorary coat-of-arms, not only for its creativeness, wholeness of
thought, depths of cognizance, courage of consciousness,
nobility of feeling. This name verily encircled around
itself an entire epoch full of th e most powerful expressions of the spirit. The style of Goethe is not only the style
of a writer, not only the style of a powerful Empire, but
the style of an epoch. Not waves of fashion, nor re-evalua-
tions, nor new achievements can affect the giants, creators,
interpreters of an epoch such as Homer, Shakespeare,
Dante, Cervantes, and Goethe. . . . It is impossible to say
that they stand as lonely peaks, for in them is fused the
spirit of their times! They have become super-personali-
ties, because they personified the most noble achievements
of the Epoch. Count A. Tolstoy, exultingly addressing

---

[*] Never would the eye behold the sun
Were it not engendered in light.

To him who himself remains,
All may be lost.

the artists and, remembering the images of Homer, Phidias, Beethoven, Goethe, writes:

"No, not Goethe this, who fashioned the great Faust
In ancient Germanic attire;
But in its truth, great and universal,
It seems the eternal image, word for word.
Or Beethoven when he created his funeral march—
Did he fashion the succession of chords which tear one's soul?
No, these sounds cried out always in the limitless space.
Being deaf to earth, he hearkened for these unearthly cries.
Be thou blind as Homer and deaf as Beethoven,
But strain more zealously Thy spiritual ear and spiritual eye
And as if upon the flame of a secret writing, faint lines emerge
*   suddenly*
Thus will the pictures suddenly emerge before thee.
And more vivid will become the colors and more perceptible
*   the paints.*
The harmonious correlation of words will interweave in clear
*   meaning.*
And thou, at this moment, behold, hearkening, holding
*   Thy breath*
And afterwards, creating—recall the fleeting vision!"

In such words, the writer desired to show the entire unearthly and superhuman substance of the creativeness of Goethe. The great lines of many secret writings were revealed to the eye of Goethe. It has been said that Goethe belonged to secret philosophical societies. This is not important. Are there not a few members and dignitaries in all other societies? The flame of the spirit, the fire of the heart, the great Agni, not through reason, but through straight-knowledge, acquainted Goethe with the secret places of the summits. The synthesis is never transmitted through societies. But it is significant to see how Goethe as a real Messenger of Truth did not deviate from life, but found a smile for all its flowers. Limitation is not befitting an all-embracing spirit.

With all justice one may call Goethe's direction of thought spatial. In it he affirmed personality, but there was liberation from egoism. Agni Yoga! Such a correlation is even inconceivable for small consciousnesses, but it is a true test of the potentiality of the personality. Did Goethe know the teachings of the East? He probably did. For Romanticism does not exist without the East. It has not reached us as to how much Goethe studied the treasures of the East. He did not insist upon them, but it is clear that he knew them; perhaps the all-embracingness inherent in him also easily opened these significant gates.

They say Goethe is an Initiate! How, then, not an Initiate, if in the flaming formula he could touch the most sacred stones without searing his hands?

How then not an Initiate into the Laws of the Foundation, if undaunted he could cross all gorges, crowded with delayed and lost travelers? How then not an Initiate, if he walked his own path, not as a seeker, but as a carrier of the treasure of the far-off worlds?

To the seer of secrets, Hoffman, it is exactly *Geheimrat Archivarius* who is a spirit of fire; Verily Goethe was a real *Geheimrat*, not a royal one but one that was pan-human. He bore this title with the ease of a giant who smiles at the fragment of a cliff which falls upon his chest. This ease in bearing the unspilled chalice of life, startles us in the paths of the greatest personalities. What would cost many wrinkles, distortions, and sighs to some, is for the giant simply another inevitability which he encounters joyously in order to hasten further onwards. Goethe himself confesses: "So unrestrainable is my striving onward that I can scarcely permit myself to inhale, or to glance back." In this powerful uplifting of the Chalice, one remembers the legend of Christopher through the stream of life. The memory of Goethe should be celebrated in a manner especially sun-filled.

As with many other standards which are not according to usual measurements, Goethe remains for some a seemingly experienced statesman; for others, an incorrigible revolutionary, for some, a foundation, and for others, a shaker of foundations. But the quality of commentaries and discussions about Goethe is itself astonishing. The entire variety of things ascribed to Goethe and demanded from Goethe reveal the scope of his creativeness.

Certainly such a mind could not have been uniform.

Goethe completed the time of Schiller, Herder, Burger, Winckelmann, Kant, Lessing. A great time! And Frankfort-am-Main is a good place! Leipzig, Strasburg, Wetzlar, Weimar—all are saturated with significant meetings. Literature, art, science, the law, government work, the entire complex of life, served only to intensify the consciousness of Goethe, not in the least burdening his powerful creative shoulders. There is time for everything and there is a smile for everything.

The years in Italy, his friendship with the similarly great spirit, Schiller, balancing and mutually complementing each other, forged an indissoluble unity. Finally, the eighty-year-old hand of Goethe inscribes the final lines of *Faust* as the synthesis of life. So to Eckermann, Goethe himself considers and expresses his understanding of the remainder of his life as a gift to, and the next year, Goethe hastens into the far-off world.

Goethe is a world spirit, *Weltgeist,* and of course world unity is one of his foundations. Creativeness and criticism manifest themselves in the creations of Goethe in an original combination: "To decide to live in all-embracingness, in Bliss, in the Beautiful."

Goethe influenced even Scott in his *Ivanhoe. The Corinthian Bride, The Earl King, God and the Bayadere, Tasso, Egmont, Iphigenie* have inspired the best minds for translations, transcriptions and musical settings.

And *Wilhelm Meister* is unforgettable as an image of culture and construction (*Bildung*), affording to many a vital lesson.

Free from didacticism and dry moralizing, Goethe gave the teachings of life through inspiring images of touching romanticism, fusing them in the symbol of *The Sorrows of Werther*.

Weltanschallung—Goethe's contemplation of the world, is irrepeatable because it is founded on his own irrepeatable rhythm of saturated, untiring action.

The influence of Goethe is not only profound in all German countries, but also in the Anglo-Saxon and Slavic world, as well as in America. *Nur rastlos betätigt sich der Mann.* He did not know the meaning of rest; he would only change the activity of the nervous centers, as Voltaire also did. His *reine Menschlichkeit* was not foreign to immortality as also his *ewig Weibliches* always soared in the pure spheres of exultation through Beauty. The Centenary of Goethe, for each broadened consciousness, must truly be the Festival of a sun-filled holiday! Goethe was close to Apollo; he was close to the light of antiquity. His key is a major one. A beautiful presentation. A beautiful Edition, in a beautiful leather binding which does not break at the first opening, with beautiful frontispieces and adornments. A dignified national festival where the noble *Meistersinger* may be crowned. Thus one envisages, contemplates, the anniversary of the glorious Goethe so near to all.

The Earl King and *Corinthian Bride* were the themes for my first sketches; and of course *Faust* was given in our Children's Theater.

We remember our study table, the school edition of *Goetz* and *Werther*; we recollect all the benevolent and beautiful thoughts which were sprung from the ballads of Goethe. Never once has it been necessary to renounce one of them and never did one have to be ashamed of the name of Goethe. One enthusiastic student often wondered: Why Wolfgang? Why not Leo, when the creator of "*Faust*" had a lion's tread!

There is no dispute about Goethe. One can only rejoice over him with strengthened and the finest reminiscence. A sun-filled holiday befits the friend of our spiritual accumulations! One desires to accompany the celebration of Goethe with something solemn, heartfelt and harmonious.

He is in the garden of life. There the Lilies of the Madonna have blossomed; there are gathered the hearkening ones. And from Solomon's beautifully wise antiquity, from the *Song of Songs* this flower-garden of life is fragrant:

"Whither is Thy beloved gone, O thou fairest among women? Whither is Thy beloved turned aside? That we may seek him with thee. My beloved is gone down into his garden, to the beds of spices, to feed in the gardens and to gather lilies."

Urusvati, Himalayas, 1931.

VII
THE BEAUTIFUL

THE REALIZATION OF THE BEAUTIFUL

PLATO has said of statesmanship: "It is difficult to imagine a better method of education than the one which is revealed and verified by the experiment of ages; it can be expressed with two rules: gymnastics for the body and music for the soul.

"In this light, the musical education has to be considered the most important; thanks to it, Rhythm and Harmony are deeply enrooted in the soul, taking possession of it, filling it with Beauty, and making of man a beautifully thinking being . . . He will be nourished and exalted by the beautiful and will absorb it with joy; he will be fully suffused with it and will co-ordinate his entire life with it."

Of course we must not understand the word music in this case as the generally-accepted concept of musical education, in its narrowest sense. The Athenians understood music as the service to all muses, and to them it had a much deeper and vaster significance than we do. In its best sense, this concept embraced not only the harmony of tone, but also all poetry, the entire field of more subtle feeling, more elevated form and general creativeness. The service to the muses was a true education of taste, which cognizes the beautiful in everything. And to this vital Beauty we shall have to return, unless Ideas of elevated constructiveness are to be completely rejected by Humanity.

Hippias Maior (Beauty) of the Dialogues of Plato is not a nebulous abstraction, but a truly living, noble concept. Beauty exists in itself! It is sensed and realized. In this realization is contained an inspiring, encouraging call to the study and implanting of all the covenants of the beautiful. The philosophical morale of Plato is inspired by the feeling of the beautiful. Did not Plato himself, who was sold into slavery by the hatred of the tyrant Dionysius, prove, later on, by his own example the vitality of the beautiful path when he was re-established and living in the gardens of the Academy,?

Of course, the gymnastics of Plato are not our contemporary football nor the breaking of a nose by fisticuffs. The gymnastics of Plato comprise the same gate to the Beautiful, the discipline of harmony and the refinement of the body to more spiritualized spheres.

We have mentioned the introduction into the schools of a course of Ethics of life, of a course of the Art of Thinking. Without education into the general realization of Beauty, the two mentioned courses will of course remain a dead letter. In the course of a few years, the lofty and vital concepts of Ethics will again turn into dead dogma if they will not be permeated with the Beautiful.

In our life, many vital concepts of antiquity have been diminished and impoverished instead of their deserved expansions. The vast and elevated service to the Muses has become, in our conception, the playing of a single instrument. Now, when one hears the word "music," he imagines first of all a music lesson, with all its accumulated limitations. When one hears the word "museum," he understands it as a storage house for various objects of art. And, as with every storage house, this understanding calls forth in us a certain sentiment of deadliness. And this limited understanding of a museum as a depository, a storage house, has been so deeply rooted in our understanding, that when you pronounce the concept in accordance with its primary significance, namely "Museum," no one understands what you mean. Yet every Hellene even those not of the highest education, would have understood that a "Museum" was, first of all, the "Home of Muses."

First of all, a "Museum" is the Abode of all examples of

the Beautiful, and altogether not in the sense of guarding these examples, but with the understanding of a vital and creative application of them. Therefore you may often hear that people cannot understand in what way a "Museum" as such can occupy itself with all branches of Art, and can occupy itself with the education of taste and the spreading of the feeling for the "Beautiful" in essence.

In this regard we recall the Covenants of Plato. So likewise we might have recalled Pythagoras with his "Laws about the Beautiful," with his steadfast foundations of resplendent universal affirmations. The ancient Hellenes reached such a level of sensitivity that they proclaimed their Pantheon as an Altar to the Unknown God. In this ascent of the Spirit, they approach the inexpressible finesse of understanding of the ancient Hindus who, on pronouncing *"Neti, Neti"*, did not thereby express something negative, but quite the opposite. In saying "Not That, Not That" they pointed out the indescribable grandeur of an Unutterable Concept.

These great understandings were not something abstract, something living only in mind and reason; no, they lived in the very heart as something vital, life-bearing, imprescriptible and indestructible. In their hearts flamed the same sacred fire which also created the fiery covenants of the hermits of Sinai. The same fire created the precious images of Saint Teresa, Saint Francis, Saint Sergius, and the Fathers of Bliss who knew so much but who were so little understood.

We speak about the education of taste, as of an act of true significance for the State. When we speak about living Ethics which ought to become a favorite study of every child, we call on contemporary hearts, imploring them to broaden their views at least to extend to the Covenants of Antiquity.

Does it seem natural that a concept which was so vividly expressed already in the times of Pythagoras and Plato, could become so narrow and lose its true significance after all these ages of so-called development?

Already in the 5th century, Pythagoras symbolized in himself an entirely harmonious "Pythagorean Life." Pythagoras affirmed music and astronomy as sister sciences. Pythagoras, who was called a charlatan by bigots, would be terrified to see how, instead of a harmonious development, our contemporary life, which is ignorant of the beautiful hymn to the sunlight, has become crushed and perverted.

In our days, even the press communicates strange formulae, as for instance the recently-pronounced formula that the flourishing of intellect is a sign of degeneration. A very strange formula indeed, unless the author ascribes to the word intellectuality some special, narrow concept. If, of course, we take intellectuality as an expression of a conditioned and dry reasoning, then of course this formula is just. But it is dangerous if the author considers intellectuality as intelligence, which must be connected first of all with the education of taste as the most active principle in life.

Within our memory in the West, a newly-coined word, "*intelligentsia*," was created. At first, people looked askance at this newcomer, until it entered literature. The question arises as to whether this concept is supposedly the expression of intellect, or does it symbolize in general, according to Ancient Covenants, a conscious education of taste?

If it is the symbol of a consciousness which is refined and expanded, then let us welcome each similar innovation which will perhaps remind us again of the ancient beautiful roots.

In a previous article, "Synthesis," I mentioned the difference between the understanding of Culture and Civilization. But each of these concepts has been sufficiently identified, even in ordinary dictionaries. Hence let us not come back to these two complementary concepts, even if anyone would be satisfied with the one lower concept of Civilization, without dreaming of Culture.

But having remembered the concept of the "intelligentsia" it will be permissible to ask, whether this concept belongs to Civilization, as an expression of intellect, or does it also embrace the highest step? To be exact, does it enter into the state of Culture, in which the heart and the spirit also act? Of course, if we would suppose that the word "intelligentsia" refers only to the stage of reason, then it would hardly be worthwhile to introduce it as a new usage. One may admit an innovation where it introduces something new, or at least sufficiently revitalizes the ancient Covenants within the frame of the present day.

Of course everyone will agree that the "intelligentsia," this aristocracy of the Spirit, belongs to Culture. Only in case of such unity can one welcome this new literary conception.

In such a case, the education of taste belongs first of all, of course, to the intelligentsia, and not only does it belong, but it becomes its duty. If this duty is not fulfilled, the intelligentsia has no right to exist, and condemns itself to a state of savagery.

The education of taste cannot be an abstraction. First of all, this is a vital achievement in all the domains of life, for otherwise where can the boundary of service to the muses as practiced by the ancient Hellenes be set? If the ancients understood this service in its entire scope and the application to life of these beautiful principles, should we not feel humiliated to clip the luminous wings of the fiery radiant angels through prejudice and bigotry!

When we suggest ethics as a subject for the schools, a subject most interesting, vast, full of creative principles, we thus offer the reformation of taste, as a fortification against ugliness.

Andromeda said, "I brought thee Fire." And the ancient Hellenes, following Euripides, understood what Fire it was, and why it was so precious. But we in the majority of cases utilize these inspiring words of guidance like a phosphorous match. We think of the high concept of phosphorous, the carrier of Light, only as a match by which we ignite our cold hearth in order to cook our daily gruel. And where is tomorrow, this luminous, wondrous Tomorrow?

We have forgotten about it. We have forgotten it because we have lost our quests. We have lost our refined tastes which propel us toward improvement, aspiration and consciousness. Aspirations have become for us passing dreams; but the one who does not know how to aspire, does not belong to the future life, does not belong to the human kinship of a higher image.

Even the simple truth that the first distinction between man and beast is the latter's capacity to dream of the future has already become trite. But the truism itself has not become the commonly-accepted truth as it should be, but only a synonym for truth about which one need not think. Nevertheless, in spite of everything, in times of even the greatest difficulties, let us not postpone or delay anything concerning the education of taste. Let us not delay our thoughts on the subject of Light-bearing Ethics. Let us not forget about the art of thinking and let us remember about the treasure of the heart.

It is said: "A hermit left his solitude and came forth with a message, telling every man whom he met, 'Thou hast a heart.' But when he was asked why he did not speak rather of compassion, of patience, of devotion, of love, and of all the benevolent principles of life, he replied, 'The main thing is that they should not forget about the heart; everything else will come.' "

Verily, can we invoke love if it has no place in which to abide? Or where will patience dwell if its abode is closed? Thus, in order not to be tormented by goodness unapplied, one must create a garden for it, which will flourish in the midst of the realization of the heart. Let us, then, stand firm upon the heart's foundation and understand that without the heart we are perishable shells. So have ordained the Wise Ones. Thus let us accept and apply these words.

Without untiring cognizance of the Beautiful; without the untiring sensitivity of the heart and consciousness, we will make the laws of earthly existence originating from a hatred of men; they will be cruel and deadly. In other words, we will help contribute thus to the basest peril.

It is said: "*Sub praetextu juris summum jus saepe summa injuria; suaviter in modo fortiter in re.*"

Himalayas, May 24, 1932.

ARTISTS OF LIFE

BY the sign of Beauty the locked gates may be opened. With song one can approach a wild yak so that she loses her fierceness and submits to milking. With a song one may tame horses. Even the serpents hearken to a song. It is significant to observe how healing and exalting is each touch of Beauty.

Often we have had occasion to write of the importance of the so-called applied arts. Many times we compared the so-called fine arts with the no less significant manifestations of all branches of artistic industry. It is even dreadful to have to repeat again that the button created by Benvenuto Cellini is not only not inferior, but undoubtedly far above multitudes of average paintings and graveyard sculpture. These comparisons are old and it would seem that reminders were no longer necessary; but life itself indicates quite the opposite.

In all fields of life, the sphere of applied art, which is blatantly stamped with some such shameful appellation as "commercial art," is abruptly separated from the general understanding of art. Instead of a gradual realization of the unity of the substance of creation, humanity seems to be striving to divide itself still more pettily, and to spread mutual humiliations. It would also seem absolutely apparent that the style of life is created not merely by the great individual creators but by the entire body of artists in the applied arts. It is not always the unusual creators who originate the character of dress, not always their hands which create a poster or a work of jewelry. By some inexplicable curiosity, the products of ceramics are considered inferior to sculpture in marble, although the charm of the Tanagra has given us ample evidence of a noble folk creation.

One may still hear the sorrowful exclamation of many young people: "I cannot live by art; I have to enter the commercial field." Thus implying that by this, the artist dooms himself to the inevitalble disgrace which is presumed to accompany participation in practical art.

What material, what circumstances, could deprive an artist of his quality? What manner of demand would compel him to do anything non-artistic in any expression of life? What type of promoter would destroy the creative fire which gushes unrestrainedly through all materials? It is important for each promoter, even for the most elementary and non-artistic one, that his product be clear, vivid and convincing and easily assimilated by the masses in their daily life. After all, which of these conditions may be regarded as disgraceful? Raphael himself, after receiving his orders, was guided by the condition of feeling. Truly the quality of feeling in no way contradicts the true artistry.

Gauguin, through sheer desire for self-expression, painted the doors and interior of his dwelling in Tahiti. Vrubel placed his "Princess Swan" on a platter. The number of examples is countless, in which the most diverse artists sought for expression through the most extraordinary materials. As we have previously noted, the material itself, by its very subtle quality, lends a special purposefulness to the object. Is there need to repeat the identical examples which have been mentioned so often in widely varying circumstances? Not discussion but action, should strengthen the attitude so necessary for culture. If we reach the expression of the unity of arts, we thereby affirm the need of the closest correlation of all branches of art in its various materials.

It would be difficult to indicate a definite order in which such workshops could be conducted together with sketching, drawing and life classes. This order must be left to life itself. In each country, in each city, and even more, in each district of the city, there are special impressions of life. Hence to these problems one must respond first. Near a large textile factory, it would be good to provide drawing and the study of the technique of this industry. Near ceramic and porcelain factories one could lend assistance precisely to this medium; thus one should correlate the practical expressions prompted by the closest demand by expanding and refining the understanding in the immediate neighborhood. Incidentally, one should not overlook the fact that the physical environment of these workshops will undoubtedly afford reciprocal assistance and provide unsuspected combinations which will offer new and fascinating results. The open mind of an instructor, unhampered by prejudice, and the broad demand for creativeness from the students, will result in that living vibration which, not becoming paralyzed by monotony, will afford to the craft workshops an endlessly practical variety and purpose.

Another gracious quality is gained through the manifestation of practical variety. It tempers the spirit, freeing it from the sense of limitation, which so often constructs the dwelling of fear. But it is from fear, above all, that each aspect of creation must be liberated. In fear, creation cannot be free; it will bind itself with every chain and forget the noble and victorious discipline of the spirit. Long ago it was said: "One must be cured of fear." One must pursue such methods consciously, in order to liberate oneself from that fear of murky pettiness and the creeping phantoms which caused even the stone that fell from heaven, aflame with a heavenly fire, to become opaque. Truly, opaque and veiled, when it could have been transparent and glowing—this Scarab of Light.

The Egyptians called artists and sculptors "Seenekh" or "Revivifiers, resurrectors." In this definition a deep comprehension of the substance of art is manifested. How immeasurably broadened this concept can become if we apply it to all manifestations of life, when we acknowledge that each adorner of daily life is an "artist of life." And this true "revivifier" of everyday life, himself, will be uplifted with new power, will become imbued with creative spirit by ennobling each object of daily life. Then the shameful and hideous understanding of "commercial art" will be cast out of usage. We shall call this noble adorner of life, "Artist of Life." He must know life; he must feel the laws of proportions. He is the creator of the needed forms, the evaluator of life's rhythms. To him, numbers, correlations, are not dead signs but the formulae of Existence.

Pythagoras calculates and creates, sings praises in rhythm, prays in rhythm because numbers were not only the earthly but also the heavenly rhythms—the "Music of the Spheres." With the name of Pythagoras, the mathematician, also resounds the name of St. Augustine, the theologian: "*Pulchra numero placent*," Beauty enchants by number. This magnet of numbers, proportions, correlations and technical consonances, necessary for each of life's adorners, precludes all diminishing or disintegration of the great creative understanding.

Do not let us fear to speak in the highest terms of each manifestation of Beauty. A cautious, exalted expression is a shield for all practical art, which is often exiled to the obscurity of the cellars. A country which is mindful of the future, should protect all—from the smallest to the greatest—for whose vindication it will be responsible at the great Judgment of Culture. Facilitating the destiny of these builders of life, the country of culture only fulfills the fundamental covenant of the Beautiful, so beautifully expressed by the poets of antiquity: "*Os homine sublime dedit coelumque tueri*": I gave to man a lofty forehead that he should perceive the summit.

With an exalted Covenant, the Bhagavat Gita confirms the multiformity of creation: "By whatever path you come to me, by that path shall I bless thee."

Himalayas, November 7, 1931.

THE MUSIC OF THE SPHERES

WOULD you restrain the Symphony of the Spheres? Would you bid the thunders of heaven to cease? Would you still the waterfalls and the whirlwinds? Would you command silence of the birds or prohibit the call of the stag? Would you deaden all human song? Would you mute the divine canticles and harmonies? What terror would prevail on earth without the Supreme Sounds! One may not even imagine what would transpire in nature, since sound and light are inalienably united. But fortunately no one can affect this devastating barbarism, since no one's forces can touch the Symphony of the Spheres which shall ring out and exalt the human spirit towards new creations. How many beautiful legends from the most remote times confirm the significance of the divine harmonies! As a symbol for all generations, the myth of Orpheus, who enchanted beasts and all living things with his celestial music has been cited. Even serpents lose their venomous intent before music, and the wild yak becomes calm and yields her milk to those who approach her with song.

It is instructive to notice how many beautiful human achievements would have remained incomplete if unaccompanied by the inspiration of song and music. Without the trumpet call, the walls of Jericho would not have fallen. Finally there is no home nor hut from which sound, as exalting and evoking harmony, may be excluded. We call the book, the friend of the home; we raise our eyes through the contemplation of superb lines and colors. Should we not, then, consider the harmony of the sound as our guide to the highest worlds? It is impossible to conceive of a temple without the harmony of voice or instruments. And King David, the Psalmist, composed his psalms with the thought of their rendition with instruments or voice. Not for the silent bookshelf did the Psalmist King create his invoking and instructive psalms. Not by accident, truly, is sound emphasized in the Bible and in other ancient writings. What can so greatly touch the human heart; what will make it immediately finer and more compassionate, completely broader in the span of receptivity? The expansion of the heart as the all-manifest understanding and the broadest striving engender creativeness in all manifestations.

My young Friends! I speak to you in the same language as to your elders, because your hearts are, if not more, equally open to the Beautiful. By your ingenuousness, your pure smile of joy, you often approach and enter with unusual ease into the Palaces of Beauty. Always, then, whenever you think of the beautiful harmony, of exalting music, always then let your hearts throb more vigorously, pre-sensing that other wondrous Gates are open for you which will lead out to a finer highway for your life's journey. Naturally, you love music. Continue not only to love it but constantly refine your understanding and approach to it. Perceive its meaning more personally; it will reveal your creativeness, will nurture your hearts and make accessible that which, lacking harmony and sound, would perhaps remain ever dormant. Regard music as the "open sesame" of your heart; and what can be more necessary, more beautiful, than a heart infinite in its power and its containment?

Each of us recalls the wonderful poem, "Beda, the Preacher," in which the stones in chorus thundered out their response to his call. If stones can concur and proclaim in harmonious chorus, will men be lower than stones? Are they only fit to quarrel and in contradiction, to mumble the unnecessary? A beautiful symphony unites human hearts. People become not merely listeners, but in their hearts they become partakers of the beautiful act.

And this uplifting call leads them to achievement and to better expressions of life.

To you, my friends, I send my thoughts for achievement, to those best manifestations of life to which each of you are destined and which only inexcusable neglect can leave unexpressed. Under the best sounds, in sorrow, in labor and in joy, hasten to the predestined Light!

Himalayas, December 1, 1931.

VIII

BANNER OF PEACE

BANNER OF PEACE

THE idea of the protection of cultural treasures of humanity preoccupied me since the very beginning of my activities. Already in 1904, addressing the Society of Architects in St. Petersburg, I outlined this idea, calling attention to the tragic condition of state architectural monuments. My extensive travels to ancient monasteries and historical cities, also the archeological excavations in such important places as Novgorod and other regions linked with most ancient traditions, gave me rich material to affirm the immediate necessity for urgent measures to protect cultural treasures. Afterwards, in 1914, I made a similar report to the late Commander in Chief, Grand Duke Nicholas, and to the late Emperor. Both reports met with great sympathy and only the extraordinary havoc of the war prevented their immediate development. Then as President of the Exhibition of Allied Nations where Flemish, French, British and the arts of other allied nations were beautifully represented, I had again a fortunate opportunity to propose this idea and was convinced that sooner or later the protection of cultural treasures would become a sacred reality in the world.

With new ardor, these thoughts preoccupied me when we were witness no longer to the vandalism of warfare but to the vandalism in times of peace. For an untrained eye it is even impossible to imagine how many inimitable cultural treasures are exposed to danger and perish without leaving any traces. One of our foremost duties is to apply all our efforts to direct the public attention to its real treasures. Each day brings news of some new destructions.

We are already imbued with the idea that precious monuments must not be carried away and must be safe-guarded on the sites, the more so because transportation facilities make even the remotest places accessible. I am deeply convinced that universal attention will be paid to the cultural treasures, and as a symbol of this, the universally unifying Banner will bring a profound and real service to the cultural development of peoples.

I am not astonished that we receive so many enthusiastic responses to our Peace Banner. The past is filled with deplorable, sad and irreparable destructions. We see that not only in times of war, but also during other eras, creations of human genius are destroyed. At the same time, the elite of humanity understands that no evolution is possible without the accumulation of Culture. We understand how incredibly difficult are the ways of Culture, hence the more carefully we must guard the paths which lead to it. It is our duty to create traditions of Culture for the young generation. Where there is Culture, there is Peace, there is achievement, there is the right solution for difficult social problems. Culture is the accumulation of highest Bliss, highest Beauty, highest Knowledge. In no way can humanity pride itself on doing enough for the florescence of Culture. For, after ignorance we reach civilization, then gradually we acquire education, then comes intelligence, then follows refinement and the synthesis opens the gates to high Culture. We must admit that our precious and unique treasures of Art and Science are not even properly catalogued. And if our Banner of Peace be that impetus which will urge such a manifestation for the universal treasures then this alone would be the fulfillment of a colossal task. How easily much of the useful and beautiful may be attained. Let us imagine a Universal Day of Culture, when simultaneously in schools all over the world the true treasures of Nations and Humanity will be extolled. The great sympathy of the Women of America must be pointed out amidst the many diverse works of enthusiasm. At a recent celebration dedicated to the Banner of Peace, the representative of a legion of women, Mrs. W. D. Sporborg, pledged their support for the Peace Banner. Vast is the list of organizations, societies, museums, libraries, schools and statesmen, which have expressed the great hope that this project will enter into life. Several organizations have already hoisted the Banner of Peace . The Museum Commission of the League of Nations under the Presidentship of M. Jules Destree, Belgian Minister, has unanimously accepted this project. And now, thanks to the initiative of M. C. Tulpinck, under the Protectorate of Dr. M. Adatei, President of the Permanent Court of International Justice, a special Conference will be held in Bruges, for which a broad program has been worked out. Of great interest in connection with this Conference, is the proposed League of Cities united under the same Banner of Peace. Mr. Tulpinck and other enlightened minds joined in this idea. A letter from Paris indicates that our friend, the poet, Marc Chesneau, will represent the old city of Rouen. I have just received an important article by Dr. Georges Schlaver "Le Pacte Roerich et la Société des Nations" (Extrait de la Revue de Droit International), which highly recommends the Pact from the legal point of view. Verily, the protection of treasures of Culture belongs to those all-unifying foundations upon which we can gather in friendship, without any petty feelings of envy and malice.

We are tired of destructions and negation. Positive creativeness is the fundamental quality of the human spirit. In our life everything that uplifts and ennobles our spirit must hold the dominant place. The milestones of the glorious path must impel our spirit to the beautiful future from childhood. One may believe that it is not a truism to speak about the imperative and urgent strivings to Culture. If some ignoramus finds this idea superfluous and unnecessary, we shall tell him "poor ignoramus, thou art outside of evolution, but remember we are legion and in no way shall we recede from our idea of a Peace Banner. If thou wilt be an obstructionist, we shall transform Thy obstacles into possibilities."

BRUGES

HEARTIEST salutations to all assembled in the name of the Banner of Peace, in the name of reverence to all cultural treasures!

I have already expressed my admiration for the noble project of M. Camille Tulpinck to convene a Conference in Bruges to spread and enforce in life our Peace Pact. M. Tulpinck will undoubtedly acquaint the honored assembly with some of the considerations, which I have outlined in my communications to him.

Now, I should like to address all present and in this salutation, to bear witness to the enthusiasm transmitted to us from countries throughout the world for this cause. To me, this Conference appears as the foundation of the long-anticipated *League of Culture*. This League will sustain the universal consciousness in its realization that true evolution is constructed only upon the foundations of Knowledge and Beauty.

Only the values of Culture will solve the most complex problems of life. Only in the name of the treasures of Culture, may humanity prevail. At the very root of this concept, so sacred to us, the entire veneration of Light, the true service to Bliss is enfolded. For it is precisely the concept of Culture that must be regarded, not as sterile abstraction, but as the virility of creativeness; it lives, nourished by the indefatigable achievements of life, of enlightened labor and of creation. Not for our own sake, because we are already mindful of it, but for the sake of those generations to come, Let us repeat again and again that during the proudest epochs of human history, a renaissance and efflorescence were achieved where the tradition of reverence for Culture grew. And we know that this tradition cannot be strengthened instantaneously. It must be nurtured daily by the benediction of Light. For even the worthiest spiritual garden withers in darkness and in drought.

Hence the Banner of Peace is indispensable for us, not only in the hour of war but perhaps, even more, as a necessity each day, when unmarked by the roar of cannons, irrevocable errors are committed against Culture.

Of universal significance are the cultural, spiritual values of mankind, and an equally peace-imparting unification is affected by the cordial handclasp in the name of the glorious treasures of all generations.

In our comprehensive program, the multifold ways of how to care for Culture are to be discussed. Multifold also will be the useful suggestions that we shall undoubtedly hear, all so needed in this universal movement. And the question which concerns us is only how best and in what order to apply them? We shall also hear of a Universal Day of Culture, when simultaneously in all schools and educational institutions, a day shall be consecrated to the full appreciation of all national and universal treasures of culture. We shall discuss which monuments of culture and which cultural collections shall be protected by the Banner of Peace. We shall discuss a universal inventory of all treasures of human genius. We shall discuss the entire complex of protective measures for Beauty and Knowledge, which must verily become the responsibility of all rational humanity, introducing firm foundations into life. There will certainly also be discussed the organizing of special Committees in all countries, the representatives of which have already expressed, or are prepared to express their endorsement of this cultural work. The organization of such a Committee has already begun in America. In our first Annual Reports, which we have had the pleasure to offer to this Assembly, the measures which have thus far been fulfilled by us for this Pact are outlined. We are of course certain that not only will the Annual Reports indicate the development of the Peace Pact, but that another edition will be issued, dedicated to all questions pertaining to the universal inventory of cultural treasures.

Beginning with this Fall, upon the basis of the sympathies and approval of the Pact by organizations numbering millions of members, we are inaugurating a Fund for the Banner of Peace. A special meeting dedicated to the Banner of Peace in our Museum in New York proved once again what powerful sympathies fortify our idea. One must also note that some institutions have already flown the Banner of Peace above their treasure, thus confirming the urgency of this decision. It is necessary to emphasize that all these actions must proceed along one channel. The concepts of Culture must arouse in us also the consonant concept of unity. We are tired of destruction and of common misunderstanding. Only Culture, only the all-unifying conception of Beauty and Knowledge, can restore the pan-human language to us. This is not a dream! It is founded upon my experience during forty-two years of activity in the domain of Culture, Art and Science. And in unison we may pronounce an irrevocable oath that we, neither we, nor our associates shall ever abandon: the defense of Culture and the League of Culture. Nor can we be deluded, for our experiences in the domains of Art and Knowledge have filled us with an unquenchable enthusiasm. Not only one nation, nor one class is with us, but multitudes, for, above all, the human heart is open to the Beauty of creativeness.

From the snowy peaks of the Himalayas, in the name of the all-embracing and all-conquering Beauty of creativeness, in its broadest conception, I greet you! I greet the friends-devotees of culture. And this Union in the Beautiful will multiply our strength; it will imbue our thoughts with harmony and with its impelling power as a Beautiful Necessity, and it will attract to us multitudes of co-workers for culture.

The conception of Culture belongs among the invincible

synthesizing ideas. Only ignorance can be hostile to Culture; and wherever it reveals itself, we must regret this dark inception. However, we must remember how slowly even the most evident ideas enter the consciousness. Let us remember that even the Banner of the Red Cross, which has since rendered incalculable service to humanity, was received, at first, with derision, mistrust and ridicule. Similar were the cases also with numerous examples of the most useful discoveries and innovations. But these deplorable facts serve to imbue us with the conviction of the necessity and vitality of the Banner of Peace and League of Culture.

After all, what we propose in no way belittles anyone or anything; it does not involve complicated measures, but is feasible making use of very simple means. Certainly, great works cannot be carried through instantaneously—long and indefatigable labor is needed. And for this we are prepared. But fire is ignited instantaneously, thus let this sacred fire, the fire of the Chalice of Ascent, unite us all without delay to join and unfurl in friendship the Banner of Peace, the Banner of Culture.

TO THE SECOND BRUGES
CONFERENCE

IT was precious to me last year to send my greetings to our first Conference and to watch the development and the dissemination in life of the Pact for the Protection of the Monuments of Art and Science.

At that time, we offered this project as based upon indisputable historical facts which imperatively demanded that public opinion concern itself with the dangers which surround the irreplaceable treasures of creativeness of the human spirit.

Since the first Conference, less than a year has passed; but from a whole contingent of countries news has come of the new unfortunate and irreplaceable destruction of art objects as well as literary treasures. These sad signs once more remind us how much the present time itself, life itself, demands that attention be paid to the safeguarding of the monuments of creation of Humanity.

At the same time one may again be convinced that although the time of war cruelly threatens the monuments of creativeness, yet also outside of formal war and during other calamities of Humanity these monuments are exposed to no less danger. I was very happy to acquaint myself with the opinion of Baron Alain d'Herbais de Thun, who wrote of our Pact that the Banner of the Pact, like the sign of the Red Cross cannot be made familiar only when military action begins. The People's consciousness, the consciousness of entire armies, must learn of the significance of this Sign, and to affirm it in their own consciousness, and for this purpose, a certain period of time is necessary.

This remark, absolutely correct, convinces one how immediately the familiarization of the essence of the Pact and its Symbol must be in the consciousness of people. For thus, the understanding of historical foundations and creative progress will be strengthened and renewed. And this constructive task is above all the nearest and most urgent duty of every cultural worker and educator for the sake of the younger generation.

Let us not evade mentioning the unusual crises and catastrophes which shake the foundations of the world. It is not necessary to enumerate these calamities, because they are known to every one of us. And not only are they known, but they are felt in a most disastrous manner. This is already not a supposition, but a truism. Therefore, the thought for the safeguarding of the foundations of the highest Civilization, of highest Culture, just now emerges with such unusual urgency.

All the sensitive minds of the world understand the seriousness of the present situation. Now the outstanding minds are remarking the need of building some new Noah's Ark, in the face of these indubitable dangers which surround humanity. All leaders of Culture have spoken of these dangers. These cries of Cassandra came from various countries under the most diverse circumstances. And the events which followed have only confirmed that these were not irresponsible utterances.

Thus we see that every day, without exaggeration— and I underline not months, but even days—brings new facts and data about the necessity to gather in the name of the Protection of Treasures of the Creative Spirit.

There cannot be a country which would declare itself unwilling to exercise the profoundest care in the protection of its most valuable Treasures. There cannot exist so insensitive a heart unwilling to understand that the flourishing of a State coincides with the flourishing of the High Principles of Civilization and Culture. Thus, I cannot see where there could be conscious opponents of our common mutual desire for the flourishing of Civilization and Culture, and, first of all, the Protection of the Monuments of the True Treasures of the Human Spirit! In daring to state that the thoughts and solicitude for the protection of the Beautiful and also for the growth of progress are unnecessary, one becomes like those barbarous destroyers who, at the moments of the downfall of civilization raised their voices and hands. Hence, let us not speak of opponents; Let us suppose that we do not live in barbaric times.

It means that before us lies the task gradually to advance and instill into the consciousness of peoples the thought about the urgency and necessity of renewing our profound solicitude for everything creative, constructive, and positive. Destruction and decay have fatigued the human spirit. They induce not only coarseness, but fatuity which has begun to be satisfied with the coarsest form of manifestation.

Cultural beginnings are in a state of neglect, because there exists an erroneous opinion that this is not the time to think about them. When the *SOS* of the human spirit shrieks out, then it is time also to think about the life-saver which will carry one again to the times of Magnificent Florescence.

For we optimists understand that the trend of thought has only to be directed in unity towards the Protection and Strengthening of constructive beginnings, and all the rest will also be added. And were not the most difficult problems solved precisely by the foundations of the highest civilization and Culture?

The history of humanity itself pleads for our consideration. Let seeming obstacles and misunderstandings represent those hidden possibilities which flourish with the conquest of impediments. In no case, shall we retreat from the idea of a profound protection of the true treasures of the spirit. We want to live, and therefore each tendency towards deadening is repulsive to us.

And we are not alone in this protection, nor are we

alone in the accumulation of the nurture of the Spirit. Before us, are the statements of many thousands of the best representatives of the World. I shall not enter into enumerations, because which of these splendid names could be omitted? And to mention them all, like the complete necklace of the most precious pearls, would mean to write a book.

Of course, these books will be written. The names of those who stand in the first rows of the defense of the most beautiful, most enlightening, most guiding, shall be preserved upon the most precious tablets. Humanity must know those who suffered and cared about the true flourishing of progress.

Let us recall the history of the inception of the Red Cross. This lofty symbol will soon celebrate the seventieth anniversary of its existence for the benefit of humanity. As a lesson to us, it will be useful to remember how much misunderstanding was shown by the contemporaries of Dr. Dunant toward this seemingly pan-human idea. And nevertheless, in spite of all shrugs of the shoulders and disdainful smiles, the idea of humanitarianism was brought into life, and even the most severe critics will not venture to say that this idea did not give remarkable consequences.

There exists a peculiar type of people of negative quality who prefer to speak only about that which they consider negative. But even these peculiar representatives of certain groups of humanity, will not utter a heretical condemnation of the luminous idea of the Red Cross.

The history of the inception of this Institution must be closely studied by us, so that we may apply it to our own many hardships.

From the history of the Red Cross we see that the idea entered into life, only because of the steadfast, irresistible, and the imperative call to action of all participants—initiators. Happily, no derision nor negation brought any destructive decay into their ranks. Let it be exactly the same in our case.

Let us remember one thing, that in no case will we deviate from our strivings. Nothing will break our united decisions about the great protection of the most Beautiful and Lofty monuments.

The means of spreading and enrooting this idea into the hearts of the peoples, into the hearts of youth—our heirs—is multifarious. They are as diverse as life itself. Therefore, I repeat with determination that every suggestion rests upon one or another foundation. Every thought must be benevolently considered. And the circumstances themselves will show us where and in what order it is possible to apply these most expediently in life.

If we speak about the safeguarding of creativeness, then we thus admit also a broad trend of thought. Let friendliness and well-wishing live in this trend of thought first of all. In the name of the luminous constructive beginnings, in the name of solicitude for everything high and best I salute you, confident of the great success which the Conference of the Pact of the Monuments of Art and Knowledge will attain.

I send my heartiest greetings to the glorious City of Bruges, which towers immortally as the symbol of a multitude of beautiful names. I salute the noble endeavors of the President of our Union, Camille Tulpinck, and of all the co-workers who think of the General Welfare. I salute heroic Belgium, which has given birth to so many beautiful creative ideas and images. I salute all members of the Conference, friends of the Protection of the True Treasures of Humanity.

Through its works and decisions, the Conference marks a luminous role in creativeness, progress, and unity.

Himalayas, August 7, 1932.

TO THE WASHINGTON
BANNER OF PEACE CONVENTION

FRIENDS:

To you, who have gathered in the name of the sacred task of Peace, I send greetings . Not without cause does the world concern itself about peace, because enmity and mutual hatred have truly reached their limits. The violations against creative life have seduced generations into the abyss of savagery. Nor can the external signs of civilization conceal the savagery of the spirit. In such hostility, in the midst of earthly unrest, the true values, the creations of the human spirit are being destroyed. Let us not look back to those dreadful precedents, when men were compelled to inscribe upon their tablets the memorable words, "Destroyed by human ignorance, rebuilt by human hope." But, precisely in the name of humanity's hope for a better future, for true progress of the spirit, it is necessary to preserve these true values.

I will not recount the history of our Pact, the furtherance of which has been actively carried forward by several Committees, by the Union Internationale and by two international conferences. The validity of our ideal for peace is confirmed by the existence of the Red Cross. If the Red Cross cares for the sick and physically wounded, our Pact protects the values of human genius, thus preserving spiritual health.

The world is thinking of peace in many ways. In each proposal for peace is contained the identical aspiration towards world progress and welfare. Each one, in his own language, repeats the benevolent formula of goodwill. Thus, we also are convinced that in safeguarding all the creative values of humanity, with a special Banner similar to the Red Cross, we are thus destroying also the very concept of war. If the entire world will be canopied with the banner for the protection of the treasures of true culture, there will be no place for war and hostility.

There have been those who have asked why we think of protection, when it would apparently be simpler to stop war completely. But at the very moment when these voices have arisen, new treasures of Humanity were being destroyed and the earth was covered with new marks of shame. Hence first of all let us sacredly protect the creative treasures of Humanity. First of all, let us agree on that which is the most simple, so that, as with the Red Cross, the Banner may significantly summon the conscience of men to the protection of that, which in essence, belongs not to one nation alone, but to the entire world, and which constitutes the real pride of the human race.

We may be asked why we think of war. But no one has ever stipulated that the Banner was needed only during a formally proclaimed war. As a matter of fact the principal of the protection of human treasures is necessary also in numerous other cases of upheaval. Truly not only war, but many other human calamities and convulsions, for some reason are wrathfully thrust against the monuments of culture. One may cite an infinite number of sad examples.

Somebody has mentioned that the Banner could hardly be a protection against the long range guns. But, the Red Cross is not visible at long distances, yet no one would deny the great humanitarian expedience of the institution of the Red Cross. Of course, we must not forget that at the inception of the Red Cross, there were many soulless critics, who argued against this highly humanitarian idea, but such ignorant condemnation is characteristic of each innovation. Let us not forget, that Edison's great invention of the phonograph was regarded as the work of a charlatan by some Academicians.

Thus let us not give importance to such limiting reasoning, for the Red Cross, with its noble benefits, has sufficiently indicated, that, even with long range guns, air attacks and the inhumanity of gases, the concept of the Red Cross still must be regarded as highly compelling and irrefutable. When a Red Cross ambulance rushes through the streets on its mission of salvation. Traffic is stopped because everyone realizes that something extraordinary has occurred, something that demands urgent measures. And now in the midst of human calamities, the *SOS* signal already resounds. The best minds have arrived at the determination of the necessity of broad measures for pacification and disarmament. But physical disarmament alone will not help. There must be a disarming of heart and spirit. Thus the World Banner, protector of the true treasures of Humanity will be a broad reminder of those forces, which must be sacredly guarded as the milestones and guarantee of a radiant future. Schoolchildren must firmly remember from earliest childhood, that wherever the Banner, the protector of human treasures flies, special measures of preservation and special care must be exercised for the dignity and friendly co-operation, in the name of Bliss!

As with the case of the International Court of Justice at The Hague, the International Postal Union, and the Red Cross, our Pact and Banner does not represent in its essence any international difficulties. On the contrary, the Pact is a summons to one more step of co-operation. A summons to the appreciation and cataloguing of religious, artistic and scientific treasures and to the establishment of a mutual respect of culture.

We need not fear, that military authorities will raise any irresistible difficulties. Strangely enough, it is just from the military milieu that we have had no opposition; quite to the contrary, we have constantly heard voices of sympathy and consideration regarding the entire practicality of the Pact. Even such undeniable authority as the former Marshall of France, Hubert Lyautey, has expressed himself very definitely in favor of the Pact. It is only necessary to familiarize ourselves with the written opinions of such scholarly military authorities as Baron de Thuen, who has already introduced lectures concerning the e Pact into the military schools, to see once again how apparently simple it is to carry out the humanitarian task of the Pact.

It is true that one scientist expressed the opinion that the Pact might impede military actions. But, if the Pact would not only impede but arrest military actions, then its indubitable merit would lie therein. For the entire World now is concerned only with the renunciation of mortal and fratricidal clashes.

People understand profoundly that no official decrees alone can transform the material crisis into prosperity. For the heart of man must consent to disarmament and co-operation. And this pan-human postulate comprises everything to remind us that the true culture of the spirit, creativeness, and constructiveness must be protected and affirmed.

We have received many thousands of sympathetic opinions regarding the Pact, from high representatives of human advancement, from governmental and educational Institutions. Organizations numbering many millions of members have done honor to the project of the Pact through enthusiastic unanimous resolutions. The Museums' Commission of the League of Nations has likewise unanimously endorsed the Pact, the President of the International Court of Justice at The Hague is the Protector of the International Union of the Pact, founded in Belgium.

Of unusual significance for me now is the Convention in America. Many formulae of a peaceful social constructiveness have emanated from America. America in her unprecedented composite of all nations has more than once been the champion of peaceful and humanitarian ideas. Hence, I consider that the public masses of America, as well as the Government, which exemplifies the high spirit of the Nation, will actively support the Pact and Banner of Peace since this agreement will be one added link towards peaceful world prosperity.

I heartily regret, that today I cannot be with you. But

with the entire power of my heart, with my entire friendship I ask you firmly and imperatively to erect one more mighty pillar for the flourishing of creative treasures of the spirit. I am certain, that the Government of the United States to which you will transmit your resolution will respond to it without delay with its customary cordiality.

If humanity recognized the Red Cross as a protection to the physically wounded and ill, then it will also recognize the Banner of Peace as the Symbol of peaceful prosperity and of spiritual health. I greet you reverently from the Himalayas and beg you to help this symbol of the health of the human spirit. I thank you, my friends.

Urusvati, 1933.

THE MISSION OF WOMANHOOD

FROM the most ancient days, women have worn a wreath upon their heads. With this wreath they are said to have pronounced the most sacred incantations. Is it not the wreath of unity? And this blessed unity....is it not the highest responsibility and beautiful mission of womanhood? From women one may hear that we must seek disarmament not in warships and guns, but in our spirits. And from where can the young generation hear its first caress of unification? Only from the mother.

To both East and West, the image of the Great Mother—womanhood, is the bridge of ultimate unification. To the Hindu of yesterday and today sings his song to the all-powerful Mother, Raj-Rajesvari. To her, the women bring their golden flowers and at her feet they lay the fruits for blessing, carrying them back to their hearths. After glorifying her image, they immerse it in the water, lest an impure breath should touch the Beauty of the World. To the Mother is dedicated the site on the Great White Mountain which has never been climbed. Because, when the hour of extreme need strikes, it is said that there she will stand and will lift up her Hand for the salvation of the world. And encircled by all whirlwinds and all Light, she will rise like a pillar of space, summoning all the forces of the far-off worlds.

In this way it happens that when the West speaks of the "Hundred Armed One" of the Orthodox Church, it is but another facet of the images of the many-armed, all benevolent Kwan-Yin. When the West exalts with reverence the gold-embroidered garment of the Italian

Madonna, and feels the deep penetration of the paintings of Duccio and Fra Angelico, we are reminded of the symbols of the many-eyed Omniscient Dukkar. We remember the All-Compassionate, the multitudinous aspects of the All-Bestowing and All-Merciful. We remember how correctly the psychology of the people has conceived the iconography of symbols and what an enormous Knowledge lies hidden at present under the inanimate lines. There, a smile appears where preconceptions disappear and prejudice is forgotten!

And as if freed of a great burden, they speak of the Mother of the World. With affection we may recall the Italian cardinal, who was in the habit of advising worshipers, "Do not overburden Christ, the Savior, with your requests, for He is very busy: Better address your prayers to the Holy Mother. She will pass your prayers on to whomever is necessary."

The images of the Mother of the World, of the Madonna, the Mother Kali, the Benevolent Dukkar, Ishtar, Kwan-Yin, Miriam, the White Tara. Raj-Rajeswari, and Niuka. All these great images, all these Great SelfSacrificing Beings merge together in one conception as one benevolent Unity. And each of these, in spite of the difference of language, comprehensible to all, ordains that there should be, not division, but construction. They say that the day of the Mother of the World has come. In the smile of Unity all becomes simple. The aureole of the Madonna becomes a scientific physical radiation, the aura long since known to humanity.

The symbols of today, so poorly interpreted by rationalists, instead of being regarded as supernatural, suddenly become subjects for investigation to the sincere research worker. And in this miracle of simplicity and understanding, one distinguishes the breath of the evolution of Truth.

A Hindu of today who has graduated from many universities addresses the Great Mother, Raj-Rajesvari Herself in full reverence.

At the same time, at the other end of the world, people sing: "Let us glorify Thee, Mother of Light!"

And the old libraries of China and the ancient Central-Asiatic centers preserve, since the most ancient days, many hymns to the same Mother of the World.

Throughout the entire East and in the entire West there lives the image of the Mother of the World, and deeply significant salutations are dedicated to this High Entity.

The great Features of the Face are often covered and under the folds of this veil, glowing with the squares of perfection, may one not see the One Great Unifying Aspect, common to Them All!

Peace be to the World! Blessed be woman, messenger of peace.

I ask you, representatives of womanhood, to support our Banner of Peace, which has as its aim the protection of artistic and scientific treasures of mankind. These treasures of the human spirit are so often endangered by destruction not only during war but also during all kinds of inner unrest.

The Mission of womanhood is great. As we have stated already: "When there are difficulties in the home, we turn to the woman. When accounts and calculations are no longer of aid, when enmity and mutual destruction reach their limits, we turn to the woman. When evil forces overcome one, then woman is invoked. When the mechanical mind becomes helpless, then one remembers the woman. Verily, when wrath obscures the judgment of the mind, only the heart finds saving solutions. And where is the heart which can replace the woman's? And where is the courage of an ardent heart, which can be compared with the courage of woman at the brink of the insoluble? What hand can replace the calming touch of conviction of a woman's heart? And what eye, having endured the pain of suffering, will respond so self-sacrificingly, in the name of Bliss?

Among these great leading missions, stands unyieldingly

the cultural mission to affirm and propagate the creativeness of mankind. Sponsoring creative thoughts, the consciousness strives towards true progress.

Three million women of America supported the Banner of Peace. All women of the world will act likewise. The Red Cross has saved many suffering ones. Thus also will the Sign of Culture strengthen in consciousness the true values of the spirit.

You, daughters of the Great Mother of the World, your hands weave the Banner of Peace unfurled in the name of the most Beautiful!

Urusvati, Himalayas, 1933.

ANGELUS

IN THE far off Himalayas the mail runner with spear, bells and horn is bringing the mail. The *New York Times* of August 12th, is precisely a month on its way and is dated precisely a year since our first Conference in Bruges.

There is a cable in the *Times* about the success of the Second Conference of our Union for the Protection of the Monuments of Art and Science. On the next page of the same newspaper there is another communication from Paris. I quote it in its entirety and in all of its starkness:

"*Unemployed Cuts Millet Masterpiece in Paris.* A mechanic slashes 'Angelus' in Louvre to call attention to his poverty. Paris, August 11th.—Pierre Guillard, 31 year-old mechanic, who recently lost his position with the electric company, has inflicted three gashes on the 'Angelus,' the famous painting of Millet, in the Louvre.

"According to his own confession, he did this in order to call attention to his miserable situation. The Administration of the Louvre reports that the restoration of the canvas will be *comparatively* easy, because it has only three cuts, one under the hand of the praying woman, another through the hip of the peasant who faces her, and the third, a long cut between these figures.

"Guillard committed this attack without warning and at first he resisted the guards who came to disarm him. Finally he surrendered and was arrested. The Ministry of Education and Fine Arts will start proceedings against him.

" 'Angelus' is the most famous work of Millet, and is regarded as one of the most celebrated art works in the world. It was painted in 1858-59 and for a time was the property of an American collector. In 1910 it was again acquired by the French dealer Chochar, who gave it to the nation."

Thus, at the very time of the Conference for the Protection of the Monuments of Art, one of the greatest masterpieces of genius was mutilated. Once again it is comprehensible why the universal recognition of the Protective Pact is so persistently and urgently needed. During the last years we have become convinced that it is not at all only the official wars that threaten the irreplaceable creations of human genius, but it is insidious barbarism and savagery that threaten, perhaps to a greater extent, the best monuments of creativeness.

Not in the skins of cavemen, but in smoking-jackets, sit these "gentlemen" who shamefully exclaim "To Hell with Culture!" Nonpunishable is their destructive arrogance and ignorance.

There is many a Herostratus! We set down the name of an insane mechanic as a most shameful stigma, but not to burden the pages of history. Criminal savagery turns first of all against the most exalted and perfect creations. Ignorance attempts to disfigure the greatest—therein is the hideous seal of darkness.

Verily, the most penetrating universal measures are needed in order to renew the traditions of Culture. Let us hope from the depths of our hearts, that the newly-formed World League of Culture will truly universally enlighten all the embittered, bewildered, obscured hearts, with a new and benevolent life.

Upon the mountain fields they are harvesting the barley, the heartfelt songs of labor ring out; and it is still more sorrowful to think that an apotheosis of labor so touching and solemn as "Angelus," is mutilated by the hand of a dark and criminal insanity. There is no vindication for it! One feels only horror before the savagery, before the chaos, of darkness!

The communication that the painting can be restored

comparatively well echoes painfully. From many years of experience in collecting, we know what a crippled painting means. What a multitude of such incurable cripples one has had to look at, regretting the inevitable consequences which sooner or later will make themselves felt. There exists no restoration which, through the ages, will not become apparent, by reason of the difference of materials. How many irreparable fissures, how many cuts, have been inflicted by ignorance. How much of that which is most precious was wiped out or turned to ashes by the barbarian destroyer. No matter how well the "Angelus" will be restored, painted over, and covered under thick glass, it will nevertheless be a cripple and the traces of this criminal attack will emerge and become apparent as the ulcers of the shame of our age.

Let us not condemn the guardians. A criminal hand will reach everywhere, if the brain and the heart are intent upon criminality. But from the earliest years of childhood, it ought to be taught in the home and in the school, wherein lie the true universal and spiritual values. If we realize that ancient China and Egypt revered creation more than we, it will seem a very unfortunate realization. A mechanic has mutilated the "Angelus." Is this not significant? Does this not recall the difference between the mechanical civilization and culture? Thank God that such a "mechanic" is not related to the true builders, investigators, and improvers of life.

Only recently we learned of the destroyed Goyas in Spain, and about the peril of a valuable library in Shanghai and of many other barbarisms. People say it is a national fury. But why does it strike the beautiful and not the ugly? Shame, shame!

All over the world the "Days of Culture" are being celebrated. This is good. Let them constitute a true homage to Light, Beauty and Knowledge, which will make the hands of the barbarians fall before the creations of the Beautiful.

Should one speak of the significance of Knowledge, of Beauty? Is it not a truism? But reality in all its ugliness forces one indefatigably and continuously to implore the affirmation of cultural foundations. Instead of the repast of labor in all its solemnity and constructiveness, there may come the night of the conflagration of destruction. You yourselves, see that it may occur in spite of all "Olympic Games," which, unlike the ancient games, sometimes finish with a wild fist fight.

The same newspaper which informs us of the mutilation of the "Angelus" communicates also about the conference of twenty-three countries dedicated to the Protection of Monuments of Art and Science. Let all the Leagues, Institutions, Museums, Societies, Institutes, Conferences, Conventions, grow and multiply in order, through enlightenment, to expel all the horrors of ignorance and darkness.

A heart which is aware of enlightenment will not mutilate the "Angelus."

Himalayas, September 13, 1932.

THE RED CROSS OF CULTURE

IN a recent cable from New York, we have read that there were about 800,000 unemployed in that city alone. In the United States the number of unemployed exceeds nine million. In addition, we know that this number does not include a multitude of professional workers, even though they are going through poverty and an unemployment no less severe. Such numbers are a true disaster; they show that the crisis has not only penetrated all strata of society, but is already a destructive factor. By the same mail we are informed that the very existence of the Metropolitan Opera House is threatened. Letters inform us not only about new curtailments of educational institutions but also about losses of many millions by people who were considered invincible pillars of financial wisdom.

When, under our eyes, such pillars of life-long wisdom are being shaken, does this not indicate a sign that these materialistic foundations have already reached their limit and are passing away? And is not this sign one more testimony that it is necessary to raise the forgotten and dusty banners of spirit out of the dust in order to counterbalance the apparent destruction with invincible values?

When, if not now, should the hearts of children be kindled by the records of heroic deeds of true education and Knowledge? Perhaps there has never as yet been a time when one needed so urgently to penetrate into the difficulties of the family and, based upon historical examples, indicate exactly what means were used to overcome the recurring crises in the history of humanity. One cannot hide any longer that the crisis has taken place; it is impossible to console oneself with the hope that daily collections will feed all the unemployed and starving. It is quite obvious that which has occurred lies much deeper.

The folk wisdom long ago had the saying, "Money lost, nothing lost; courage lost, all is lost." Now we must remember this wise proverb, because we have gotten into the habit of speaking about the crisis; those who have suffered as well as those who have for some reason suffered only a little, equally blame the crisis, equally blocking all their initiative and creative efforts.

Thus, if basic counteraction is not begun, this crisis may be only a prelude to something much more colossal.

We optimists must primarily divert any panic, any despair, whether on the stock market or in the Holy of Holies of the Heart. There is no horror which, after a greater tension of energy is evoked, cannot be transmuted into a luminous solution. It is especially horrifying to hear people who are not ill-intentioned but burdened by the crisis, begin to say that now is not the time to think of Culture. We have already heard similar words, inadmissible, in their cowardice and despair.

Know, my dear readers, that now one must think with particular urgency, not only about culture as such, but about how to apply this source of life for the new generation. One may imagine how the trend of thought of youth, which has just begun to form, will express itself, if it hears in school and at home about the horrors of despair, only about the necessity of renouncing that which is most vital, and forgetting the very sources of Light and Progress.

The terrible expressions "One cannot," "This is not the time," "Impossible," lead the new consciousness into a dark prison. And nothing, nothing in the world will illumine these obscurities of the heart if they are once admitted. Nor must we think only of youth; we must at the same time also think about childhood. Every educator knows that the foundations of a person's attitude towards the world, often ineradicable throughout one's entire life, are being laid, not during adolescence, but far earlier. It is often only the silent gaze of a child which reveals that the surrounding conditions are not at all beyond his comprehension, as it seems to adult conceit. How many basic problems are being solved in the brain and heart of a four or six-year-old child!

Everyone who has watched the development of children will of course remember those remarkable definitions, remarks, and counsels which have been uttered by the child quite unexpectedly. But besides these spoken expressions, what innumerable sparks of consciousness are also revealed in the silent look of a child. And how frequently these little ones divert their gaze from the grown-ups, as though protecting some decisive thought which, according to the opinion of children, the grown-ups would probably not understand.

And now one should fill this agile mind of a child with the most luminous thought, not with empty hopes, because idealism is expressed not in nebulous words, but in an immutable force, which can be proven by historians as a most exact mathematical problem.

Is it not now the time in our schools, beginning from the lower classes, to bring in the attracting and inspiring message of the heroic deeds of humanity, of its most useful discoveries and of that luminous Bliss, which of course is predestined, but which has not yet been consummated because of the absence of vision.

We began with the mention of New York, amazed by the last newspaper reports, amazed by the fact that in the seemingly wealthiest city, the municipality is in immediate need of dozens of millions, in order to prevent starvation.

We are quoting this newspaper communication because it is not only far from the truth, but in its essence, it doesn't even express the entire truth. That which was communicated about New York refers of course to all cities, not only to those of America, but of the entire world. Often these communications are concealed either by conditioned limitations or by the dark dust of eruptions as is now being reported from South America, in the accounts of airplanes that were sent to places stricken by cataclysms where "nothing was to be seen." Verily from many parts of the globe "nothing is to be seen", and when the darkness of the eruption disperses, then we see a still greater calamity of the human spirit.

He who now considers the inevitability of the crisis is in no way a Cassandra, uttering ominous prophecies, "which at least in the case of Cassandra were fulfilled." He who now points out the crisis is assuming a role analogous to the flagman of a train who, seeing the impending catastrophe, waves his flag of warning, hoping with his entire heart that the engineers will be vigilant and see his warning. Let us be such flagmen.

Let us raise the banner for the protection of Culture! Let us remember the Universal Day of Culture suggested last year as a day in schools when recitations of the greatest achievements of humanity, instead of the ordinary lessons, would kindle young hearts, through their luminous message. If last year we had in mind a League of Youth and at least one day which would manifest the Beautiful Garden of humanity, then we now ask that the urge for this manifestation be increased. A single day will no longer strengthen the consciousness which is now shaken by social and family misfortunes. One must speak more frequently about the saving, creative, and inspiring source.

To educate, does not mean to give a record of technical information. Education, the forming of the world-consciousness, is attained by synthesis; not by the synthesis of misfortunes, but by the synthesis of the joy of perfection and creativeness. But, if we shut off all flow of this joyous illumination of life, then what type of educators will we be? What education can the pedagogue offer who spreads around him sorrow and despair? Not far from despair is also the pretense of joy; here, it is, that each forced smile that has been called, not without reason, the smile of the skull. It means that we must convince ourselves how necessary and vital the program of Culture is as a salutary beginning, as a giver of life.

From the medical world we know that the so-called, vitalizing remedies cannot act suddenly. Even for the best vitalizer, time is needed so that it should penetrate to all nerve centers, to stimulate them not only mechanically (because each stimulant induces a reaction) but truly to strengthen and revitalize the nerve substance. If we see in all examples of life, the necessity of a certain period for the process of revitalization, then how urgently necessary it is to think and to begin to act under a sign like the Red Cross of Culture.

Humanity has become accustomed to the sign of the Red Cross. This beautiful symbol has penetrated life not only in times of war, but has afforded to all existence an affirmation of the concept of humanitarianism. And the same realization of humanitarianism, the same immediate necessity from small to great, must surround this sign of Culture similar to the Red Cross. One must not think that it is possible only to think of Culture at certain times when digesting the tasty food of a dinner. One should know that it is just as needed during hunger and cold. As the sign of the Red Cross shines luminously to the wounded, so should the Sign of Culture burn ardently to the physically and spiritually hungry.

Is it now the time to obstruct, to protest, to disagree and to wrangle in a petty manner? When a Red Cross ambulance hurries through the streets, all traffic stops to make way for it. Likewise for the urgent Sign of Culture, Let us also give up at least some of our usual habits and all the vulgar sediments and dusty limitations of ignorance from which, in any case, we will sooner or later have to purify ourselves.

For people who have not come close to questions of education, the Sign of Culture may seem only an interesting experiment. Of course, we will not hide our opinion that people will thus show their lack of education in history. But if it seems only an experiment to some we also will agree to this, because no one may say that this experiment can be destructive or create decay. Creativeness of thought about Culture is so apparent that it is even ridiculous to speak of it.

During serious danger on a ship, the command is given "Act according to your ability."

And also now thinking about Culture one must say to friends and enemies, "Let us act according to our abilities." It means let us double all our forces for the glory of the creative concept of Culture whose vitality cannot be deferred.

Himalayas, April 17, 1932.